PROFIT FORECASTS

Other publications by C.A. Westwick:

A study of profitability in the hosiery and knitwear industry, National Economic Development Office, 1971.

Accuracy of profit forecasts in bid situations, Institute of Chartered Accountants in England and Wales, 1972.

Investment appraisal for the clothing industry, HMSO, 1973.

Accounting for inflation: A working guide to the accounting procedures, Institute of Chartered Accountants in England and Wales, 1973.

How to use management ratios, Gower, 1973.

Investment appraisal and inflation, Research Committee Occasional Paper No. 7, Institute of Chartered Accountants in England and Wales, 1976 (with P.S.D. Shohet).

Property valuation and accounts, Institute of Chartered Accountants in England and Wales, 1980.

Sources of British business comparative performance data, Institute of Chartered Accountants in England and Wales, 1980.

Current cost accounting, Oyez Publishing, 1980 (with P.R. Hinton).

Do the figures make sense?: A practical guide to analytical review, Institute of Chartered Accountants in England and Wales, 1981.

Profit Forecasts

How They are Made, Reviewed and Used

Edited by

C. A. WESTWICK

Gower

© Gower Publishing Company Limited, 1983

Published by
Gower Publishing Company Limited
Aldershot, Hants, England

 British Library Cataloguing in Publication Data

Profit forecasts.
   1. Business forecasting
   2. Economic forecasting
   I. Westwick, C.A.
   388.5'44   HB3730

ISBN 0-566-02207-9

Contents

Preface

The aim of this book is to show how profit forecasts are prepared in today's business world, how they are made public and how they are used. While most of the book is about the United Kingdom, practices in the United States, Canada and the European Economic Community are also described.

Most of the contributors write from first-hand experience. My object as editor has been to make this book thoroughly practical and therefore useful to businessmen, directors, investors, analysts, accountants and auditors. Reading these chapters has given me, as I hope it will you, a fascinating insight into what happens within the companies, firms and organisations concerned.

The book is in four parts. In the first part the senior financial men from diverse companies in a wide range of industries describe how forecasts are prepared, for how far ahead, and how they are co-ordinated, monitored and revised within their own companies. How they deal with the problems they encounter in this process is also described, as are some of the forecasting techniques.

In the second part a reporting accountant and merchant banker describe the work that lies behind their brief reports when a forecast is published in the UK. The role of the Stock Exchange and City Panel is also explained.

How a stockbroker sets about making his own forecast of a company's profit, and how accurate these forecasts, and the forecasts of managers themselves, have proved to be in the UK and the USA, is the subject of the two chapters in Part Three.

In Part Four we move further outside the UK and look at practices in the USA, Canada, France, Germany, The Netherlands, Belgium and Luxembourg.

Each part is preceded by an overview which outlines the highlights of the chapters in it. Finally, there is a comprehensive bibliography for those who want to study the subject of forecasting further.

Forecasting, with its associated activities of planning, budgeting and target setting, is at the heart of the management of all successful modern businesses. But it is a paradoxical process: the most certain thing about a forecast is that it will prove wrong, but it must be made and acted upon nevertheless. The monitoring of results and their comparison with the plan then lead to new forecasts, plans and action.

That management needs forecasts is almost indubitable. But to what extent these forecasts should be published more widely (eg to share- holders and employees) on a regular basis is a matter of debate, as is the role of the independent accountant and financial adviser in reporting on them. If I may venture my own forecast, this is an area, together with the use of more sophisticated statistical and interactive computing methods, where significant developments should be expected in the Western world in the next decade.

C A Westwick

Acknowledgements

First of all I am most grateful to the contributors, all of whom are busy men or women, for giving us the benefits of their practical experience of the subject matter.

I also wish to thank the authors and publishers of the articles referred to in Chapter 12 for giving their permission to reproduce the extracts which I have quoted.

I am very grateful to Ray Hinton, Pat Thomson, Marilyn Murray, Ralph Cantelow, Paul Edwick, and Iain McKinnon of Arthur Andersen, and the staff and students of the Department of Accounting and Business Finance at the University of Manchester, for help of various kinds with the chapter on accuracy.

I am indebted to Michael Bywater, Librarian of the Institute of Chartered Accountants in England and Wales, for contributing the major part of the Bibliography and to R.W. Heley, P.J. Hughes, M. Murray, G. Mulcahy and P. Thomson for additional contributions to it.

I am also grateful to my wife Wendy for her encouragement, and for help with the chapter on accuracy, for collating the bibliography and compiling the index.

C.A.W.

Notes on Contributors

A V Ashton, FCA *(The role of the reporting accountant).* Alan Ashton is a partner in Deloitte Haskins & Sells' London Office. He is principally concerned with the review of all Stock Exchange and other public documents issued by clients and is responsible for all technical matters relating to prospectuses and take-overs and mergers.

K G Bishop, FCA *(Forecasting in the retail industry).* Kenneth Bishop was educated at Richmond Grammar School and Cambridge University. He qualified in 1955, having been awarded a Certificate of Merit and the Plender Prize for auditing. Since qualification his career has been spent in commerce and industry: as a Management Consultant with Harold Whitehead and Partners for four years before joining Yardleys as Chief Accountant; as a Director of Morganite Crucible and, prior to his present appointment, as Divisional Director, Finance, of Rothmans/Carreras. He was Finance Director of Debenhams Limited from 1971 until his appointment in November 1979 as a Managing Director. He was also appointed Chairman of Hamleys in the same year.

He joined the Committee of the London Society of Chartered Accountants in 1966 and was elected Chairman for 1971/72. He was elected to the Institute Council in 1974 and re-elected in 1975. He has been a member of the Technical Committee and until 1981 served on the Parliamentary and Law Committee and the Accounting Standards Committee. He has also been involved with the IASG with a particular interest in current cost accounting and taxation.

Dr J B Coates, ACMA, FRSS *(Forecasting in practice: an overview).* After National Service in the Royal Navy, Dr Coates became a graduate apprentice with J Lucas (Electrical) Limited. He then became a member of the Sales & Production Planning Department with responsibility for special planning projects and monitoring short-term production forecasts. He has been a lecturer at the Nottingham Regional College of Technology and the University of Birmingham. He is now senior lecturer in finance and accounting at the University of Aston Management Centre. He is co-author of Cost Control for Production Management and has contributed chapters to books by the Institution of

Production Engineers as well as having many articles published in professional and academic journals.

P M D Gibbs, MA, FCA *(How an investment analyst uses a profit forecast and makes his own)*. Martin Gibbs took a degree in engineering and economics at Cambridge before qualifying as a chartered accountant. He joined Phillips & Drew's research department in 1959 and became a partner in 1964. After many years as senior research partner he was appointed partner in charge of corporate finance in September 1980. In the last few years he has been particularly interested in inflation accounting. He has lectured and written a number of articles on this subject. He is a member of the Accounting Standards Committee.

R M Grainger, ACMA *(Forecasting in a nationalised industry)*. Mr Grainger is a qualified management accountant with many years' experience of large business organisations and has been mainly concerned with business planning, corporate strategy and general management information. He currently holds the position of Chief Planning Accountant with the National Coal Board.

R W Heley *(The role of the merchant bank)*. R W Heley is a director in the corporate finance department of Hill Samuel & Co. Limited. After a first degree in economics and a period as a research officer in manpower planning, he joined Phillips & Drew, stockbrokers, in 1969, where he researched and wrote books, papers and memoranda on many aspects of the implications of British entry to the European Communities, including portfolio investment opportunities for UK investors.

In 1974, he joined the corporate finance department of Hill Samuel & Co. Limited and has since been engaged in financial advice and the conduct of takeovers and mergers and of capital raising operations for UK and overseas companies.

P J Hughes, FCCA, FCIS *(Forecasting in a service industry)*. Mr Hughes worked initially in industry and qualified as a Chartered Secretary. He then moved into the accountancy profession and qualified as a Certified Accountant while working for Peat, Marwick, Mitchell & Co.

He joined C. E. Heath & Co. Limited in 1975 as Group Accountant, and in 1976 moved into the Insurance Broking side of the Group's operations as Chief Accountant and subsequently as a Director.

J R Knight, MA, FCA *(The role of the stock exchange)*. Jeffrey Knight was born in 1936 and educated at Bristol Cathedral School and St. Peter's College, Oxford, where he obtained an Honours Degree in

Philosophy, Politics and Economics. He was articled to a City firm of Chartered Accountants and qualified in 1966. He joined the Quotations Department of The Stock Exchange in March 1967, was appointed Deputy Head of the Department in June 1970 and succeeded Mr. W. S. Wareham on his retirement as Head of the Department in May 1973. More recently, Mr. Knight has been appointed Chief Executive of The Stock Exchange, having been Deputy Chief Executive since 1975.

Jeffrey Knight is an official Stock Exchange delegate to the International Federation of Stock Exchanges and was a delegate to Working Party No. 2 of the Financial Markets Committee of the Organisation for Economic Co-operation and Development. He has frequently represented the United Kingdom at meetings with the Commission of the European Economic Community and is a Special Adviser to the Department of Trade on EEC matters. He was a member of the City Company Law Committee and is a member of the Department of Trade Panel on Company Law Revision. He is also an Adviser to the Council for the Securities Industry.

G Mulcahy, MBA, FCA *(Profit forecasts in Canada)*. Gertrude Mulcahy was born and educated in Ontario. She graduated from the University of Toronto and started her business career as a member of the internal audit staff of the Head Office of the Bank of Canada in Ottawa. Later she qualified as a chartered accountant with Clarkson, Gordon & Co., in Toronto. She joined the staff of the Canadian Institute of Chartered Accountants in 1949 where she is now Accounting Research Director. She has been the author or co-author of several research studies and articles in professional accounting journals. She received a Master of Business Administration Degree from York University in 1969. In 1962 she was the first woman to be elected a Fellow of the Ontario Institute of Chartered Accountants (an honorary designation for distinguished service to the profession).

H Norris, FCA *(Forecasting in the construction industry)*. Mr Norris qualified as a Chartered Accountant in 1939 with a small firm of Manchester chartered accountants. From then until 1946 he worked with Deloittes. His subsequent career included becoming Deputy Chief Accountant of Vickers Armstrong Limited, managing director of Rank Overseas Films Distributors Limited and joint assistant managing director of the Rank Organisation Limited. He joined George Wimpey Limited in 1963 and became the finance director; he retired in 1980. He is also deputy chairman of the Stock Conversion and Investment Trust Limited. His book on accounting theory was published in 1947 and he has written numerous accounting and economic articles. He has served on various Institute of Chartered Accountants and film and construction industry committees.

J Pearcy, CA *(Forecasting in the chemical industry)*. Mr. Pearcy qualified with Thomson McLintock in 1948 and joined ICI in 1952. He worked on taxation and in management accounting both at Head Office and in an operating Division. He was until recently Deputy Chief Accountant. He is a past member of the Council of the Institute of Chartered Accountants in Scotland and a member of various committees, including currently, the Accounting Standards Committee. He has lectured and written frequently on various accounting topics, particularly inflation accounting.

J M Renshall, OBE, MA, FCA *(Profit forecasts in the EEC)*. Michael Renshall, a chartered accountant, was educated in Wales and at Cambridge. He trained with a firm of accountants in public practice in Liverpool. After qualifying as a chartered accountant he worked in industry as an assistant to the group chief accountant of Pilkington Brothers Limited before joining the technical staff of the Institute of Chartered Accountants in England and Wales in 1960. In 1969 he was appointed technical director of the Institute, with overall responsibility for the Institute's work on research, accounting and auditing standards and company and fiscal law and practice. He became a partner of Peat, Marwick, Mitchell & Co. London in 1977, where he is partner in charge of the firm's Professional Practice Department. He has written and lectured widely on professional subjects.

C A Schaller, BASc, MASc, CPA *(Profit forecasts in the USA)*. Carol Schaller is an audit manager at Ernst & Whinney. Before joining E&W, she spent six years on the staff of the American Institute of Certified Public Accountants. Carol holds a Bachelors and a Master of Accounting Science degree, both from the University of Illinois. She served as editor of the Accounting and EDP column in the *Journal of Accountancy* and has published articles on various auditing topics. She is one of the co-authors of the revision of the book 'Auditing and EDP'.

W T Seward, B Sc (Econ.) M Sc *(How and investment analyst uses a profit forecast and makes his own)*. Bill Seward took a first class degree at the University College of Wales, Aberystwyth, in Economics, followed by a Master's degree in Accounting and Finance at the London School of Economics. He joined Phillips & Drew, the City Stockbrokers, as a trainee investment analyst in 1970. Specialising in the motor industry and consumer durable sectors, he joined the firm's partnership in 1979. In addition to the firm's own limited circulation publications, he writes regularly for the financial press on his areas of specialisation.

R A Wade, BD, FCA *(The role of the city panel).* Mr Wade was educated at Kings College London. He qualified as a chartered accountant with Coopers & Lybrand in 1972. He was seconded to the Takeover Panel for two years from 1977-79 before returning to the Investigation Department of Coopers & Lybrand in London. He is now with Coopers & Lybrand in Zambia.

C A Westwick, B Sc (Econ.), FCA *(How accurate are profit forecasts?).* Chris Westwick was educated at St Paul's School and the London School of Economics. After graduating and qualifying as a Chartered Accountant he worked for 12 years as a management consultant, first with the Centre for Interfirm Comparison and then with Associated Industrial Consultants. From there he went to The Institute of Chartered Accountants, where he launched the Accountants Digest series of publications and the Interfirm Comparison for Auditors. He also worked on profit forecasts and spent a substantial amount of time on inflation accounting. He was seconded to the Inflation Accounting Steering Group as its Secretary and helped produce ED18 on Current Cost Accounting before returning to the Institute as Technical Director. He then became a Research Fellow at the London School of Economics. He is now with Arthur Andersen & Co.

R Whittington, BBA, MS, PhD, CPA, CMA *(Profit forecasts in the USA).* Ray Whittington is an Academic Fellow at the American Institute of Certified Public Accountants. He is an Associate Professor of Accounting on leave from San Diego State University. He received a BBA degree from Sam Houston State University, an MS degree in Accounting from Texas Tech University and a Ph.D from the University of Houston. He is both a CPA and a Certified Management Accountant. He has published articles in the *Accounting Review, CPA Journal, Management Accounting* and *Journal of Taxation.*

PART ONE

PROFIT FORECASTING IN PRACTICE

Overview

The first part of this book consists of descriptions by the senior financial men involved, of how forecasts are made, assembled, co-ordinated and revised within a deliberately diverse group of companies.

First ICI, a major world diversified chemical company, is described by Jeff Pearcy, until recently Deputy Chief Accountant. The features which distinguish the chemical industry are: huge investment in plant which is highly specific, has a long life, but is vulnerable to technological change; heavy research expenditure; the need to recoup investment by selling some products worldwide; and the integrated nature of the petro-chemical business. Forecasts are prepared on three time horizons ranging from twenty to one years ahead. Mr. Pearcy describes how these are prepared, revised and monitored. He identifies ICI's major problem areas as inflation, exchange rates, the trade cycle, volume/capacity balance, oil prices and technological changes, and provides a fascinating description of how these problems are tackled with the aid of on line interactive computing — although as he points out 'the back of an envelope still has its uses'.

Ken Bishop, Managing Director, Finance of Debenhams describes forecasting in the retail industry. Here, too, there are problems of different timescales: it takes from four to five years to open a new retail outlet but some fashions change almost over night. When forecasting, the retailer has to contend with the linked problems of stock levels, margins, space, staffing, promotions, and marked seasonal patterns of trade. Mr. Bishop paints a picture of an exciting and dynamic business. For example, actual results are measured against forecast weekly so that the necessary action may be taken quickly.

The National Coal Board was chosen as an example of a nationalised industry, although obviously each nationalised industry is different, with the additional problems that this brings of meeting (changing) government objectives. The NCB is a very large business (295 000 employees compared with ICI's 143 000). Two of its major customers are also nationalised industries (Electricity and Steel). Its major competitors are oil and gas. Forecasts are made over the long, medium (one to five years) and short term and are discussed with the Unions and the Secretary of State for Energy. There is a continual two way flow of information between the 200 collieries of the NCB, but monitoring need not be so frequent as at Debenhams. Ron Grainger, Chief Planning Accountant of the NCB, mentions the problem all forecasters face of trying to evaluate forecasts from optimists (mining engineers in the coal industry — in most industries it is salesmen) and pessimists (accountants), those seeking to impress and those protecting themselves against possible future criticism for under achievement by being unduly cautious.

In some ways forecasting in the construction industry is easier than in other industries as work is usually carried out to order and less often 'for stock', (e.g. speculative house building), but the industry is especially vulnerable to the weather and political changes of direction. Harry Norris, until recently Financial Director of George Wimpey, also contrasts the difference between the results reported to management based on the progress of the work programme and the more prudent reporting to shareholders based on the relevant Standard Accounting Practice. He makes the point that the size of the order book and the bid margins secured are better guides to the future than any trend derived from past results.

Dr J. B. Coates, who worked on forecasting for J. Lucas of Birmingham before joining the staff of the University of Aston, describes in simple terms some of the techniques of forecasting: statistical methods; market research; and cost estimation. He stresses the need to integrate all the plans, forecasts and targets within an organisation and the advantages of computer based financial modelling in this process. Forecasts lead to plans for action and these need to be compared with the actual results on a timely basis so that remedial or adaptive action can be taken.

A complete contrast to the others is provided by C. E. Heath — a worldwide insurance broker selling a service rather than products. Many factors which affect an insurance broker are outside his control. (e.g. movements in foreign exchange and interest rates, speed of payment by underwriters) so Heath forecasts for a relatively short period (up to three years) ahead. As well as foreign exchange movements, premiums required and commission paid by underwriters, inflation and the level of world trade all affect a broker's forecast. How these are dealt with is described by Heath's Finance Director, Paul Hughes.

C.A.W.

1 Forecasting in the chemical industry

J. Pearcy, formerly Deputy Chief Accountant, ICI

ICI Background

The forecasting processes and timing in any business are related to the needs for managing that particular business. Consequently, before describing the procedures in ICI, it will be useful to sketch a picture of the group.

Imperial Chemical Industries Limited is the parent company of an international chemicals manufacturing group, with its principal manufacturing sites in the UK, continental Western Europe, USA, Canada, Australasia, India and Malaysia. The products are sold throughout the world. Some dimensions are given below:

Table 1.1
ICI Group Statistics

	£ million — 1980
Total assets employed	4 698
Sales	5 715
Trading profit	332
Numbers of employees	143 000

The group is probably the most diversified of the world chemicals manufacturers, both geographically and in its product range. An indication of the latter is given by the classes of business table included in the 1981 annual report (Table 1.2).

A number of features of the chemical industry have a special bearing on forecasting. First, this is a processing industry in which each plant is usually designed to make just one product or a range of co-products. A single plant can involve as much as £200 million fixed capital investment with average life expectancy of twenty years. Consequently, one is concerned with long term trends in the consuming industries and in the world economy.

Secondly, the industry is in an area of high technology with large sums spent on research — especially in pharmaceuticals — and continual

Table 1.2
Contribution to ICI group sales and profits of main product ranges

| | Sales | | Trading Profit | |
| | 1980 | 1981 | 1980 | 1981 |
	£ million		£ million	
Agriculture	1,071	1,245	151	182
Fibres	432	444	(86)	(36)
General chemicals	1,143	1,232	99	75
Industrial explosives	210	258	19	35
Oil	770	1,056	**97	**83
Organic and speciality chemicals	520	573	(34)	(30)
Paint and decorative products	449	455	27	27
Petrochemicals and plastics	1,588	1,746	(79)	(54)
Pharmaceuticals	346	407	66	90
Miscellaneous	90	118	8	−
	6,619	7,534	268	372
Inter-class eliminations	(904)	(953)	19	(2)
Royalty income	−	−	24	32
Government grants	−	−	21	23
Total as in profit & loss account	5,715	6581	332	425

** After provision for petroleum revenue tax

change in the products and manufacturing processes. A major plant is seldom rendered completely obsolete, but regular modification is vital, to incorporate the latest technology.

The combination of large scale plants and heavy research expenditure means that many products have to be sold worldwide to be profitable. This is not true of heavy basic chemicals such as fertilisers and caustic soda, but it does apply to the high value products such as dyestuffs, pharmaceuticals and crop protection chemicals.

The third feature to mention is the integrated nature of major areas of the business, particularly those based on oil feedstocks. Petrochemical products are sold to other industries or, as petrol, direct to the public. They are also used as intermediates for many other products, notably synthetic fibres and plastics. Thus, plans and forecasts must be balanced carefully to ensure that they are compatible.

These diverse but important features call for a range of forecasts with differing time horizons. While parts of the forecasts can be based on reasonably well established trends, other parts are subject to much uncertainty. Contrary to popular belief, the management of a world-wide group has only limited freedoms to decide its future and has no special crystal ball.

Forecasting periods

Given the needs for a range of forecasts with differing time horizons, let us now try to identify these needs more precisely and see how they are met by the forecasting periods which are used.

The first requirement is for very long periods: to look well ahead and get some feel for the shape of things to come in twenty or more years' time. As is often said, the one certain thing about a forecast is that it will be wrong, but curiously enough these very long range forecasts often prove proportionately less wrong that the shorter term ones. They are, of course, constructed in very broad terms and are concerned with wide segments of the industry and with economic and political development in whole continents. They are needed for strategic purposes, to identify which areas of the business are likely to grow and which to decline and to decide where the growth points of the business should be sited. Once a chemical production complex has been established at a particular site, it becomes very difficult and costly to switch new plants to another location.

The second need is for forecasts in a range of three to five years ahead, to match, approximately, the length of the trade cycle. Until the OPEC oil price rises in 1974 there was a well established trade cycle of about five years, but it was disrupted at that time and as yet it is too early to say whether the traditional pattern will re-emerge. Medium term forecasts are needed principally for purposes of planning the capital expenditure programme and the related finance. The capital programme determines the size and shape of the growth of the group – what amount can be spent in total and which projects should be selected to meet the long term strategies. A chemical plant may take two years to design and three years to build, so the timing of a project in relation to the expected market is critical.

Finally, the third time period is for the next calendar year. These one-year forecasts form the basis for the budgetting and monitoring processes: they set the short-term targets of the operating units in the light of current trading conditions and they govern short term financial and tax planning. In practice, they provide the first year of the three-year medium term forecasts.

5

Frequency of forecasts

In determining the frequency of preparing forecasts, a balance has to be struck between the desire on the part of the top management to have up-to-date information and the cost and effort involved in preparing any forecast. In general, the longer the time horizon, the less frequent the forecast. In ICI, the short term forecasts are prepared in the autumn and revised quarterly in the following year (they always relate to the calendar year, not to a rolling twelve-month period). The medium-term forecasts, also prepared in the autumn, may be revised once or twice a year. Thus, a particular year is forecast no less than eleven times over a three-year period; it will also be included in the last two years of the five-year forecasts, these two years being covered more informally by central estimates on an *ad hoc* basis.

The long range forecasts are not prepared regularly in detail, but a computerised financial model of the group is used to identify trends on various assumptions. The results of these studies are used in conjunction with operating units' own strategic forecasts in order to identify which products are growing, which should be held steady, and which are candidates for divestment.

Methods of forecasting

In ICI there is a planning cycle which may be said to start with the preparation of the medium term forecasts which are considered in the autumn. For each of the main groups of products there is a sub-committee of the Main Board called a Product Policy Group and there are also Territorial Policy Groups for the main territories. The autumn forecasts are considered by these Policy Groups and, accordingly, they are called Policy Group Reports. They cover the development of the particular product group (or territory) for the following three years and include forecast profits and cash flows and the proposed capital expenditure programme, together with a range of items such as manpower and research expenditure.

The actual forecasting process starts well before the autumn with the issue of forecasts of economic indicators by the Economics Department, including indicators for major customer industries as well as the chemical industry itself, and for a number of overseas countries. They also include forecast exchange rates. The Personnel Department issues estimates of UK salary adjustments.

These various estimates give the framework within which the operating units make their more detailed forecasts. If significant changes occur during the compilation of the forecasts, they are taken into account by broad scale late adjustments.

The forecasting procedures used by the operating units follow a general pattern, namely, sales volumes and prices by the marketing departments, then a balancing of volumes to production and forecasts of production costs. Fixed costs, both direct and overhead, are, of course, forecast independently of projected volumes. The main operating units are divided into product groups, each of which is a profit centre, and these are the basic forecasting units. The interdependence between different units requires a process of agreement of volumes and transfer prices between them. Nowadays, there is an increasing use of interactive computing to process the numbers. In this method of using computers, the user can key in data via a terminal, the data is processed using the pre-programmed financial model and the results are displayed on a screen within seconds. The user can amend data in order to answer 'what if' type questions, and results can be printed out as required.

The forecasts are presented in the Policy Group reports in a standard format which covers the main items — sales, profits, cash flows, capital employed. They are consolidated in the centre to produce the aggregate group forecasts, and the centre adds its own view as to whether these totals are acceptable.

Once the forecasts have been discussed and agreed (or adjusted) at the Policy Group meetings, the first year of the forecast becomes the plan for the ensuing year.

In principle, the basic process for revising the forecasts is the same, but if the assumptions have not changed and actual results are not significantly different from forecast it may be possible to make adjustments without repeating the whole process. The autumn forecasts will commonly form the basis for revising the detailed product standard costs, and subsequent adjustments will normally be incorporated by way of forecasting the variances. However, if costs change substantially, it may become necessary to revise this item again.

Monitoring

The profit plan of each operating unit constitutes the benchmark for monitoring, but a number of more detailed budgets and targets are used for monitoring purposes. The principal periods used for comparing actuals with plans are the calendar quarters, but approximate profit figures and a number of other indicators are watched on a monthly basis. These more detailed indicators include sales, trade debtors, capital expenditure, stocks and major raw material prices.

The regular quarterly monitoring at main board level is carried out by way of reports to the board, the directors responsible for the product areas having a particular remit to keep themselves informed of progress in their areas. Down the line, there is more detailed monitoring at profit centre level within the operating units.

In addition, there are spring meetings of the Policy Groups which are concerned with longer term progress against the agreed strategies and consideration of the capital expenditure programmes. These meetings are also used to examine selected areas of the business such as the long term raw material supply situation, energy conservation, etc.

Problems

It will be seen that the whole forecasting procedure is an iterative process, starting with broad estimates which, in the long term, may be qualitative rather than quantitative and gradually narrowing down until the actual result is known. Even after an accounting period has ended one may still be making forecasts of the result because the actual figures are not yet to hand.

A group such as ICI faces the same problems as any business — the status of a large multinational does not confer inherently greater wisdom. Actions of God and governments, economic forces which are still little understood, moves by competitors, successes or failures by its own staff, can all upset any forecast. In another category, there are also practical problems of ensuring consistent assumptions and assembling a manageable package of key information from the available mass, including devising reliable group variance analyses.

The problems to which ICI's forecasts are particularly sensitive can be listed as:

(a) Inflation
(b) Exchange rates
(c) Trade cycle
(d) Volume/capacity balance
(e) Oil prices
(f) Technological change.

(a) Inflation

Figure 1.1 shows UK rates of inflation over the period 1970/1980.

Up to a rate of about 4 per cent, inflation seldom merits separate identification because it is within the degree of error introduced by

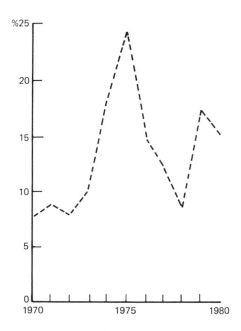

Figure 1.1   UK inflation rates

other variables. Above that rate, and particularly if it is fluctuating, it demands very careful consideration. Three things are needed: a forecast of the rate which can be used consistently by all units, a means of adjusting the forecasts for changes in the rate, and a means of separating real from inflationary results and trends.

It is not too difficult to make a forecast of the rate of inflation (which may or may not turn out to be right); but it is more difficult to ensure that the forecast is used by people down the line when making their detailed forecasts which will eventually be incorporated in the total group forecast. For example, it is tempting and natural for a sales manager to make his own judgements about future selling prices for his products without paying too much attention to some central calculation. To overcome this difficulty one relies heavily on good communications with the chief financial officers to ensure both that they understand what is required and keep a watchful eye on the consistency of the forecasts compiled in their units.

To adjust for changes in the rate of inflation is not easy because there are two main kinds of effects at work. There are direct first order effects − if the projected average rate of inflation falls from 15 per cent

9

per annum to 5 per cent per annum it can be assumed that rates of increase in costs and prices will fall correspondingly. But there are also second order effects. Inflation bears more heavily on some sections of the community than on others — for example, it favours those businesses which have a short time horizon and quick turnover of their capital because they can adjust to change more rapidly. Because of this uneven incidence, some parts of the group may have less difficulty in managing in times of inflation than others. Similarly, certain costs and income may be more affected than others.

These second order effects are not well understood by anyone — they may be explained fairly simply in a relatively undeveloped and isolated community such as one finds in Latin America, but the complicated network of variables across the developed countries so far defies human analysis. One is driven back to judgement and hunch: Western countries have been through an intensive learning process since World War II. Perhaps one explanation for the West German economic success is that, by experience, they know more about inflation than the other developed countries.

Whatever the practical difficulties, it is nevertheless essential that a view should be taken of the effects of inflation. It is also vital that the 'real' trends of capital employed and profits should be revealed. For this purpose, current cost accounting has to be used, allied to the conversion of the figures for different years to a common purchasing power base. This introduces problems of calculation and communication, but they have to be faced if management is to be given a realistic picture of the business.

Having set up the forecasts for, say, the year ahead, the problem then is how to monitor the actual results against them. If, for example, standard costs have been revised to a predicted mid-year average then in the first half of the year there should be favourable cost variances and in the second half there should be unfavourable variances. But if the actual inflation rate proves materially different from the forecast rate comparisons become meaningless: there has to be a system of updating the forecasts in the light of changing rates of inflation. This makes the whole process more complicated and the results more difficult to grasp, but there is no way out — one of the biggest problems of coping with inflation for an accountant is the added complexity it brings to his systems.

(b) Exchange rates

Changes in exchange rates are closely allied to inflation — in fact, if they are completely free and if there are no time lags, it can be demonstrated that changes in exchange rates between two countries

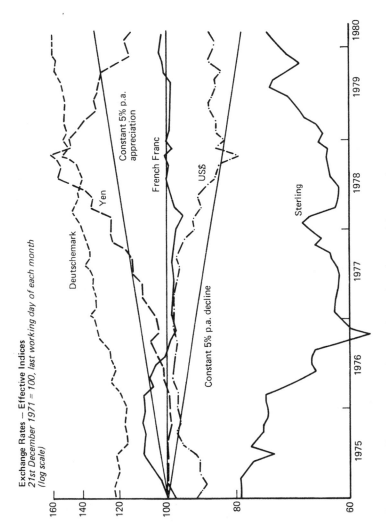

Exchange Rates – Effective Indices
21st December 1971 = 100, last working day of each month
(log scale)

160

140

120

100

80

60

Deutschemark

Yen

Constant 5% p.a.
appreciation

French Franc

US$

Constant 5% p.a. decline

Sterling

1975   1976   1977   1978   1979   1980

Figure 1.2   Exchange rate fluctuations of major world currencies

mirror the relative rates of inflation. Problems arise because there are time lags in the system and because, for political reasons, governments manipulate exchange rates artificially. The diagram on page 11 shows how major currencies have moved in recent years.

Consequently, one cannot take the forecast rates of inflation and apply them automatically to forecast the exchange rates. Once again, judgement has to be brought to bear. Hardly anyone succeeded in forecasting the paradoxical combination throughout 1980 of UK inflation and a strong pound, which has so damaged British industry.

As in the case of inflation, it is necessary in practice to produce central forecasts of exchange rates to which the units will conform when making their profit forecasts. In ICI, these central forecasts are produced in collaboration by the economists and the cash management team. The former know of the broad economic factors which obtain, and the latter have close working experience of the foreign exchange markets. The freeing of exchange controls in the UK has, of course, caused problems: it is salutary to realise that when this happened, probably no one working in this sphere had first-hand experience of life without exchange controls.

A particularly difficult problem with exchange rates is that no one has yet agreed on how exchange differences should be treated in accounts. The ideal would be a system which reflected in the accounts the actual exchange exposures which have to be managed and the degree of success which has been achieved. Given the complexity of modern cross-currency financing operations and the extra dimensions added by the freeing of the UK foreign exchange markets, this is not easily achieved. It is possible to construct a logical treatment in conjunction with inflation-adjusted accounts, but these are still not fully established and understood.

A practical problem when dealing with exchange rates is the extent to which the management of exchange exposures is made a responsibility of operating units rather than being kept as a central responsibility: there are arguments both ways. In one sense, it can be said that operating units are responsible for running their business and this should include the management of any exchange exposures which arise. On the other hand, it can be countered that management of group finance is a central responsibility which includes management of exchange exposures: by this means, offsets between operating units can be made, central expertise can be brought to bear, and the full group weight can be applied. ICI uses a compromise arrangement: exchange exposures are managed centrally on a group basis and individual operating units are usually treated as covering their separate exposures by application of forward exchange rates. However, if special exchange exposures affect a particular operating unit, such as its main raw materials being priced in US dollars, then special arrangements can be made with the centre to deal with them. By this means, operating units are alerted to the effects of movements in exchange rates on their trading position but the outcome of group exchange cover operations which are not their responsibility, is reflected in the centre.

Having decided on the division of management responsibilities and the accounting arrangements which reflect it, then it follows that the responsibilities for forecasting are similarly divided and the accounting structure of the forecasts is identical to the management accounting structure of the final results.

(c) Trade cycle

Until the OPEC oil price rises in 1973 there was a regular four or five year trade cycle round a steady long term trend in the world chemical industry, and this could be relied on when making forecasts. Since then, the cycle has been uneven, with no regular pattern established.

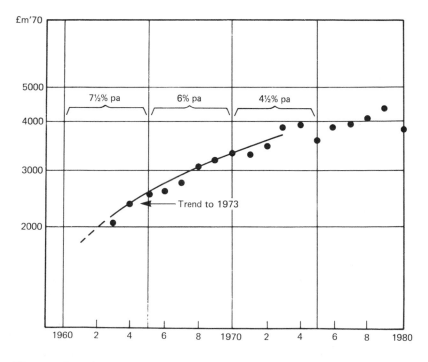

Figure 1.3   UK chemicals sales and traditional trade cycle

Nevertheless, over 60 per cent of the ICI group business is in overseas markets and sales by ICI's UK divisions and major overseas units are closely related to changes in world chemical industry activity.

Consequently, it is necessary for each operating unit to monitor world trends in its business, which in turn entails constant awareness of trends in the chemical using industries. For example, a material proportion of paints goes to the motor car industry so that changes in the demand for motor vehicles have to be watched closely. Similarly, synthetic fibres sales are dependent on the health of the textile industry, where added problems are created by the long supply line between the fibre producer and the retail shop. A fall in retail sales will leave increased stocks in the hands of wholesalers, which in turn will lessen the demands on garment makers, creating an increase in their stocks. This will be reflected back to the cloth makers and ultimately to the fibre producers. The effect tends to become exaggerated at each link in the chain so that quite a small change in retail demand can have a disproportionate effect on fibre sales. Fashion also adds its complication: the craze for hula hoops produced a brief bonanza for plastic tube manufacturers. The lesson is to know your customers, and their customers, right down the chain.

In dealing with the effects of trade cycles and other longer term trends it is most useful to construct a central view as a cross-check on the totality of each separate operating unit's views. In ICI, the central view takes into account the general economic growth trends forecast for the UK. ICI's UK business is closely linked to the UK economy as a whole, so that the forecasts for ICI have to show a close correlation with the forecasts for the UK. In most overseas markets, ICI's market share is smaller and the trends in the chemical industries are more significant than the economic trends. Expectations of growth in market share can be particularly important: sometimes an apparently reasonable assumption turns out to be unrealistic when translated into capital requirements and when competitors' likely actions are taken into account.

(d) Volume/capacity balance

There are two aspects to the problem of the balance between sales volume and capacity. One is the technical one of deciding the optimum timing of expansions in capacity, bearing in mind that demand tends to rise steadily whereas capacity increases in steps. Temporary shortages of capacity can frequently be made good by purchases from fellow manufacturers, but some complicated calculations have to be made to determine the most economical size and timing of new plants.

Forecasting total world demand for a product is much less complex than working out what the competition is likely to do — remembering that they in turn will be assessing ICI's position. Unfortunately, one consequence of free-for-all competition in an industry such as chemicals, with long lead times between the decision to go ahead and the start-up of production and with relatively low marginal costs of production, is a tendency to install too much capacity. The manufacturer who gets in first with his capacity will tend to capture the market; consequently, everyone tries to get in first. The result, particularly if demand does not rise as fast as anticipated, can be that too much capacity is installed and prices are forced down to uneconomic levels in the fight for sales volume.

So correct prediction of competitors' actions is important. It is also important to seek ways of reducing the risks, for example, by establishing some kind of competitive edge such as an improved process or product, a strong market presence, and so on.

Coming back to the forecasting process, the danger to be guarded against is that of making the forecasts without looking hard enough outside the group. One safeguard is central scrutiny of the units' forecasts and questioning the assumptions which lie behind them. Another safeguard is to have at least one person whose specific job is to keep an eye on the competition.

(e) Oil prices

The spiralling cost of oil over the past decade provides an extreme example of the problem of forecasting the prices of natural commodities. Other raw material values which affect the chemical industry are phosphate rock, sulphur and fluorspar, but oil is by far the most important because so many chemicals are now based on oil and its derivatives. Because it is so politically sensitive it is also particularly difficult to predict.

Faced with the need to forecast in such a situation, one has to make one's best guess at future prices and also calculate carefully the sensitivity of the forecasts to changes in oil values. This is not easy for a commodity which is the raw material for so many downstream products, many of which have competing alternatives so that an increase in price will cause a fall in demand if the alternatives are not affected to the same extent.

In ICI, we are feeling pleased that the decision to go into oil production ourselves was taken some years ago, thus laying off some of the risk.

(f) Technological change

In a high technology industry, the rate of technological change is a basic factor in any forecasting or planning process. In planning for the group as a whole, it can affect the rate and direction of capital spending, the predictions of asset lives and the predictions of profitability of existing assets. If one also includes the effects of consumer preference on the acceptability of existing and new products and processes, it can have even more far-reaching effects. It may be possible to average out some of these effects for the group as a whole – for instance, it is calculated that technological progress is reducing the capital cost of chemical plants by some two per cent per annum – but they can loom very large in relation to particular products and processes. The timing of a change, as much as its likelihood, creates the problem. For instance, in the 1950s it was fairly easy to predict that the production of ammonia in the UK would change from being coal-based to a process based on oil. However, when the change would take place depended on a host of factors, including relative prices of coal and oil, other cost relationships such as wage rates and capital construction costs, growing pressure to reduce atmospheric pollution from coal, agreement with trade unions on reductions in job numbers and changes in working practices, and so on. A more recent example relates to chlorine production where it is necessary to take a view on the continuing acceptability of a process involving the use of mercury, on the costs of preventing contamination beyond an acceptable level and on the costs of alternative processes.

The general effect of technological change on the forecasting process so far as accountants are concerned relates more to long term than short term forecasts. Forecasts for the current year are hardly affected, because decisions have already been made about changes in processes, new capital expenditure and so forth. However, long-term forecasts may be radically affected and the accountant has to keep in close touch with the technicians and ensure that technology is included in his checklist of matters to be considered.

Other forecasts

This chapter has focused on the routine forecasting and monitoring process, but, of course, many ad hoc forecasts are also made. These will usually relate to specific areas of the business and will frequently be connected with capital expenditure proposals, but they are also required for make or buy decisions, long term commercial contracts, rationalisation plans, and so on. For all these purposes the basic principles and methods are the same, but whereas the routine forecast is concerned with the general progress of the business and is closely related to the ultimate presentation of the actual results in published accounts, these *ad hoc* forecasts each have their own particular objectives. Consequently, it is always necessary to start by defining the objective and hence specify the accounting information required and the degree of accuracy needed. Less frequently, forecasts may be needed for a prospectus. Once again, the processes involved do not change and the objective needs to be defined. A special feature of these forecasts will be the involvement of outside parties, including auditors and merchant bankers. It is essential to agree with them beforehand, and preferably in writing, the extent of their involvement, their requirements, the timetable and the respective responsibilities.

Use of computers in forecasting

In these days of online interactive computing, the time and clerical effort required to produce a forecast can be reduced dramatically. Benefits can be reaped in two main areas: in the processing and compilation of the basic forecast data on sales, costs, and similar items, and thereafter in manipulating the results to answer 'what if?' questions.

The first, number-crunching, area is best handled by using the system which produces the actual results. By using identical processes but working on forecast data instead of actual data, one ensures that the identical accounting policies and practices have been applied so that the results are truly comparable with actual results. One also does this at least cost, assuming there are means of short-circuiting the full process so that forecast data can be inserted at appropriate levels of detail. Whether or not the forecasting system parallels the system for the actual results, the regular formal forecasts must be prepared in a disciplined way, using defined procedures and proper documentation.

The 'what if?' area demands a fully interactive system if acceptable response times are to be achieved. This will need careful design to make sure that the right data to answer the questions are fed in and that the programs perform the correct calculations. However, it may well not be necessary to design one's own system: a number of suitable packages are available from software houses and computer bureaux.

A word of caution is called for: nowadays it is very tempting to use a computer for almost any arithmetical process and this can be very expensive, particularly if it involves bureau charges. The back of an envelope still has its uses!

Conclusion

Much of what has been written above applies generally to any business. An attempt has been made to emphasise the things which specially affect forecasting in the chemical industry; undoubtedly there will be different emphases in other spheres. To put together a forecast is a demanding and satisfying exercise of accounting skills, but the accountant must beware of calling it — or letting others call it — 'his' forecast. The responsibility for any forecast rests with management.

2 Forecasting in the retail industry

K G Bishop, Managing Director, Finance, Debenhams Limited

Factors which affect forecasting in the retail industry

One cannot produce company forecasts oblivious to the nature of the industry within which one is operating, or of the trends within that industry. One may argue that longer term industry trends are irrelevant to a particular company's immediate fortunes; indeed, in retailing I find myself often wishing to ignore monthly government statistics when examining my own company's performance. Unfortunately, City analysts continually insist that if sales have not increased in line with the retail prices index a company has suffered volume reduction, notwithstanding the effects of low priced imports, the pattern of demand in fashion items as against household goods or cars, for instance, and even mortgage payments. In 1980 the price inflation in my own company's range of products based upon internal rated statistics was 4 per cent lower than the central statistical office index for the relevant sector. This variation could mislead both analysts and a company as to its performance in volume terms. The advent of current cost accounting is making us all much more aware of the need for accurate measurement of changing prices which, in turn, must lead us to measure volume changes more precisely. I welcome this development heartily.

Nevertheless, company planners must learn the effects of national, geographic and economic trends on their industry and temper their forecasts accordingly. These trends will form the background for strategy papers and longer term plans, for annual consideration by the board. Although retailing is very much an industry of the present, in that conditions can change quite quickly and give rise to shifts in direction, the lead time for opening new retail outlets of any size is many years. The need for planning permission and possible compulsory acquisitions, with consequent public enquiries, is inevitable in the development of major shopping precincts, and it is often four or five years from the time negotiations start until the first customer crosses the threshold. In recent years consumer spending as a proportion of the gross domestic product has remained relatively stable. In 1971 it was 62 per cent and in 1980, 60.3 per cent. But the rise in personal savings from 5.1 per cent of GDP in 1971 to 10.9 per cent in 1980, during a period of high inflation, shows how careful retailers must be in assessing spending power.

Consideration must also be given to shifts in spending patterns over a period, as may be seen from the following table which analyses consumer spending in 1971 and in 1980 by major categories:

Table 2.1
Main analysis of consumer spending

	1971 %	1980 %
Food	20.2	17.6
Clothing & footwear	7.9	8.7
Household durables	4.0	5.6
Other goods	15.2	16.6
Drink & tobacco	10.9	11.2
Housing	14.5	14.0
Fuel & light	4.6	4.3
Cars & motorcycles	3.9	3.1
Other services	18.8	18.9
	100.0	100.0

Spending must be translated into a volume pattern, because so many of the retail industry's costs relate directly to this factor. For example, floor space, warehouse costs, staffing levels and transport capacity are all volume related. The DTI's figures for retail volume changes from 1971 to 1980 show the following:

Table 2.2
Volume changes in retail trades

	% volume change 1971-80
Food shops	−11.7
Non-food shops of which	+36.7
Clothing and footwear shops	+10.9
Durable goods	+50.6
Others	+21.1

20

Various categories of retailer have achieved very different rates of volume growth over the same period:

Table 2.3
Retail traders' volume growth

	% volume change 1971-80
Mail order	+54.9
Department stores	+12.5
Multiples	+32.2
Co-ops	+ 6.9
Independents	− 0.9

The above figures demonstrate some of the external factors which must be borne in mind when producing company forecasts. Many more statistics are available from government sources, trade associations and the City. Company forecasts, however, need to be much more sensitive, even intuitive, if they are to reflect the individual performance of various trading departments and to meet the demands of a board of directors.

The problems of adjusting indices based upon sterling figures are obvious, but difficult to overcome. The adoption of current cost accounting will go some way towards reflecting changing price levels, but in a retail business with a wide range of products, and where specifications or designs of products are constantly changing, the adjustments by way of government indices will be somewhat crude. Ideally, an internal index should be developed for each separate department, and the close involvement of buyers sought in its compilation, but I am not aware of any large retailing organisation which has achieved this.

The role of forecasting in a retail company

The retail trade is an incredibly complex business due to many outside influences, not least the attitude of the customer. To be successful the retailer must use a crystal ball several times a day, and balls of different magnification.

If the fashion buyer can anticipate the new season's colours (at least two seasons ahead), and the kind of material customers will want, can she also predict whether there will be a move back to dresses instead of separates, and what the weather will be like? Cold and wet summers demand different garments from hot, dry months. Then, if a cold snap has not arrived by November maybe the customers will make do with last winter's coats and buy new ones in the following spring.

A forecast of demand for all types of merchandise will precipitate conflicts for space. When one visualises the wide range of goods carried by department stores, one begins to understand the problems associated with forecasting — stock levels, footage, staffing, promotions and so on.

The most important is probably stock turn. If the stock level is out of line with sales:

(a)   the space devoted to various ranges will be out of balance resulting in lower sales where goods in demand are not adequately displayed

(b)   inadequate stocks mean lost sales

(c)   high stocks mean high markdowns and loss of margins

(d)   timorous ordering means low buying discounts

(e)   over optimistic ordering involves excessive handling, warehousing and interest charges.

However much flair the retailer has, he must depend upon good information covering past performance, so careful analysis of departmental, item, colour, or price point information is essential. The pattern of sales is also critical, adjusted for the changing holiday pattern — Easter is constantly moving!

The sales pattern must therefore be quantified and a carefully designed promotional calendar superimposed upon it. This will set out both the normal sales and other promotional events to stimulate demand and the advertising programme geared to buying patterns. Bridal outfits don't sell in midsummer — nor do fur coats.

The determination of stock turn in relation to the sales pattern is the key to calculating the extent of 'open-to-buy' — the sterling value of orders that may be placed by buyers — for each accounting period, normally four weeks; but buying management must be kept informed of new footage either through the refurbishment of existing outlets, or new stores or shop units which are coming on stream. The buyers will also have their say in determining the most appropriate time to open a new unit — if new autumn stock does not arrive until September it does not give a store a good start to fill it with sale residues in August.

So far I have outlined basic considerations in forecasting related to annual budgets. Before considering the construction of such forecasts in detail I must emphasise that every week some of the factors which influence such forecasts will change. Anticipation of the change in the factors affecting forecasts and the resulting action makes forecasting such an integral part of retail management.

Retailers like to know their daily sales. Half way through a week they will have a fair idea of the percentage increase they will achieve over the previous year and in relation to their forecast. As far as sales information is concerned, it is difficult to prevent retailers from using the previous year's figures for comparison, even though they have detailed forecasts, plans or budgets, for the current period. I, for one, would not wish to abandon either of the comparatives to current performance.

By Monday morning most retailers will know the 'flash sales' for the previous week, analysed departmentally. If the forecast has not been met in any areas, action can be instituted immediately, through sales promotional material, markdowns, advertising. But the impact of performance will be evaluated, not only in relation to current profitability, but also to the forecast profits. Similarly, the margin performance, which is a combination of buying efficiency and sales mix, will have been extrapolated so as to indicate the likely result for the period.

A more formal reappraisal of the previous forecast will be undertaken every four weeks when the management accounts are produced and presented to the board. A simple deduction of results to date from the new forecast for the year gives the board a clear indication whether the target for the remainder of the year is at all feasible. Most managements are reluctant to reduce their forecasts, hoping that any initial shortfall will be made good in the remainder of the year. The percentage performance of the remaining months in relation to the budget for that period, compared with achievements to date, will certainly catch out those reluctant heroes.

If the sales and margin estimates are realistic, regular preparation of new forecasts for the year will allow management to take effective action over costs to maintain profitability. Costs are easy to control and adjust provided sufficient warning is given. Staff can be reduced by natural wastage if sales trends are falling short of forecast, whereas sudden redundancies might be intolerable. Redecoration or replacement of plant or cars can be postponed provided contracts have not been placed. Yet it is often surprisingly difficult to ensure that sales management, or buying management, face realities soon enough.

Of course, emotion is strong in the retail field. Constant failure to achieve forecasts can lower morale and therefore turnover and profits, but the emotion of achievement and success wins sales. A retail outlet where morale is high will achieve better results than one where the forecast of achievement is low. You can see how tempting it is therefore to use the forecast as a means of boosting morale and how profitable such a course of action can be.

Construction of the profit forecast

In the interests of simplicity I propose to deal with four principal
constituents of the cost structure of a retail company — sales, margin,
wages and expenses — highlighting the important and difficult areas in
each category. In aggregate they determine *the most important factor
in retailing* — profit.

It can be well argued that cash flow is vital. With its fluctuations in
demand a profitable retail company can verge on collapse with inadequate cash flow, but low profitability can be tolerated for a considerable period provided the cash position is under control.

There may be occasions when the profit forecast is built up from the
bottom line — decide on the profit achievement required and cut
expenses in order to bring it about — on the basis that management will
naturally be cautious in reducing costs and will build into its cost
structure a safety or contingency margin, which will almost certainly be
spent anyway. Whichever way one approaches the problem, a reliable
sales forecast is needed.

(a) Sales

We first must decide whether:

- to generate a sales forecast from a build-up of individual assessments in each sales department from every retail unit,
- to derive the figures from an examination of trends within the
  buying function, or
- to determine a desired market share for a particular department or product.

The store assessment will take account of local competition, changes in
layout or position within the store, or changes in the square footage
allowed to the department. It may reflect new fixtures which improve
display, or new security arrangements which reduce shrinkage.

On the other hand the buyer is in a better position to judge the
strength of his particular market, and the products or new technology
which may have an impact upon his buying department. The introduction of skate boards necessitated new areas to be devoted to them —
the lack of good forecasts encouraged some manufacturers to build
factories to produce skate boards after the demand had melted away.
The buyer will also know the effect of changing commodity prices on
his own area, and the impact the resulting cost changes may have on
demand.

A pre-determined market share may be a necessary target if it

24

promotes a marked improvement in cost structure especially if, in order to be represented in a particular field or product group, contracts have had to be placed demanding new machinery or absorbing the output from whole factories.

In my view, the sales forecast should be built up in all three ways where applicable, and reconciled by senior management. An examination of the results from different points of view will often reveal weaknesses not otherwise apparent. The timid buyer will be exposed before he has the opportunity to buy inefficiently. Inadequate sales promotion or staffing will be evident if the sales side falls behind the growth potential envisaged by the buyer, or insufficient space and promotion has been allotted to take up the large contracts placed.

(b) Margin

Senior management must review the sales forecast continually in the light of the profit mix. Many traditional profit margins operate in the retail trade and the profit to turnover ratio shows wide variations. Achievement of total sales targets does not necessarily attain the profit goal. The margin mix demands careful analysis so as to generate sufficient sales effort on higher margin lines to maintain the income percentage.

Departments with different margins normally have identifiable cost differences. A low margin department must have a high stock turn, for the interest cost of holding stock is considerable. The cost of holding stock at the point of sale is much higher than holding it in a warehouse due to the inflation in high street rents and rates in recent years. A high margin department will normally be fashion orientated and demand a big markdown provision to clear stocks, particularly if the buyer's fashion acumen has slipped for once.

Accurate forecasts of the gross profit percentage can only be made if the 'commitment' and 'linked' margins are monitored continuously. When each order is placed, the cost and selling value is recorded and allocated to a commitment margin for the period or week when the stock is scheduled for delivery. In this way, buyers can be controlled and future pricing regulated. The commitment margin, however, is not used for stock valuation where such valuations are based upon counting stock at retail prices and reducing to cost by the cumulative margin. This latter margin is the 'linked' margin derived from comparing the cost and selling values of invoices in respect of delivered merchandise. While the commitment margin and linked margin on each individual product should be the same, the linked margin on a cumulative basis for each dissection of sales will reflect the sales mix as goods are received to replenish stocks at the point of sale.

With sophisticated computer systems, duplication of such an exercise can be avoided but even so it is valuable to compare the two separate monitors.

In the case of the commitment margin, management's attention is drawn immediately to selling prices long before items are ticketed. It is also a measure of the buyer's ability which can be used for the incentive award where targets are clearly set. The comparison between the commitment and linked margins will also highlight hidden costs such as freight and insurance on overseas purchases, or demurrage and packaging costs, which buyers sometimes neglect.

The record of the cumulative margin, or as it is sometimes known, the cumulative mark-up, is critical where stocks are valued by applying such a percentage to the retail value of stocks held in a sales unit to reduce them to cost. Nevertheless it is important that the cumulative margin does not become the primary goal of management; achieved margin (after necessary reductions in price or markdowns have been taken) is an essential indicator of profitability.

For this purpose, a record which requires constant attention is that of markups and markdowns. Even the best buyers require some markdown provisions to clear surplus stocks, because of the effect of circumstances outside their control, and these markdowns are normally made during the special sales periods. Nevertheless the sales organisation will always be alive to competitive pricing, and if a retailer suddenly meets price competition he may need to react swiftly. So the markdown budget will need to be allocated over the year and allowances given to each buyer. The effect of markdowns is reduced by markups, hated by customers and yet necessary at times. It is bad practice to markup goods on the sales floor in a way that is apparent to the customer but perfectly fair in the stockroom; it is essential to markup standard lines at the end of the sale. The forecast of the amount of the markups will normally correlate to the size of the stock holding.

(c) Wages

Wage costs are not difficult to forecast, provided they are derived from detailed establishment budgets, and the impact of part-time employees is carefully thought out. Economies can be made if the establishment budget is broken down to periods, and the full time equivalent numbers reflect the volume of sales to be achieved. It is difficult to engage or dispense with the services of full time personnel, and yet a retailer cannot afford to carry the same staff complement in February as in the January sales period. The flexibility must therefore arise from the use of part-time staff for peak periods of the year, and of the week or day.

Other costs associated with staff are more difficult to forecast. Insufficient analysis can certainly lead to funding pension costs at a higher rate than necessary and the development of special programmes of interrogating payroll records is essential for a proper analysis of pension information. Introducing an accounting standard which requires the split of pension contributions between the cost of pensions on current salaries and the cost of funding future increases would call for more accurate forecasts. In my view much of the pension cost at present charged in accounts is more properly a payment in advance of a liability which will accrue when salaries rise and should be charged against the profits of those years in which such increases occur.

Staff discount is another associated staff cost which can increase unexpectedly. Rules can ensure that only those staff who are entitled to purchase goods at a discount do so, but they seldom limit the amount so purchased for personal use, and staff recognise value for money in new stock even more quickly than customers. While an excess over budget on staff discount account may indicate an improvement in the style, quality and value of goods for sale, it upsets those responsible for profit forecasts.

(d) Expenses

Most expense forecasting is a routine affair, but interest does not come into this category. The forecast of interest costs depends upon a well established system of cash flow forecasting. This, in its turn, can be affected materially by stock movements and the length of credit taken. Inevitably there is a conflict between the buyer who is striving to improve his margin and often achieves that marginal increase by negotiating a rebate or cash discount, and the accountant who is seeking to take as much credit as possible (without the supplier noticing) in order to reduce his interest costs. The buyer is unlikely to be successful in negotiating ever increased rebates if the supplier can politely suggest that he pays his bills on time.

Careful planning of sales, purchases and stock movement is also critical to the forecast of VAT payments, a surprisingly large factor in present day cash flow forecasting. The mix of departments where zero rated merchandise is sold must also be reflected.

Validity of profit forecasts and external uses

Many retail companies make up their accounts to the end of their peak selling season, in most cases after the Christmas period and the January sales. The low stock levels at this time not only make stock counting easier, but also show the balance sheet in its most favourable light.

The obvious disadvantage of such a year end lies in the vulnerability of profit forecasts which depend to such an extent on the last eight weeks' trade. This is particularly true of department stores, less so with fashion retailers and to a smaller extent with food shops. The January sales also affect the markdown/markup situation and the stock shortage provision.

Recent years have also seen the threat of industrial unrest from major industries, such as power or transport, in January, and this can deter shoppers at a critical time. Thus, there would be a good case for a different year end, were it not for the resultant upheaval in investment appraisal.

While profit forecasts are essential for effective management control, their publication could lead to chaos. The forecast for management is a tool to enable changes to be made in the operations of the business, but disclosure of regular monthly adjustments in the figures would shake analysts' confidence in management. Non-accountants seem to think that because figures have been calculated and set down formally they are fact − accountants are not nearly so confident and use figures as a means to an end, to bring about change in working methods or in direction, so as to improve profitability or cash flow.

The problems associated with an annual profit forecast and its vulnerability to certain peak periods of trade are also applicable to interim statements. The purpose of an interim statement is to show investors the progress being made towards the year's results, although, most retailers will have earned only a minor proportion of the year's profit by that time. Any dealing in shares on the basis of a retailer's interim announcement could prove misguided unless great care had been taken to understand the pattern of that retailer's trade. The further imposition of demand for quarterly figures on the retailer would be even more misleading.

Within a retailing company, however, forecasts are the responsibility of every executive. You cannot ask a retailer about his past performance, for instance last week's trade, without following with a question about the rest of the month, or season, or year. His assessment of the future becomes his new forecast and upon that rely a host of decisions with regard to stock commitment, stock clearance, staffing levels, space requirements and pricing policy.

Retailing is one of the most dynamic industries where a professional approach to forecasting is imperative.

3 Forecasting in a nationalised industry

R M Grainger, Chief Planning Accountant, National Coal Board

Introduction

Like most business enterprises the National Coal Board has responsibility for managing existing production facilities and for providing new capacity so that market requirements can continue to be satisfied. Coal mining is an extractive industry where production capacity is continually being worked out and replacement capacity is needed. By the nature of the business both planning and mine development are fundamental to the continuity of coal production and the satisfaction of energy demands. Physical mining developments have lengthy leadtimes requiring months or even years to complete and the right investment decisions are crucial. Colliery underground layouts are relatively inflexible, mine roadways (tunnels), transportation and communications providing little scope for rapid or short term changes of operating policy. In view of the practical limitations, planning decisions must take into account the likely future economic trends, opportunities for new technology, changes in energy requirements and general business prospects both inside and outside the mining industry.

Being a nationalised industry means there are clear legal obligations (Nationalisation Act of 1947 etc.,) requiring that the business be operated in a manner which satisfies the coal requirements of the country, ensures that the industry is viable after charging interest and that borrowings are contained within limits set from time to time by the government. Additional government objectives (White Papers) include the achievement of minimum required rates of return on all investment and that internal sources, principally profit and depreciation, move towards financing at least 50 per cent of capital investments. External borrowing requirements are also subjected to government limitations through the Public Expenditure Survey and the Financial Statement and Budget report.

Managing a business is largely a matter of decision taking and prospects for taking the right decisions are improved when regard is shown for all the options and their likely implications. Although the future cannot be foretold it can be predicted, on various assumptions. Well prepared business forecasts can aid management to identify opportunities and examine prospects for alternative decisions. The needs for forecasts are extensive but to be of value they must be relevant, feasible, flexible, comprehensive, manageable and yet understandable to the user. The structure and reliability of forecasts are very important when they form the basis for taking decisions.

The extent of detail in a forecast depends on its purpose and the timespan covered. Short timespans generally allow and require more detail than do longer term forecasts and such patterns generally apply within the National Coal Board.

The National Coal Board

The Coal Board has been in existence since 1947 and is responsible for some 99 per cent of all coal mined in the United Kingdom. It is the largest coal producer in the European Economic Community and currently produces around 123 million tonnes per annum. As well as coalmining it also operates coke ovens, manufactured fuel plants, by-product plants and other supporting activities.

The business is organised by profit centres, the main groups consisting of 12 Mining Areas, an Opencast Executive and 2 non-mining companies (Coal Products Ltd. and Ancillaries Ltd.). There are some 220 operating collieries employing 230 000 men with a further 40 000 men employed providing services and also 25 000 non-industrial staff. Each Area has its own directorate responsible for between 10 and 30 collieries which together produce an average of 9 million tonnes per annum with a turnover in excess of £300 million.

Considerable coal reserves still to be mined can last 300 years at present extraction rates. The main types of coal produced are general purpose steam coal, coking coal and low volatile anthracite. Methods of mining coal have changed considerably since nationalisation with old manual operations now replaced by fully mechanised coal getting machines with self-advancing hydraulic powered roof supports. A typical longwall coal face will be 200 yards long and 6 feet high with 200 powered roof supports each capable of supporting loads up to 400 tonnes. The investment required to equip such a coal face will be between £2 million and £3 million.

Local colliery management is responsible for day to day operations including operational development planning. Pay rates and selling prices are controlled and settled at the centre on a national basis. Operational management accountability is exercised through action programmes, annual budgets and regular projections of operating prospects. Budgets for all sections and levels of business management activity are framed to cover the 12 month NCB accounting year ending with March. Major profit centre activities, centrally controlled non-operational expenditure and capital investment budgets all get board approval while lesser operational profit centre and departmental budgets are approved by the level of management which has the delegated authority and is held accountable. Meetings also take place with officials of the Department of Energy and the Secretary of State.

Most sales of coal are to United Kingdom customers but there are some exports. The biggest consumers of British coal are the electricity generating authorities, with their annual consumption of some 85 million tonnes. The next major consumer is the steel industry but demand has declined recently because of the sharp recession in that sector. The other main users are general industry, local authorities and the domestic market. Competition in the energy field has been mainly from oil but OPEC oil price rises have dramatically changed the position and competition is now mainly from gas in the domestic market and from imported coal in the electricity and coking markets. Nuclear power is slowly developing as an alternative source of energy to help satisfy the expected growth in demand.

Accounting and information services are provided through an extensive computer network, including on-line printers and VDU's, with inter activity processing. An integrated accounting system gives financial and management accounting information from the same source data and provides comparisons as appropriate for local management, middle management and the Board. Management accounts are produced monthly for each profit centre together with budget and previous year comparisons.

Following a period of low investment during the 1960's the Middle East oil crisis of 1974 triggered off a major new investment programme in the British coal mining industry. Two investment programmes were framed by the Board — 'Plan for Coal' and 'Plan 2000' — both with the the aim of restructuring and modernising capacity and creating a new industry with expanded output and higher productivity. The Department of Energy requires frequent monitoring and control of investment with regular reporting against phased budget and follow up discussions. The current level of investment in the industry is in excess of £700 million per annum and the biggest single project is the new Selby coalfield which at current prices is expected to cost around £950 million.

Range of forecast routines

There are three basic types of forecasts in use which can be summarised as:

Strategic   —   long term — 5 years and beyond
            —   medium term — 1 to 5 years
Tactical   —   short term — up to 1 year

Forecasts are prepared for all the main business functions such as production levels, sales patterns, sales income, changes in stocks of products, manpower requirements, earnings and related costs, consumption of stores, use of services, stocks of stores, non-operational expenditure, research and development, depreciation, interest charges, investment expenditure and cash flow movements. It is very important that there should be a proper correlation between internal forecasts and external economic indicators.

Major mining investment takes time to bring into production with some 'greenfield' projects requiring years to construct. Many factors which must be considered at the planning stage include the likely demand for the product, market preferences, the alternative fuels likely to be available, whether technological developments will alter demand patterns and if so, when, whether the required labour will be available when needed, what changes might be expected in union attitudes and whether conservation and environmental pressures will affect the business. Internal matters to consider include the situation of coal reserves, their qualities, whether they are workable, the best methods of extraction, the investment cost, when production can be expected to start and whether an acceptable return can be achieved from the investment. Other vital issues which have to be resolved are approval to explore, approval to establish new workings and the provision of infrastructure necessary to support a modern coalmine.

Long term strategic plans and forecasts covering five years and beyond are updated at least every two years but are structured to accommodate the probability that some future circumstances will be anticipated incorrectly. Considerable importance is attached to the robustness of long term forecasts. Because of the many future uncertainties, all key basic assumptions are varied over a range of possibilities until they affect the central plans or forecasts significantly. The identified range of variability for each basic assumption then enables a view to be taken on the strengths and vulnerabilities of the long term forecasts.

Medium term strategy covers the period from one to five years ahead and deals with investment projects, revenue profit and loss results, cash flow, financing requirements and external financing needs. Many of the investment projects will have received Board approval, particularly those scheduled for the earlier years of the period, but others will be included on the basis of outline approval only. Medium term planning is based on a five year rolling programme with the first year dropping out at each annual review and a new fifth year added.

Short term tactical forecasts and plans are concerned with operating circumstances during the current and following year. These forecasts include capital and revenue finances, price and wage policy, annual budgets, annual projections of prospects, cash flow movements and borrowing requirements. They are generally prepared at local management level and are fairly formalised procedures with review dates linked to regular accountability timetables. In addition to regular short term forecasts it is often necessary to provide *ad hoc* forecasts for specific situations such as wage and price negotiations and decisions. Other forecasts are used in project appraisal and for board policy issues.

Timetable

Long term strategy forecasts deal with broad market and investment opportunities. Accordingly, they are not subject to regular time-tables for preparation or review. Revisions are usually dictated by significant changes in factors which determine assumptions.

Medium term forecasts form part of a regular investment and financial planning review procedure. As a nationalised industry, the Coal Board is required to comply with the government's public sector investment reviews which take place annually and influence internal timetables. The annual cycle begins in early summer when local managements review physical plans for each activity together with alternative plans, where these exist. The views that emerge are examined and approved by Area management before being transmitted to headquarters where all options are considered and selections are made. The operational aspects of medium term forecasts are agreed before the end of November when work is completed on the full financial implications. Evaluations are made in terms of revenue expectations, capital spendings and financing requirements as well as manpower recruitment and training needs. The whole business forecast summary for the five year period is submitted to the Board by early December. It is then forwarded to the Secretary of State for Energy by the end of December. Further discussions follow between the parties before a five year strategy is accepted.

Short term forecasts relate to the current and following year and are part of the budget planning cycle. The annual cycle begins in the autumn when local managements have completed their contribution to medium term planning. The first year of the medium term plan provides a basis for the next year's budget. Each operational activity also has an action programme which deals with the eighteen months ahead and forms part of the detailed physical planning for that activity. Action programmes are updated and extended every three months and along with the medium term plans and headquarters policy guidance they enable a budget estimate to be produced.

The NCB accounting year runs to the end of March on a 4:4:5 week accounting period basis. Revenue budget estimates, evaluated at current year prices, are transmitted to headquarters by early January. They are then appraised prior to budget review meetings which take place during early February between Board representatives and Area management. Subject to changes agreed at these meetings and to subsequent board approval the activities must then convert their budget estimate to outturn price levels in accordance with specified inflation guidance. Budget estimates at outturn price levels reach headquarters by late March and are ratified by the Board in early April. As the year progresses, results are monitored and compared with phased budgets for all profit and cost centres through to a national comparison. At the end of each quarter activities are required to submit projections of prospects for the current year based on results achieved to date and estimated results for the remainder of the year. These projections are used at quarterly accountability meetings and for reports to the Board.

The timetable of events relating to cyclic forecasts can be summarised as follows:

July	— local review of medium term plans and investment programme commences.
mid-Sept	— medium term plans and investment requirement details sent to headquarters.
end-Oct	— headquarters complete scrutiny of medium term plans and seeks board approval of the investment programme.
early-Nov	— preliminary work starts locally on next year's budget estimates.
early-Nov	— financial evaluation of medium term plans completed.
early-Dec	— central policy guidance issued to all activities for next year's budget estimates.
early-Dec	— medium term investment forecasts agreed with unions and submitted to the Secretary of State for Energy.
mid-Jan	— budget estimates at current prices sent to headquarters.

Feb	— budget estimate review meetings take place between Area and Board representatives.
end-Feb	— activities make agreed amendments to budget estimates.
mid-March	— budget estimates converted to outturn prices and to headquarters.
early-April	— budgets approved by the Board.
end-June	— colliery action programmes updated and quarterly projections of annual prospects produced for each main profit activity.
end-Sept	— —ditto—
end-Dec	— —ditto—

Methods of preparation

The cornerstone of colliery budgets is the action programme. This sets out planned actions and operations necessary to ensure that the available resources are deployed effectively, and that the required production levels can be attained. Colliery action programmes are phased to weeks and detail the coalfaces to be available, the times when they can be expected to work, the required manning levels, the equipment to be used and the output performances expected. They also cover a programme of supporting mine development work which will be needed to ensure that replacement capacity is available when required.

Preparation of annual revenue budget estimates begins early in November with local management considering the physical aspects of the activity for the next budget year. This done, the financial evaluations can be completed by including sales estimates, selling price levels, earnings rates, manpower recruitment and wastage patterns, service departments and non-operational expenditure. Specialist contributions are provided by the various functional departments through a budgeting team which has responsibility for ensuring that all contributions are compatible. Then, completed budget estimates are examined for feasibility by Area managements to see if they should form part of the Area budget estimate. Even though individual colliery estimates may appear realistic they are unlikely to produce an acceptable aggregate for the whole Area. The likelihood that unforeseeable difficulties will arise at some collieries means that a realistic Area output estimate is usually less than the aggregate of individual collieries. This problem is normally resolved by introducing an Area output relaxation which avoids arbitrary amendments to individual colliery budget estimates and maintains colliery budgets at the levels agreed by local management.

At this stage financial budget estimates are revised in terms of current year prices and reconciled with an up-to-date projection of results for the current year so enabling differences to be identified in 'real' terms.

Local and Area management consider budget estimates jointly and endeavour to achieve a balance with area objectives before sending estimates to headquarters. This position is reached by mid-January when budget estimates are examined and appraised at headquarters prior to budget meetings held early in February. In addition to Area budget meetings, similar meetings are held with officials of the Opencast Executive and the two non-mining companies, again with a view to making sure that budget estimates are realistic and fulfil the board's key objectives. A consolidated summary of budget estimates at current year prices together with suitable comparisons and headquarters' own assessment of the effect of inflationary factors is considered by the board and, if appropriate, is then approved.

Subsequently the Board's views are notified to Area management together with guidance on the treatment of inflation for the budget year. Budget amendments accepted at the meetings are calculated at current price levels, then inflation provisions are added. New budget estimates at outturn prices are sent to headquarters by mid-March, again in the form of a reconciliation which analyses 'real' and inflationary changes since the previous submission. Provided these revised estimates satisfy national objectives, Board approval is sought early in April. After approval all activities are advised that budgets can be used for control purposes.

During the course of the year each activity endeavours to operate according to phased budget and progress is fully monitored both monthly and quarterly. An up-to-date projection of results expected for the year forms an essential feature of quarterly monitoring. Comparisons are made with budget and explanations are sought for important deviations, together with details of actions being taken to return to the budget course, where this is desirable. Budgets are seldom revised during the year, although there have been exceptions when a major policy change has substantially affected prospects for the majority of activities. The effects of changed key physical factors on operating costs are monitored and controlled through a system of flexible budget costs.

Preparation of five year estimates (medium term development forecasts) starts with mine development and investment plans for each colliery. These plans are agreed by late October and are evaluated in terms of revenue, capital spending and cash flow forecasts. Evaluations are made at constant prices over the full five year period using assumed outturn price levels for the first year, which also happens to be the next budget year. First evaluations rarely produce satisfactory estimates and changes are often required before the desired national objectives are met. Even so, it is not always possible to achieve financial objectives without amending selling prices though such changes are usually a last consideration. This routine helps to identify options which will need to be explored further before the next wage and price reviews. When acceptable national forecasts have been produced at constant prices, these must be converted to outturn prices for each year to provide estimates for the government's Financial Statement and Budget report.

Investment estimates are normally produced at Area level where most project applications originate. They are prepared at current year prices considering each situation with and without the proposed project and comparisons are made with the previous year's actual performance, suitably revalued to current year price levels. Existing revenue budget information is also used to check that project estimates are realistic. Alternatives are examined and project applications are subjected to discounted cash flow rate testing. Control of capital spending is not without difficulties such as slippage, technical change, planning delays and cost inflation, all of which tend to affect revenue results and external financing requirements.

Most forecasts are produced either at local or Area levels, but experience has shown a need for independent national forecasts produced at headquarters. These provide cross checks for the aggregate of individual activity forecasts. Producing national forecasts on an independent basis is not difficult, because the larger the sample involved, the more likely it will be to conform to average expectations and experience. These forecasts embrace working capital requirements and interest charges but tend to be confined to short term periods and annual projections.

Most of the administrative workload is involved with short term forecasting with its many individual activities and considerable detail. Computer budget systems are used to handle routine processing and the production of budget statements.

Frequency of updates

Each forecast pictures the likely situation under a given set of circumstances. Inevitably, the passage of time will modify or revise previous assumptions due to changed circumstances inside or outside the business. The extent to which updates are carried out will depend on the nature of the forecasts.

Longer term forecasts can usually accommodate quite wide variations around the basic assumptions. Though the Board does not set

a timetable for reviewing these forecasts there is a general understanding that they will be examined at least every two years.

Medium term forecasts are more specific and there is an annual
programme of review and updates except on the rare occasions when
earlier reviews are dictated by a special re-examination of policy.

Generally the Board does not revise or update annual budgets but
there have been occasions when changes have had to be made. Usually
these have been precipitated by policy changes affecting all or most
activities. The effect of operating changes is quantified through the
procedure for projecting annual results and this is a useful management
discipline because it ensures regular re-examination of the future for
their part of the business and comparison with targets. Local management commonly prepares projections more frequently than every
quarter, particularly as the year advances.

Special policy forecasts can be required at short notice and at
irregular intervals. They are normally produced centrally, using a
combination of headquarters' knowledge of circumstances and routine
forecast information which is readily available. Routine forecasts and
projections produced at headquarters are updated at the same time as
Area equivalents although additional requests can be made, particularly
towards the end of the fiscal year.

Use made of forecasts

Long and medium term forecasts relate to the investment and general
business framework necessary for a corporate strategy. They are of
major importance to the Board when considering policies for market
share, production levels, resources to be employed and financing
arrangements. For a nationalised industry they also form a basis for
reviewing strategy with government departments where particular
emphasis is placed on investment and funding requirements.

Medium term forecasts also involve area management and decide
strategy for each of the major operating activities over the next five
years. They can be used to communicate central policy to lower business formations and, in reverse, to check that central policy is being
followed. The involvement of operational management in preparation
work ensures that they understand the policy implications, can see how
their own part fits into the whole and know why they are required to
operate in a particular way. Preparation of forecasts also allows management to consider a range of alternative options and examine the 'what
if' possibilities.

Annual budgets and projections are concerned with operating the
sections of the business and are management tools for control and

accountability. They give detailed specifications of the resources to be deployed and the performances that are expected.

Due to the nature of the business and its national structure, the Board operates centralised banking and national marketing arrangements. This means Area and local management are not directly concerned with financing though they produce budgets, forecasts and monthly management accounts on an operating profit and loss account basis and control investment expenditure within capital budgets. By this means they are kept fully aware of the profitability of their activities and of the need for an adequate flow of funds.

Many situations require separate forecasts, some relating to national policy issues and others concerned with investment opportunities. National policy forecasts are used for central decision taking and can involve wage negotiations, price policy, market policy, manpower needs, research and development expenditure, mining technology and capital investment programmes. Separate investment project forecasts are part of the authorisation procedure and are considered by authorisation committees. In the operations field many technical forecasts are used by engineers of all disciplines and most involve computer models. Applications include geological surveys, mineral clearance systems, air ventilation flows, optimum product preparation levels, future plant and equipment needs and stores stock holding levels. There are many more applications too numerous to mention but which are well established as essential aids to operational management.

Reliability of forecasts

Opinion on the reliability of forecasts tends to be subjective and can be conditioned by the nature and purpose of forecasts. To make a reasoned judgement it is necessary to consider why actual performance differs from forecast and to pay particular attention to the validity of the basic assumptions and parameters. The feedback from such examinations is most useful in helping to improve reliability of new forecasting work. It would seem obvious that the nearer the event the more reliable the forecast should be, and annual projections and budgets do tend to be more reliable than medium and long term forecasts. However, in practice, dealing with short term detail can involve many complications which do not arise with longer term broad assessments.

Correct analyses and research into the forecast subject will invariably reveal that some aspects are more predictable than others because they either follow a fairly regular pattern or correlate to some other factors.

In the mining industry it is fairly simple to establish labour cost estimates once the constituent elements of manpower, shifts per man, productivity levels, base earnings rates and incentive payments have been agreed. Related employment costs also flow from the same base data together with other items which make up labour related expenses. On the other hand patterns of production, the use of some types of equipment and consumable stores usage are less regular and more difficult to forecast.

Reliability is also a factor of sample size with Area and national forecasts tending to be more reliable than those for individual activities. The uncertainties of mining operations can sometimes cause major fluctuations at individual collieries, but these may be relatively insignificant within Area and national totals. Such situations are well recognised and contingency relaxations are commonly included between individual coal faces and colliery totals and between individual colliery totals and Area totals.

Problems can arise from the personalities of people responsible for preparing forecasts. Many forecasts originate at local management level and with some 220 colliery managers plus many times that number of engineers, marketeers, employment personnel, accountants and others involved there is a fair risk of personal bias. Some disciplines tend to be natural optimists (mining engineers) while others are more pessimistic (finance people) and in their own ways they either seek to impress their superiors or cover themselves against future accountability. This problem applies particularly to short term budgets and forecasts which involve many people of widely differing interests. To combat the risks of bias it is necessary to check past records of personal performance, compare forecast performances, complete statistical analyses and vet by higher management. The aim with both short term budgeting and forecasting is to ensure realisable targets. From a budget view point the chances of lower management taking budgetary control seriously are greater if budgets are not set beyond their reach or are not achieved too easily. Short term forecasts are intended to assist higher management to control the business and therefore need to be realistic and reliable. In both cases attainment in the very short term and maintenance over the full timescale are vital objectives.

Provisions for inflation present particular problems and it is important to control these from the centre. Nearly all selling prices and wage/salary pay rates follow national agreements and are usually settled for about twelve months ahead. Mining is still quite a labour intensive industry with employee and related expenses responsible for some 60 per cent of all operating costs. Bought-in inflation affects goods and services which embrace some 25 per cent of costs and as the mix of the Board's buy is unique, it has long been the practice to monitor price movements and produce internal indices of purchase price changes. These indices form the basis for fairly reliable bought in inflation forecasts up to eighteen months ahead.

Initially medium and long term forecasts are prepared at constant price levels so as to establish the 'real' movements and ignore the effects of inflation. Subsequently, however, it is necessary to convert to assumed outturn prices. By this method, finances in each year are expressed at different value levels in accordance with assumptions made about future movements in product prices, labour pay rates, bought in goods and services, price inflation and interest rates. These conversions can create problems, especially when government (Treasury) methods impose an across-the-board effect of inflation whereas some cost items are not affected in the same manner as others, for example, historical depreciation and funded interest payments. Considerable importance is attached to reconciling these different approaches, otherwise the external financing limits might be set incorrectly.

Budget preparation can be used at all levels for 'political' purposes: to persuade management (or government) to take a particular course of action, for example, to obtain finance for projects, to extend areas of responsibility, or to impress management of efficiency or ability. Therefore the reliability of budgets must be considered with these possibilities in mind. Conversely, budget officers may accept budgets imposed on them (sometimes for personal reasons such as individual weakness of character or cynicism) which are impossible to achieve and are therefore totally unreliable.

Forecasting problems

External influences play an important part in the future of modern businesses such as coal mining. Apart from coal itself men, money, machines and markets are the main constituents of the industry and they are all susceptible to social, political and economic change. It is therefore essential to maintain a close watch on all potential external influences and to anticipate the likely impact on prospects. Changes are inevitable and as the pace of change quickens more frequent updates of forecasts are demanded. The reasons for such pressures are understandable but there are dangers in overdoing the number of updates as these can confuse and destroy management's confidence in forecasts as a basis for control and accountability. At all times realism and relevance are essential but so is a balance between continuity and revision.

When budget and forecast preparation is devolved to local management it is important to ensure that forecasts are compatible before they are aggregated. In this respect clear basic guidance is essential and procedures need to be well structured, with inbuilt checking routines where possible, so as to limit the areas of personal judgement.

Care must be exercised in the use of forecast information. The needs of control and accountability are quite different to those required for policy and investment decisions. Forecasts must not be allowed to mislead a user at any level in the organisation.

Worthwhile business forecasts draw on information and ideas from all relevant management functions. A balanced contribution must be obtained from each functional department through a central co-ordinating body which ensures that all requirements are covered. In practice, the right co-operation can be difficult to obtain, but a large organisation can improve matters by identifying a clear planning responsibility within each main functional department which provides a link with the central planning group.

Conclusion

Few businesses today can prosper without considering the future and its likely impact. The complexities of our modern world serve to increase the emphasis on future-orientated information covering all key aspects of a business. Forecast information provides a valuable management aid to the decision taking process by narrowing or even eliminating some of the future uncertainties. Such information can also test the sensitivity of different courses of action and quantify the effects of taking particular decisions.

Forecasts are used throughout the National Coal Board to help management at all levels and to provide estimates to government in the form of Medium Term Development plans, the Financial Statement and Budget report, the Public Expenditure Survey and so on. They cover all aspects of the business including technical applications, revenue performance, capital investment, cash flow and external borrowing requirements.

Medium term forecasts play an important role in planning for future investment in industry within the framework of an overall corporate strategy. Short term forecasts and budgets are widely used to direct central policy into the various operations of the business. This is achieved through objectives for separate activities which set operating patterns, availability of resources and required performance levels. The short term forecasts also provide a basis for operational control and management accountability. Other applications include option forecasts which can involve Board policy and very many technical applications are used by engineers of all persuasions, marketeers, purchasers, manpower recruiters, research and development staff.

To be of value budgets and forecasts must be soundly based with full co-operation of all the various functional interests and made as realistic as possible. They must be produced with integrity and must not mislead or confuse.

Budgets and plans provide models which tend to concentrate on one future view owing to the sheer clerical effort involved in working out alternative scenarios. Computerised models have the capabilities to try out different assumptions, to enable 'what if' questions to be examined and to test the sensitivity of the various factors. Modern computer technology is helping models to become more interactive and useful to strategists. Clearly, even greater capabilities will be built into forecasting models as technology and experience advances, so permitting keener insights into the factors which influence business performance. It may not be possible to foretell the future, but well constructed forecasts expose possibilities and narrow uncertainties.

(The views expressed in this chapter are those of the author and do not necessarily represent the views of the National Coal Board.)

4 Forecasting in the construction industry

H Norris, former Finance Director, George Wimpey Limited

The special characteristics of the construction industry in relation to
forecasting vary from those which contribute to a firm view (such as
the length of the order book and of advance work programming) and
the converse (weather, accidents, political upheavals, and so on).
Another element of vulnerability is that profits are a thin proportion of
turnover, and thus, being highly geared in a special sense, are more
liable to sizeable fluctuation. The relative number of projects is important as a swings and roundabouts factor, a firm with one or two
dominant projects being particularly susceptible to forecasting errors.

Management/financial accounting distinction

In construction, we must distinguish management accounting from
financial accounting to a much greater extent than in other spheres. I
will deal largely with the former, but a few words on the latter are
important — particularly with reference to the chapters on publication
in part 2. Despite SSAP9, considerable disparity persists between the
contract accounting procedures of different companies, although the
need for a partially-defined policy for any individual company does
exist, and exerts substantial discipline in terms of consistency if not in
logic. The second 'S' stands for Standard, but in no way does SSAP9
merit the word.

For management use, however, a much more immediate measure of
effectiveness of operations is needed, without the constraint of the
prudence required when reporting distributable profits. In general, each
month's work is valued by reference to the unit prices in the original
bid. These might be the contract rates, where a measured work contract
exists, or the in-house rates for various elements of the job where a
lump sum price contract is concerned; that is, the rates used for various
elements in the build-up of the fixed price bid. Since a programme of
work is designed for each job, the monthly amounts of estimated
revenue and estimated cost are fairly readily available. The schedule

would extend to the end of the job, which might be a matter of years ahead. The programme must be in very great detail with the periods of employment of the various sub-trades (bricklayers, carpenters, etc.,), with the planned employment of sub-contractors, delivery of materials (nearly all purchased specifically for each contract), hiring of plant and so on. Despite publicity on individual delays of well-known projects, these plans are generally close to experience and the translation into financial terms for each specific job is therefore generally fairly accurate.

The first estimates of aggregate results, therefore, are based on existing contracts and the major element of uncertainty within a year is the introduction of new bookings. In any given year ahead, forecasting for a company engaged on sizeable jobs will only involve a small margin of estimation of new work — say up to 25 per cent — so that the margin of error in gross revenue projection, ignoring complicating external factors, is not large. This, however, is not to say that the margin in profit prediction is quite so firm!

Long term contract work/short term

The foregoing comments relate to longer term contracts. Of course, many shorter term jobs exist, which involve greater uncertainty in annual turnover estimation. These include private house sales, repair work, and road surfacing, for all of which there is a different degree of estimation. However, in general, a reasonably accurate estimate of company profit a year ahead is achievable, and an estimate for the following year is worth attempting. Apart from exceptional circumstances, these figures would perhaps be more reliable than similar estimates for other types of activity. For management use, such figures are invaluable, but the impact of many uncertain factors remains as a contingency. The bad weather of early 1979 had a great impact on work programmes in the UK. The problems in Iran affected a number of companies. A spread of work — in type, and geographically — is a safeguard against a punitive impact. As mentioned, the number of large projects is significant and a large company with well diversified contracts has an advantage in terms of a swings and roundabouts factor.

Budget procedure

A programme for preparing budgets of revenue, profits and cash for the following year is normally compiled by the commercial/quantity surveying personnel and accounting staffs in the tenth and eleventh months of the current financial period so that a forecast of comprehensive figures for the year ahead can be presented shortly before its commencement. Monitoring is normally on a monthly basis, though re-assessment of the year's budgets may be much less frequent. A marked variation against budget in any month may prompt an unscheduled re-assessment, but otherwise such re-calculation may not be undertaken more than two or three times in the year.

Preferably, in the first half of the year, the succeeding year should be assessed to some degree. Some companies operate on a moving annual total basis, but seldom more than quarterly or even half-yearly. One element of re-calculation arises where a contract runs into a loss situation. Management accounts as such may show simply the month by month valuation and accruing losses, but an assessment of loss to complete is certainly needed, first as additional essential management information, and secondly, at the year-end, for full provision in the financial accounts. This aspect emphasises the differing approach to management and financial figures in long term contract accounting.

The assessment of current results involves a physical assessment of monthly progress and a valuation of this by reference to bill rates, i.e., the contract price make-up. In this country this procedure is carried out by quantity surveyors, and is frequently part of the procedure of claim against the client for payment. However, where such interim payments are not on a measured basis, for example, on a staged or fixed instalment schedule, then it is still a necessary procedure. Some companies carry out a cost-to-complete exercise every month, but these are in the minority, and most concerns calculate this figure only for jobs which have run into a loss position.

In budgeting contract work there is no substitute for calculation job by job. Every company will have a miscellany of jobs in commercial terms, notably as to price escalation coverage. The rise in the rate of inflation produced a tendency to have escalation clauses, thereby, to that degree, paradoxically reducing escalation risks below the level existing when inflation rates were lower. But there are always some fixed price contracts, and here the incidence of the date of wage negotiations (probably in July) is significant. Certain building materials have been even more erratic in price than the generality of industrial raw materials — timber and bitumen being notable examples in recent years.

External influences

Work overseas can, in some, though not all, countries involve greater uncertainties than in the UK. Rising nationalism, coupled with arbitrary acts by foreign governments, has taken its toll of many international construction companies. In the UK, the impact of governmental decision is extremely important to the industry which for years has complained of being used as a regulator, by falling first victim to a Stop Go policy. This has, indeed, been true on many occasions. Normally, the effect is greater in the medium (or perhaps longer) term than in an existing year. Projects take a long time to gestate before a contract award is made, but there have been occasions of cancellation at a very advanced bid stage. The converse, a great unexpected burst of new government work, never arises!

In housing, the decline of local authority work has been precisely measurable within an annual time span. For private development — houses for sale — the forecasting problems are greater. General confidence, inflation, building society money availability — are all variables of consequence. Again, size is a boon. A company planning for many thousands of house sales spread over the country is better placed for accurate estimation than one with possibilities of 3-500 exclusively in the North-East — or the West Country. Also, 2 000 at £20 000 is more likely to prove a correct forecast than 800 at £50 000. With the larger companies, an error margin in numbers of more than 10 per cent would be unusual, though a larger factor would apply to the total profit margin.

Manufacturing/construction contrasts

Perhaps it is worth noting a few points on which construction work involves fewer problems, than, say, manufacturing work — or even no problems!

The overhead allocation problem is almost non-existent as nearly everything is treated as a direct job cost, including site office personnel. General overheads are a smaller percentage, and, indeed, may well not be charged to contracts at all.

Very little speculative work exists, everything being expended for specific jobs — there are hardly any general stores. Private house development and land are obvious exceptions, not affecting all construction companies. In general, therefore, valuation is clearly tied to known contract prices rather than possible sale prospects.

As a broad generalisation, I feel that estimates for a year ahead should normally be within 10 per cent of actual — a fairly close correlation, I suggest — except in an occasional special situation of an adverse event — political or otherwise. Consciousness of the risks of special events tends to produce a degree of caution in operators' estimates giving rise generally, though not invariably, to a modest surplus variance.

Financial accounts — SSAP9

Much of these observations relates to the management accounts. Reverting to the differential of the financial accounts, rather different factors are involved. The profit recorded in these accounts is essentially related to work at a relatively late stage in execution. When financial accounts were prepared on a closed contract basis, the main problem was to assess which jobs would be completed within the year. The profit on each of these was normally fairly accurately known at the beginning of the year. The incidence of factors such as wage awards and price inflation was therefore of less consequence. For uncompleted work (subject to the procedure for dealing with loss-making contracts) the incidence of these various factors did not affect the profit and loss account. The inclusion of profit on well-advanced jobs (SSAP9) has modified this situation somewhat, but it is still legitimate to say that the forecasting of financial accounts profit is marginally safer than that of management profit.

Trend significance

Perhaps it is not too much of a digression, in view of the analyst's approach to the subject, to consider the relative significance of profit figures — actual or forecast — in relation to trends. Even with the inclusion of some profit on work on hand and even with full provision for losses to completion, the published accounts of contractors are less valid as underlying trend indicators than, say, the accounts of retail traders. The internal management accounts in construction, plus knowledge of the size of the order book and the bid margins secured, are of more immediate significance to the board than the results in the financial accounts, important though these may be.

A fishmonger, or a restaurant chain, has the trend expressed in simple cash terms — day by day, in fact. For a construction company, even a year's figure may not give a reliable indication and, indeed, many chairmen have said as much. I would regard the division of information available to management and that available to shareholders as inevitable and proper. The former involves a good deal of estimation — and conceivably even intuition — and only on the exceptional occasions of capital raising or amalgamations can management be expected to bare its soul. But perhaps other contributors will prove to have different views.

I close with an expression of sympathy for the external financial analyst hopeful of achieving accurate profit forecasts. The task of doing so without inside job-by-job knowledge is a difficult one!

5 Forecasting in a service industry

P J Hughes, Finance Director, C E Heath & Co. (Insurance Broking)
Limited

Insurance broking: Introduction

As insurance brokers we represent the interests of our clients in obtaining for them the best insurance cover available at the most
favourable rate. In law and practice the broker is the agent of the
insured and is therefore independent of any insurer, though he is
remunerated by the insurers who pay him a percentage commission of
the premium written. In addition to placing business with underwriters,
the broker also represents his client in agreeing claims with underwriters
and arranging the collection and payment of those claims to the
assured.

In the United Kingdom, there are about a dozen publicly quoted
insurance brokers, together with approximately 300 other Lloyd's
brokers, and 9 000 non-Lloyd's brokers. In common with many of the
other major brokers, C. E. Heath manages a number of Lloyd's syndicates and has interests in both underwriting agencies and insurance
companies in certain parts of the world. However, insurance broking
produces the most significant part of the group's income and it is therefore the broking side of our business upon which I wish to concentrate.
The expertise which has developed over the years within the major
insurance brokers permits almost any type of risk to be insured at a
competitive rate. By virtue of its historical development, London is still
the most important centre of the insurance world, with its ready access
to Lloyd's, to the UK tariff companies and to the global insurance
markets.

Our insurance broking company operates world wide in all classes of
insurance, placing risks both directly with insurers and also through a
network of broker correspondents. We deal in both insurance and
reinsurance and although the procedures are substantially the same, the
responsibilities differ. Where direct insurance is concerned, our client is
the insured, who is often represented by an intermediary broker and it
is our responsibility to advise on the type of cover best suited to our

client's requirements, to obtain the best possible terms, and to offer technical assistance.

Reinsurance comes in when an insured company which has already underwritten a risk wishes to reduce its liability by reinsuring part of the risk. In such cases our main responsibility is to find an acceptable market and often we have little or no say in the premium to be charged. Besides reinsurance of individual risks, known as faculatative reinsurance, many insurance companies reinsure on what is called a treaty basis whereby a proportion of all risks of a certain class are ceded to another insurance company.

Insurance is clearly a service industry, with no tangible product other than policies and cover notes. Nevertheless, as a large company we have responsibility for ensuring that the business is run both professionally and profitably. To this end, the planning of future growth is treated as an important matter. If planning is to be realistic, the assumptions upon which it is based must be considered very thoroughly and the balance between the relative factors must be weighed in the light of past experience and future expectations. Once completed, the profitability plan or profit forecast in all its ramifications represents a vital part of our corporate objective.

Forecasting difficulties

As a public company one of our principle objectives is to satisfy the expectations of our shareholders. In normal circumstances this requires profit growth and an annual improvement in our earnings per share. However, profit forecasting in the insurance broking sector is not at all straightforward due to many factors outside the broker's control which can materially affect results. These factors generally arise from the international nature of insurance broking. For example, the relative strength of the currencies in which income is earned against our base currency of sterling can have a major effect on our income.

The highly competitive nature of the business can result in some accounts moving between different brokers very frequently. Indeed, certain clients use the price of cover as their sole criterion for placing their business, instead of balancing this factor against the quality of the cover provided. When claims arise, it is invariably far easier to collect from the better markets, (i.e., Lloyd's and the major companies) than from small and perhaps less reputable overseas underwriters. This factor can affect the interest earnings of the broker who is required to finance claims to his client on behalf of the underwriters.

As stated, certain fundamental factors are outside the broker's control and therefore any attempts to produce profit forecasts rely upon the basic assumptions used proving to be correct. This uncertainty has led us to concentrate on planning profits for relatively short periods ahead and to amend our forecasts frequently. By keeping the detailed forecasting period short, we believe that we can monitor our progress and take prompt corrective action where and when required.

However, long term planning is necessary when considering our world wide representation and the need to have either offices or correspondents in countries with the greatest development potential. Also as major brokers, we must keep to the forefront of the technical side of our business, particularly to the way in which risks are organised and placed in the most advantageous way both to underwriters and our clients. In addition, planning for staff requirements on a long term basis is always under consideration.

Forecasting methods

Budgetary control is used by the group as being the best means of controlling events against a plan and dealing effectively with variances where necessary.

It has been found that the most constructive method of producing a forecast in our group has been to require the management of our subsidiaries to complete a detailed forecast at the same time that the annual budget is prepared. The budget is produced in the final quarter of the current financial year, together with a profit forecast for the two years following that budget period. Therefore in our financial year to 31st March, 1980 the budget for 1980/81 was produced in February/ March 1980, together with forecasts for the financial years 1981/82 and 1982/83. We therefore have a three years forecast or plan against which to monitor results, evaluate performance and deal with variations.

Figure 5.1 illustrates the method used to prepare each forecast and the way in which each individual year's forecast is amended annually to reflect any material changes in the situation.

The schedule assumes that the planning programme commences in 1980/81. You will see that in March, 1981 the forecast for 1981/82 (Forecast (ii)) will be amended to become the Budget (iv) for that year and the forecast for 1982/83 (Forecast (iii)) will also be revised (Forecast (v)). The figures are revised because the closer one gets to a forecasting period, the less doubt remains about the major factors which will influence the forecast and therefore the more accurate one can be. Nevertheless, the adjustments necessary to Forecast (ii) and (iii) to produce Budget (iv) and Forecast (v) are carefully considered and evaluated for future reference.

PLANNING PROGRAMME

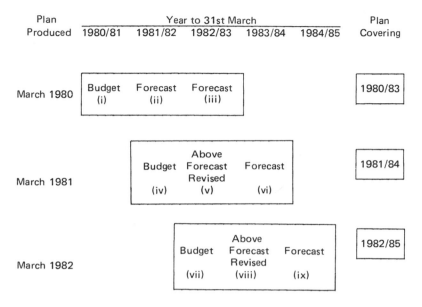

Plan Produced	Year to 31st March					Plan Covering
	1980/81	1981/82	1982/83	1983/84	1984/85	
March 1980	Budget (i)	Forecast (ii)	Forecast (iii)			1980/83
March 1981		Budget (iv)	Above Forecast Revised (v)	Forecast (vi)		1981/84
March 1982			Budget (vii)	Above Forecast Revised (viii)	Forecast (ix)	1982/85

Figure 5.1 Budgetary control plan

No forecast or plan is inviolable and the accuracy or inaccuracy of the plan matters less than the evaluation and understanding of deviations as they arise. In this way, budgeting and planning provide management with a means of monitoring and controlling the activities and growth of their company.

Problems encountered

Exchange differences

As London remains a vital centre for the world insurance market, the business coming to London must be written in many different currencies. An assured resident in Brazil will generally require his claims to be paid in Brazilian cruzeiros and not in any other currency. As international brokers, therefore, we have to deal in numerous currencies, although as a general rule only business written in the major world currencies is settled to underwriters in the original currency. The remaining currencies are accounted for in either convertible pounds sterling or convertible US dollars.

Our London based broking operation receives in excess of 70 per cent of its brokerage income in foreign currencies, all of which must at some point be sold for sterling since ours is a UK company. In addition, we incur the majority of our expenses in pounds sterling, together with our tax liability and dividends to shareholders. For many years the parity between important currencies was fixed against the US dollar and devaluation or revaluation of any major trading currency occurred very rarely. In those times, exchange fluctuations were not material and were generally ignored.

However, in recent years, with floating rates of exchange between currencies, the exposure of a company dealing in any currency other than its domestic currency can be considerable. The point is illustrated by the effect of a falling US dollar against pounds sterling on a UK broker.

Table 5.1
Depreciation of US earnings when converted to sterling

	1977	1978	1979
Brokerage	US$2m	US$2m	US$2m
Average rate of exchange for year	1.76	2.00	2.15
Sterling equivalent	£1.136m	£1m	£.930m

Despite maintained brokerage income, the relative value of the US dollars when sold for pounds sterling has declined considerably.

Nevertheless, the expenses of operating the company in the UK, assuming no exceptional circumstances, will generally continue to rise so that more brokerage must be earned to compensate for the adverse effect of the decline of the US dollar against the pound.

The following example illustrates the effect on profit where income is earned in a falling currency, yet sterling expenses are rising.

Table 5.2
Profits squeezed by depreciating currency and rising expenses

	1977	1978	1979
Brokerage income	US$2,000,000	US$2,000,000	US$2,000,000
Average exchange rate	1.76	2.00	2.15

	1977	1978	1977
Sterling	£1,136,000	£1,000,000	£ 930,000
Expenses (increasing at 10% per annum)	636,000	700,000	770,000
Profit	£ 500,000	£ 300,000	£ 160,000
Percentage decrease in profits		40%	47%

It follows from the above that a UK broker who is heavily reliant on his US business must take decisive action in this situation if he is to maintain his profitability. In fact, to show a relatively modest increase in profits, of say 5 per cent per annum, his income would have to be increased as follows:

Table 5.3
Necessary increases in income to combat currency depreciation

	% Increase	1977	1978	1979
Brokerage income		US$2,000,000	US$2,450,000	US$2,840,687
Average exchange rate		1.76	2.00	2.15
£ Equivalent		£1,136,000	£1,225,000	£1,321,250
Expenses	10%	£ 636,000	£ 700,000	£ 770,000
Profit	5%	£ 500,000	£ 525,000	£ 551,250

Brokerage income in the above case would have to be increased by 22½ per cent in 1978 and by 16 per cent by 1979. This illustrates the very material, yet disproportionate effect which exchange fluctuation can have on the profitability of a UK broker.

Resulting from the importance of exchange rates, a broker must form an opinion as to the likely average exchange parities between sterling as his base currency and the various currencies in which he earns his income, before attempting any profit forecast.

This is a very difficult area, as acknowledged experts rarely agree on the future parity of currencies. The uncertainty arises because the underlying economic fundamentals between two countries — growth rates, inflation rates, mineral resources — rarely dictate the relative parity of their currencies. Exchange markets are highly sensitive to political factors which often override economic factors.

Another area in which exchange fluctuation can cause great concern is in the group accounting for overseas subsidiaries and associates. An overseas subsidiary can make significant profits, but present a loss situation in the group's consolidated accounts due to the impact of exchange fluctuations on the values of overseas assets when converted to sterling. If we assume that a company has a South African subsidiary with a net worth of SA Rand 5million in 1979, then the position could develop as follows:

Table 5.4
Effects of currency depreciation on book values of overseas subsidiaries

	1979	1980
Net worth	SAR.5,000,000	SAR.5,490,000
Exchange rate	1.60	1.80
Consolidated value of subsidiary	£3,125,000	£3,050,000

The above assumes a profit of SAR 490 000 in 1980. In this case the group profits must be reduced by £75,000 to recognise the lower net worth and therefore carrying value of its South African subsidiary.

Exchange differences of this type can, of course, produce big profits as well as losses, and UK accounting practice dictates that these differences must be dealt with in the profit and loss account in the year in which they arise. There are ways of reducing exchange exposure by entering into forward currency transactions but it is impossible to obviate them completely.

Premium rates

The major source of income for a broker is commission or brokerage which is generally calculated as a percentage of the premium payable. Therefore the amount of premium which an underwriter requires to cover a certain risk determines the remuneration which the broker receives for his part in the transaction.

The rate at which premium is calculated varies between different classes of business, — Aviation, Marine, Fire — and also according to the claims experience of the underwriters specialising in any particular field. Competition between underwriters for certain classes of business can also affect the rates which are charged. New insurance companies wishing to establish a portfolio of business, may decide to write at low rates for a limited period, in order to attract business. However, the rating of each class of business is generally based upon an extensive study of the premium and claim statistics over a number of years both in respect of individual underwriters and the market as a whole. There is therefore a direct relationship between the premium charged and the broker's income. On occasions, particularly after a large loss, under-writers will adjust their rates upwards in order to avoid future losses by catering for their increased exposure. Although brokers follow the rating of business closely, it is impossible to predict when a change in the rating of a particular type of business will occur. When forecasting profits, it is necessary to make assumptions in this area, but all too frequently changes do not occur as predicted, due to the complex nature of this highly competitive market.

The following table illustrates the significant effect of rating on the income of an insurance broker. I have assumed that a number of massive aviation losses have arisen in 1980 which have resulted in underwriters increasing their rates by an additional 10 per cent.

Table 5.5
Effects of rating on brokerage income

	1980	1981	1982
Forecast			
Aviation premiums	£50m	£55m	£60m
Brokerage, say 5%	£2.5m	£2.75m	£3.0m
Actual after 10% Rerating			
Aviation premiums	£50m	£60.5m	£66m
Brokerage, say 5%	£2.5m	£3.0m	£3.3m

It also follows that the rates which underwriters set are sometimes reduced and the broker receives a smaller income on the same volume of business in consequence.

Inflation

The rate of inflation also has a marked effect on insured values and therefore on the premium charged by underwriters and the related commission earned by brokers. The rate of inflation is never predictable in any country in the world, but it clearly is vital for a broker to make positive assumptions as to likely rates and the consequent effects on brokerage.

The rate of inflation in a country rarely has a direct effect on, for example, property values which tend to rise in sudden surges as opposed to gradual growth. The inflation rate in the USA has a very material impact on most major London brokers' incomes, as a large proportion of the insurance business which comes to London emanates from the United States.

Inflation provides insurance brokers with a valuable growth potential but the unpredictability of the rate makes it difficult to forecast profitability in future years. Inflation similarly affects the cost of operating an insurance broking company in the UK.

The nature of insurance business generally dictates that the industry is labour intensive. Staff costs, which represent a very significant part of the operating expenses, must be kept in line with the rise in the cost of living. Another major expense is the cost of travel. This is necessary to maintain existing client relationships as well as to develop new business. The other principal expenses are telex and telephone charges, communication being vital for servicing international business.

World trade

The level of world trade as represented by the rates of growth in the major countries and general economic activity, also strongly influence the volume of insurable assets. The more factories and construction projects undertaken, the greater the potential for the insurance industry. This is why the developing areas such as South America, the Middle East and Far East offer such important opportunities for insurance brokers.

In addition, the greater technical sophistication of present day commercial and industrial life helps to produce new business as people endeavour to protect themselves from the growing litigious philosophy.

The increasing cost of replacing assets following the high annual rates of inflation in recent years, has compelled more businesses to insure their assets on a replacement cost basis, the risk of not insuring being considered too great.

Interest rates

Premiums paid to brokers are held in trust prior to being settled to underwriters and are generally invested in the short term money market pending payment. Holding these premium funds permits the broker to advance a claim to the assured prior to the full collection of the claim from the underwriters concerned. On occasions it is also necessary for insurance brokers to fund very large claims — for example, a jumbo aircraft hull worth in excess of US$ 25million — before they can collect any of the claim due from the underwriters. In days of high interest rates, such financings can represent a considerable interest cost to the broker.

The investment potential for the broker obviously depends upon the rate of return available in the money market. Again, this presents a problem when attempting to forecast future profits as interest rates depend upon a number of contingent factors and are difficult to predict. For example, in the past few years sterling interest rates guided by the MLR, have varied from 5 per cent to 18 per cent per annum. The fact that many brokers' investment incomes can equal between 5 per cent and 10 per cent of their brokerage, highlights the materiality of interest rates.

Market organisation

The great importance of the USA as a producer of insurance through the US brokers to London arises from a lack of capacity in the United States to underwrite the business which it generates. There are a relatively small number of major US brokers, most of which have well established ties with the larger London brokers. These links between major broking houses have developed over the years and tend to be very strong; in many cases joint ventures are undertaken in various parts of the world by the UK and US companies concerned.

However, recent years have seen a number of very significant mergers and regroupings of insurance brokers on both sides of the Atlantic with the result that large portfolios of business have changed hands. This situation can arise, for example, when a major US broker acquires another important US broker and in the course of rationalisation business is moved from one London broker to another London broker.

Major US brokers have in recent years taken sizeable shareholding in London brokers in the course of the next few years, so that they can benefit from the profits earned in the UK on US business placed in London.

The insurance market is constantly changing and each small reorganisation can influence the profitability of London brokers in future years.

Conclusions

Within the insurance world continuous reassessment is undertaken by all the larger brokers as part of the effort to achieve maximum profitability. The insurance broking sector of the stock exchange has a somewhat speculative reputation, and the bigger firms of stockbrokers monitor all the factors which can influence the brokers' profitability and share prices dramatically.

It is unlikely that many firms of brokers anticipated the longer term ramifications of the Fisher Report in their profit forecasting for future years. This report was prepared by a working party appointed by the Committee of Lloyd's under the chairmanship of Sir Henry Fisher and contained certain proposals for self regulation at Lloyd's. It considered the potential conflict of interest which could arise from the ownership of managing agencies by Lloyd's broking firms and recommended that in order to demonstrate complete independence, the brokers should divest themselves of these interests. While commission and fee income from this source is not generally very material to the major brokers, the probable long term effect of this report will be to reduce the brokers' earnings.

A further outside factor is the Insurance Exchange in New York and those planned for Chicago, Illinois and Florida. They are organised using Lloyd's of London as the model, the intention being to underwrite reinsurance, foreign risks and any other risks which cannot be placed elsewhere within the USA. The insurance exchanges will be in direct competition with Lloyd's and over a period of time could easily reduce the premium flow to London and thus the earning capacity of Lloyd's brokers.

The insurance business is complex and highly organised. By its nature it is always changing and adjusting to new circumstances. Therefore it is up to each broker to be as flexible as possible, to seek new markets constantly and to monitor and react quickly to the many factors which can affect his profitability.

6 Forecasting in practice: an overview

J B Coates, Senior Lecturer, University of Aston Management Centre

Forecasts, plans and targets

As a general rule a forecast is regarded as a value derived from some form of extrapolation of a model based on past data and relationships. A plan, on the other hand, can be devised without any reference to the past. In developing a plan, an organisation need not necessarily be constrained or guided by the past: it can attempt to draw up a strategy which will ultimately make a substantial break with its past history. It is also probably true that there is a degree of disenchantment with the use of forecasts as the main predictions of the future since even in experienced hands they may prove expensive and inaccurate [1]. However, a plan refers to the future and will be regarded by many as a predictor of it, if the strategy laid down for its achievement is followed.

The term profit forecast may also convey the misleading impression that profit is being directly forecast. In accounting, profit is basically a residual element and in the internal forecast it will be the revenues and expenses which are directly estimated. The possibility of a profit target being imposed can be appreciated in this context. The logic in terms of revenue and expense of a forecast or the best researched feasible plan may prove unacceptable to a management whose success is likely to be seen ultimately in the context of its profit record. The ratio of profit earned to capital employed or even an absolute level of profit are frequently used measurements of management performance, so there may well be some temptation to establish future plans around a profit target which gives, on paper, the kind of results required. There seems little point in such deception, especially if it is totally at variance with basic expectations: calculating a range of future outcomes will indicate the scope for aiming at results different to the most likely outcome, yet remaining within the bounds of reality.

For present purposes a profit forecast is deemed to have been reached via the middle of the road approach, using both forecast and researched data as input and requiring management expertise to blend them together. Thus a profit forecast and profit plan may be regarded as much the same thing in terms of their derivation, though still different to a profit target.

We must also differentiate between a profit estimate and a cash forecast. In the usual accruals basis of accounting profit is not generally synonymous with cash, though longer term projections are frequently produced on a cash flow basis. In the short run as well, a cash forecast could well be more important to an organisation than one for profit.

Developing a profit forecast

The principal means used to arrive at a profit forecast are as follows:

(a) Application of statistical forecasting models,
(b) Market appraisals, including market research and scene setting appraisals. Market research can include statistical analysis of sample data.
(c) Cost estimations
(d) Assessment of the implications of information from (a), (b) and (c) with respect to policy decisions on, for example, products, investments, finance and financing.

In a large organisation, the forecast may be produced for the company as a whole as well as segments such as divisions and profit centres within it. Unless the latter are totally independent of each other, further considerations, such as transfer prices, will have to be settled before sectional profit forecasts are agreed. Further, it will probably be necessary to incorporate macro forecasts from outside, such as forecasts for the performance of the economy as a whole, into the internal forecast, rather than attempt to define the general economic framework for the forecast from within the company [2].

An adequate, consistent series of historic data is generally required for the models of (a). Market research also utilises past data, but is by no means so reliant on it, nor, in terms of the conclusions drawn from the research, is market research so dependent on the logic of something as precise.

(a) *Statistical forecasting* methods vary greatly in complexity [3] but can be categorised as:

(i) *Automatic methods*: where a functional relationship is established between the variable to be forecast, for example sales, and time. Projections of future values are obtained simply by inserting the appropriate time value as the independent variable value in the functional equation and reading off the extrapolated value of the dependent (in this case, sales) variable. There is no attempt to explain an economic process; the time factor is the sole determinant of the relationship.

A useful first step here is to divide the original time series into its component parts (Figure 6.1):

> the long-term (secular) trend
> cyclical (business trade cycle) fluctuations
> seasonal (within the year) fluctuations
> irregular (random) fluctuations.

Simple moving averages are often used for this purpose.

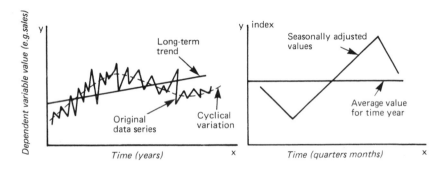

Figure 6.1   Time series divided into component parts

Moving average models may also be used for forecasting, but in general other models are considered preferable on such grounds as ease of handling and relevance. Again, they can be broken down roughly on the basis of the future period to which they relate:

Exponential smoothing for short-term forecasting; incorporates a range of different models under the general heading, simple exponential smoothing being of the form:

$$\text{New forecast} = a \,(\text{new data}) + (1-a)\,(\text{old forecast}),$$

where 'a' is known as the smoothing constant and takes a value between 0 and 1 (a low value heavily damps the fluctuations of the original data, whilst higher ones reflect these to an increasing extent). There are many other models [4] of increasing flexibility and complexity.

Trend curves [4] for medium to long term analysis; simple linear regression is an example of this class of technique where

$$y \text{ (sales)} = a + b \text{ x (time)}$$

and 'a' + 'b' are constants which fit the intercept value and slope of the line. It is computed by the least squares method to give a line of best fit; an error term is calculated from sample data which can be used to assess the degree of confidence in the results, that is, having obtained an estimated value from the line, what interval of values can it be expected to lie within.

A parabola takes the form
$y = a + b x + cx^2$, but x remains the same (time) variable in this group of forecasting methods. Others in the same class are:

    modified exponential curves
    logistic curves
    gompertz curves

(ii) *Econometric models* [4] Here the forecaster attempts to model the real economic variables which affect the value of the variable (e.g. Sales) being forecast. In theory such models are more sound than others, since they incorporate economic relationships which are expected to hold. They vary greatly in complexity; for example a simple product sales model may show it as being linearly related to the general level of industrial production:

$$y \text{ (product sales)} = a + b \text{ x (index of industrial production)}$$

Refinements added to this may show a relationship to a particular sector of industrial sales production, lagged by a certain time period; for example, sales of spares to vehicles may be partly directly dependent on new vehicle registrations of two years ago and partly on the total stock of vehicles. One problem which arises is that it is often necessary to forecast one or more of the independent variables in these models.

The *basic* statistical technique employed is multiple linear regression, taking the form:
$$y = a + b_1 x_1 + b_2 x_2 \ldots + b_n x_n$$
when   y = dependent variable to be forecast
    $x_1 \ldots x_n$ = independent variables
    $a, b_1 \ldots b_n$ = the coefficients of the model.

One should distinguish the use of econometric methods from multiple regression on the grounds that although the latter may contain economic variables they may have been selected for inclusion purely through the mechanics of computational methods, for example as with the application of a straightforward stepwise regression. The development of an econometric model, on the other hand, may well involve a less than optimal equation from a statistical point of view since the forecasters may require it to accept certain relationships judged to have a real influence in the model. Computer packages now available greatly extend the possibility of use of these techniques.

(b) *Market research* involves both desk-based analysis of market reports and statistics and active sampling of the market, whether for consumer or industrial products. The results are brought together in reports which are to some extent subjective in the final assessment of market conditions. The general economic climate affecting demand in an industry; the impact of alternative policy decisions made by a firm's management in that market; the assessment of the strength of competition at home and abroad are examples of factors which are all capable of formal analysis with the aid of statistical techniques, but eventually a quantification of their effects on the demand for a product(s) of a particular firm will contain an element of judgement. Results of surveys carried out on the basis of sound statistical principles can be interpreted in terms of a range of outcomes within defined statistical limits, but here too an analyst and/or a company's management may impose its own judgement when interpreting the survey outcomes for future planning purposes. New and existing product/service lines can be analysed with the aid of market research techniques, though the former may have to go through a more extended series of appraisals of demand with the aid, for example, of a test marketing.

As the market under analysis lies further and further in the future, the use of standard market research techniques gives way to long term planning. The aim of such planning is to establish a realistic market scene for the future within which the company can expect to operate.

Besides supplying estimates of market demand for goods and services, analysts should seek to:

> identify changes in economic and social trends which will affect a company's commercial and technological policy.
> identify factors to which the company's future is significantly sensitive.

(c) *Cost estimation* presents problems which are sometimes simpler, but often just as difficult to deal with as those of assessing markets and market demand levels. The introduction of new technology is one obvious example, and analysis of the likely range of costs should form part of any appraisal before profit forecasts/plans are presented or finally approved. Forecasting methods of the kind described for demand analysis may be relevant to cost assessment in some cases, but special cost estimation methods [4] may also be used.

(d) Data produced by the methods described in sections (a) − (c) are the raw material for a profit forecast. It will need further evaluation and assessment before eventual use as the basis of a company's operating programme: for example, would it be realistic for the company to attempt to carry out a programme purely in line with the forecast? can it recruit the necessary skilled manpower? raise finance, etc.? The raw data should be used by management to investigate a range of possible future programmes:

> forecasts of revenues and expenses will enable a company to study relative product profitability on existing ranges and the potential for new products. Formal mathematical programming models could be employed to establish a 'best' range of products within identified boundaries.

> the need for new investment in plant, buildings, research and development programmes can be defined or possible alternative paths considered whereby assets are purchased through mergers and acquisitions of other companies.

> supporting finance requirements will be spelt out: how much cash is needed, where it is to come from, at what cost and what risk does it carry? Tax angles, including government assistance programmes for example in special development areas, [5] must also be investigated.

As a comparative base for tentative future programmes, an analysis of a company's current strengths and weaknesses should raise some useful questions. This analysis should cover not only indicators of its present financial performance such as:

> return on capital employed
> gearing
> liquidity

but also operating ratios such as value added [6] per man, machine, and per unit of floor area, and the profitability of existing products and services.

By the end of this process, a framework will have been developed within which all important factors have been investigated as thoroughly as any view of the future will permit; and the resulting profit forecast should be as realistic as possible. Also, since the longer term future will have been analysed, the profit forecast need not progress in a series of practically unco-ordinated annual steps. Having said that though, provision should be made for monitoring results as well as updating all relevant information.

Computer based financial modelling

Any set of formally established relationships constitutes a model. A profit forecast is developed through a series of separate, but linked models. The availability of computer assistance together with a properly designed package of programmes greatly facilitates all aspects of a profit forecast and the subsequent monitoring of actual results. Particular advanges are:

(a) the ability to carry out rapid appraisals of forecast and alternative plans, testing areas of plans of special importance for their sensitivity to the uncertainty of future outcomes.

(b) the ability to monitor actual outcomes closely and provide re-appraisals of plans in the light of these disclosures and other new information.

An example of the general planning and forecasting sequence which management may adopt is outlined in Figure 6.2. A number of the sections of the diagram comprise a set of sub-elements, with their own routines. Linking the short and medium term plans to the long term objectives is an important feature, but rigid adherence to a long term plan is not implied: continuous monitoring of actual events and new ideas as they arise subjects long term plans to regular review, though not with the degree of frequency applied to the short term results.

Methods and techniques employed in preparing the information required in the sequence may be more or less formal. The same point applies to the way in which the information is finally put together to produce the profit forecast. In practice, management application of these techniques appears to vary widely from willingness to accept them, probably with reservations, to a belief that they cannot be applied. The latter is often due to ignorance of their availability and potential benefit. The more formal the analysis though, the more necessary computer assistance will be to carry out this process.

Among the techniques referred to are those based on mathematical programming [7], where the objective may be to produce an optimal ('best') sales/production schedule to gain maximum profits; applications may be in long term (capital budgeting) or short term time periods [8]. Formal techniques of analysis are also employed when the objective is not so much to achieve peak profits or reduce costs to a minimum, (i.e. the optimisation of the value of a given variable) but to attain a satisfactory result in relation to the objectives and the actual circumstances faced by a company [9], [10].

A forecasting and planning cycle such as that illustrated in Figure 6.2 can be used whatever methods are employed to forecast and analyse information for it. Given the scepticism often expressed with respect to forecasting it is notable that companies, especially those with computer based company models, often use a scheme similar to this but expressing only general goals: various alternative policies and their results can be reviewed and tested quite quickly and at relatively little expense. Inevitably the same proviso applies as for inputs of a more formal nature; all information used should be within the bounds of feasibility and realism.

The acceptability of both the long and short term plans may be measured on the conventional basis of the rate of return on capital employed. This ratio, together with other commonly used ratios such as liquidity and gearing, can be computed as part of the total financial model package to facilitate broad assessment of policy objectives.

Implementation of a long term programme has immediate financial effects as new plant and equipment are acquired or old plant sold. This will affect both the profit and loss account — through tax allowances — and the cash flow statement. Test runs of the latter are vital before acceptance of any policy for short, medium or long term objectives, since the method of finance — assuming funds can be raised — influences the degree of risk attached to a policy, for example, through financial gearing/leverage increases.

The tests of the significance of proposed amendments to original plans, related to the short term planning cycle of Figure 6.2 are paralleled by similar tests at the corresponding level of the longer term planning scheme, remembering their interconnection. Some of the variables which are obvious candidates for study would be:

inflation rate
sales volumes/market structures
period of adjustment of prices to cost increases
sales to areas of high political risk
raw material supply difficulties.

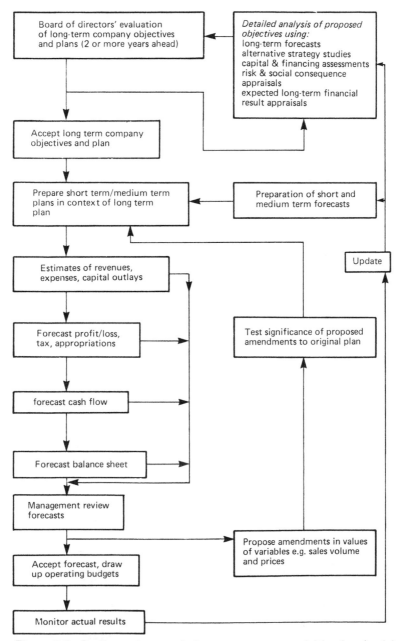

Figure 6.2 Outline scheme of the management activities involved in the preparation of profit forecasts

Variations in the quantities of these variables from initial estimates may be tested singly or — probably more realistically — in combination. This approach really amounts to posing a simple 'what if' question, basing the procedure for enquiry on those areas considered most important and a carefully considered pattern and progression of questioning. If formal mathematical models have been employed, the output solutions for the models provide information about the sensitivity of the output to parameter inputs; in other words, how robust the model is to variations in input parameter values.

Administration of a profit forecast

Adoption of a system for producing a profit forecast must be backed by parallel administrative systems for translating the forecast into plans for action and subsequently monitoring and controlling the actual results. Depending on the size of the company, its belief in the profit yardstick as a motivational device and similar considerations [11], the overall profit forecast may be broken down to give individual forecasts for divisions of the company, product lines or any other defined profit centre. While profit is not always the sole yardstick of performance, it will be frequently linked to capital employed for this purpose.

The estimates of activity, revenue and expense detailed in the final agreed profit forecast are prepared by the higher management team responsible, in collaboration with the managers of the individual operating areas, production units or departments. Discussion of possible alternative strategies and activity forecasts between the two groups is vital to secure a viable operating plan and commitment from managers to work to it. At whatever level within a company a profit forecast (or budget) is defined, it should not simply be imposed by some agency acting on behalf of a central management.

The basic document from which other detailed statements are developed and with which they must be integrated is the agreed statement of overall forecast profit (which may be referred to now as budgeted profit) together with the linked cash flow and balance sheet. Figure 6.3 is an example of this document, showing actual results to date and planned results for future periods. The same basic document applies at the level of the total company and subsections of it, though with differences of detail. For example, dividend payments will feature in final accounts only, while allocation of head office costs will appear only in divisional statements, as will the definition of capital employed.

The use of ratios to assist evaluation of forecast results is indicated at the bottom of Figure 6.3; as the degree of detail in planning increases, the use of ratios can be extended beyond the normal financial management ratios to include specific operating and value added ratios [6]. These would be contained in documents supplementing the main ones shown in Figure 6.3.

The forecast columns may be derived partly from external input forecast data, as for the sales forecast, or from links between items built into the financial planning model on the basis of established practice within a company and between a company and its customers or suppliers. The results of any operational plans put forward naturally lead into the cash flow statement, and so to the ultimate problems of how a given future operating programme (including long term and short term implications) is to be financed. Clearly, it will not always be practicable to finance all projected operating plans, however attractive they may seem. In addition, it should be remembered that financing conditions may impose their own constraints on operating plans; for example, the proportion of loan capital and related interest costs can affect the risk level of a particular plan.

Actual Results for Previous Periods (by value & % breakdown)			Forecast/Budgeted Profit & Loss Account	Future Planning Periods (by value & % breakdown)	
		1	Sales Value		
		2	Less: Cost of goods sold		
		3(1—2)	Gross Profit		
			Gross Profit %		
		4	Less: Selling Costs General Administration Research & Development etc.		
		5(3—4)	Net profit before interest		
		6	Interest		
		7(5—6)	Net Profit after interest Pre tax profit %		
		8	Taxation		
		9(7—8)	Net Profit after interest & tax After interest & tax profit %		
		10	Other appropriations		
			Forecast/Budgeted Cash Flow		
		11	Opening Cash Balance		
		7	Profit before tax		
		12	Depreciation		
		13	Tax payment		
		14	Dividend payment		
		15	Other cash inflows/ outflows		

71

			(e.g. capital asset purchases/sales)		
			Movements in working capital items		
		16	Change in stocks		
		17	Change in debtors		
		18	Change in current liabilities		
		19 (Σ7,12—18)	Net cash flow		
		20 (11 $\pm$ 19)	Closing cash balance		
			Forecast/Budgeted balance sheet		
			Employment of Capital:		
		21	Current assets (detailed)		
		22	Less current liabilities (detailed)		
		23 (21—22)	Net working capital		
		24	Fixed Assets: Land & Buildings (net) Plant and Equipment (net)		
		25 (23+24)	Total net assets *Financed by:*		
		26	Share capital		
		27	Reserves		
		28	Loan capital		
		29	Minority interest		
		30	Deferred tax		
		Egs. of ratios			
		5:25	% Return on capital employed		
		1:25	% Sales: capital employed		

Figure 6.3   Profit forecasts: Forecast final accounts for total company or profit centres. This provides the broad framework for establishing detailed operating budgets.

Two final general points:

1. Companies usually break down the annual planning statement into monthly figures. This is necessary to obtain more precise information on cash flow and to incorporate expected seasonal variations.

2. Volume as well as value forecasts should be given; the former are

essential to enable the responsible departments of the firm to go ahead and plan resource procurement (materials, personnel, equipment etc.).

Having discussed analysis of the total plan into monthly data and volume/quantity data, each related to individual profit centres where appropriate, it remains only to indicate other main supporting documentation in the administration of the profit forecast. This will relate to:

1. *Sales forecast* information broken down by value, volume, new products, market shares by value and volume, prices and margins (with reference to cost data).
2. *Fixed asset, current asset and cost allocations* or apportionments to profit centres showing bases of allocations and valuation.
3. *Planned stock levels, debtors and creditors* wherever these are required as separate, independent inputs to the profit statement. Allocated to profit centres as indicated above.
4. *Total company and divisional analysis of capital expenditure* requirements, detailing type of asset, estimated cost, life, depreciation rate, date or period of introduction. This includes acquisition of all types of fixed asset including land.
5. *Research and development budgets.* Frequently these will be related to the capital expenditure budget, but where projects are entirely concerned with or are to be developed from an early stage within a company or one of its divisions, it is valuable to plan the project over time as accurately as possible. In addition, finance must be provided for pure research. Accounting for Research and Development Expenditure can significantly influence forecast/reported profit [12].
6. *Education, training and recruitment budgets.* Separate items of course, but well worth providing detailed information for: type of course/training required, cost; personnel needs for the development of the company.
7. *Marketing and market research budgets*: details of special campaigns and surveys related to special studies of products and markets; added to the basic budgets for these activities.

Control

Monitoring the profit forecast and its constituent elements is a relatively simple process, provided the administrative routines for collection, processing and examination of results have been established.

The block diagram in Figure 6:4 outlines the sequence of control from agreement on the operating budget:

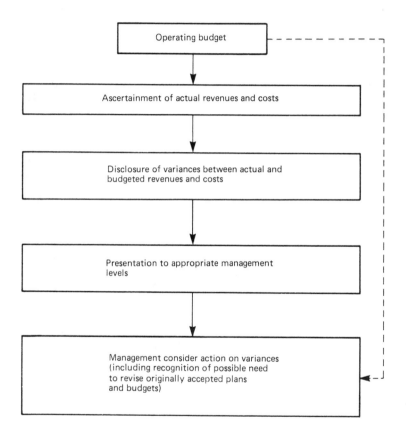

Figure 6.4   Outline of the control monitor sequence for a profit forecast plan

Deciding the point at which the size of the reported variances justifies intervention is not so easy. While the variances are simple arithmetic differences obtained by subtracting actual from budgeted revenues and expenses, investigation as to their cause could involve a costly process.

A rule of thumb sometimes applied to cost variances is to calculate the ratio, variance : budgeted cost. Investigation is indicated when the ratio looks too large, this point being supported by reference to a plot of the trend in the ratio over time. More formal schemes akin to quality control procedures and charts are sometimes proposed, but these are seldom employed in practice. Management judgement will be the final arbiter of the course of action to take, especially where this involves substantial revision of the accepted profit plan.

References

[1]   Christopher Lorenz 'How Shell Plans to Cope with an Era of Surprise', *Financial Times,* Wednesday, 19 November, 1979. (As an example.)
[2]   As examples of externally produced macro-forecasts, sources are:
      (a) National Institute for Economic and Social Research
      (b) London Business School
      (c) Henley Centre for Forecasting
[3]   (a) M. Firth, *Forecasting Methods in Business Management.* Arnold.
      (b) I. Scott-Armstrong, *Long-Range Forecasting from Crystal Ball to Computer.* Wiley — Interscience.
[4]   'The Report of the Steering Group on Development Cost Estimating. Vol. 2 — Handbook of Procedures, Programming, Estimating and Control of Development Projects'. H.M.S.O. 1969.
[5]   Department of Industry Publications on Incentives for Investment in Development Areas. H.M.S.O.
[6]   B. Cox, *Value Added*, Heinemann, 1979.
[7]   L. R. Amey, *The Efficiency of Business Enterprises.* George Allen and Unwin. 1969.
[8]   L. R. Amey, 'Budget Planning: A Dynamic Reformulation'. *Accounting and Business Research.* Winter 1979; and K. Bhasicar, 'A Multiple Objective Approach to Capital Budgeting'. *Accounting and Business Research.* Winter 1979. (See also in relation to [10]).
[9]   H. A. Simon, *Models of Man.* John Wiley and Sons, 1957.
[10] P. H. Grinyer and V. Wooller, Corporate Models Today. I.C.A.E.W.
[11] G. A. Hofstede, *The Game of Budget Control.* Van Gorcum, 1967.
[12] Statement of Standard Accounting Practice No. 13. *Accounting for Research and Development.* Dec. 1977.

PART TWO

MAKING A FORECAST PUBLIC

Overview

Not all forecasts are made public but in the second part of this book the process of publishing a forecast in the UK is described, as are the safeguards for an investor. If a forecast is made in a prospectus or during a takeover bid it must be reported on by independent accountants and by the issuing house or sponsoring brokers or financial advisor. If a forecast is made with the interim results it does not have to be reported on unless the company subsequently becomes involved in a bid.

Alan Ashton of Deloitte Haskins and Sells explains in detail the work and responsibilities of the reporting accountant. This type of work was pioneered in the UK.

Richard Heley of Hill Samuel describes the role of the merchant bank in flotations, rights issues, and takeovers (offers and defences). He sets out the work the merchant bank performs and how this relates to the role of the reporting accountant.

All those concerned with producing or using forecasts will find these two chapters most useful guides to the nature and extent of the considerable amount of work required to compile the brief reports which eventually appear from the reporting accountant and merchant bank. Even if a forecast is not to be published these two chapters will be useful as a suggestion to directors as to the steps that should perhaps be taken to review internally forecasts which form the basis of management's plans and actions.

This part concludes with two authoritative chapters on the roles played by The Stock Exchange and the City Panel in the UK to safeguard investors when forecasts are published. They have been written by Jeffrey Knight, Chief Executive of The Stock Exchange and Richard Wade of Coopers & Lybrand who, until recently, was seconded to the Takeover Panel.

Mr. Knight emphasises that The Stock Exchange does not require a profit forecast as such but that prospectuses should contain a statement as to the financial and trading prospects of the company. The advantage of this approach is its flexibility. Often companies do publish a forecast and if this is not achieved The Stock Exchange requires the company to publish an explanation.

The Panel on Takeovers and Mergers was set up in 1968 by the Bank of England to interpret and enforce the City Code on Takeovers and Mergers which deals with a wide range of matters. Companies are not required to publish a forecast in a bid situation (though just under a half do) but must provide shareholders with adequate information upon which to exercise their judgement. The City Code emphasises that forecasts are the responsibility of directors but requires them to be reported on by independent accountants and the company's financial advisers. Any published but unaudited profit figures and any forecast made before the bid are also required to be similarly reported upon.

Richard Wade describes the Code's application to forecasts in detail, how its working is monitored, how it is enforced, and the treatment by the Panel of failed forecasts.

C.A.W.

7 The role of the reporting accountant

A V Ashton, Partner, Deloitte Haskins & Sells

Introduction

The preparation of profit forecasts as an aid to management has been common practice for many years and some of the larger groups of companies regularly forecast five or ten years ahead. However, the publication of such forecasts was a rare occurrence in the United Kingdom prior to the 1960s, when their use as a weapon for, or defence against, a takeover bid began to be common practice. Before the 1960s prospectus documents frequently contained a form of words indicating the likely outcome of the current year, which nowadays would be regarded as a forecast.

The City Code on Takeovers and Mergers, first issued in the United Kingdom in March 1968, required directors using profit forecasts in takeover negotiations to have those forecasts examined by independent accountants. This rule was amended shortly afterwards to require the publication of the accountants' report. The Stock Exchange followed this lead by requiring profit forecasts included in prospectus documents to be reported on by independent accountants and their report to be published.

Prior to these developments, examinations of forecasts by independent accountants were carried out during investigations or for prospectus purposes, but although reports were occasionally prepared, accountants generally were reluctant to allow those reports to be published. The requirement to publish the report in certain instances has led to the production of a short report, appropriate for publication, often backed up by an unpublished longer report. Outside the United Kingdom independent reporting on profit forecasts has met with considerable opposition and is only gradually gaining acceptance.

The circumstances in which accountants may be asked to report on profit forecasts

The reader must understand clearly at the outset that there are no requirements in the United Kingdom for companies or other organisations to make or to publish profit forecasts in the first instance. Misunderstandings frequently arise over this matter and boards of directors often think that when making, or faced with, a takeover bid they have to make a profit forecast. This is not so. If, however, a company has already issued a forecast or even published a form of wording which may be construed as a profit forecast, and subsequently the company becomes involved, willingly or unwillingly, in takeover negotiations or in the issue of a public document, it may be required to confirm or amend such a forecast and have it reported on by accountants.

Furthermore, there are often circumstances in which, when communicating with existing or potential future shareholders, it is the responsibility of directors to ensure that they provide all the information necessary for an informed judgement to be made. In discharging this responsibility the directors may consider it necessary to publish a forecast of the probable outcome of the current financial period and sometimes the succeeding period as well.

The circumstances in which independent accountants may be approached to report on forecasts are normally:

(a) When a company subject to the regulations of the City Code (normally UK public companies whether listed or unlisted) proposes to publish a profit forecast in connection with a takeover or merger.

(b) When a company proposes to publish a forecast for inclusion in a prospectus, offer for sale, or other document, the issue of which is subject to the regulations of The Stock Exchange.

(c) When the accountants are appointed to carry out an investigation or review of a company or unincorporated business, commissioned either by the proprietors or by a potential purchaser or lender and the terms of appointment include a review of profit forecasts.

In circumstances (a) and (b) the accountants would be required to produce a short-form report for publication. In the circumstances described in (c) the report, generally referred to as a long-form report, would be in greater detail and would not be intended for publication. Long-form reports may be required additionally in circumstances (a) and (b).

The term 'reporting accountants' is used in this context for any firm of independent accountants (including the auditors) acting in connection with a profit forecast. In the case of a prospectus document The Stock Exchange requires the auditors to report, but the issuing house may ask another firm of accountants to act jointly with the auditors. Generally speaking it is better for the auditors to be appointed as reporting accountants. Familiarity with historical forecasts and the impact of changing business conditions on profits can probably be assessed better by auditors who know the management and the reliability of their forecasts. The time pressures associated with take-over bids and mergers place a premium on the instant knowledge that auditors have regarding their client company; knowledge that could not be acquired hastily by another. If the audit partner deals with the forecast he must recognise, however, that a conflict of interest may develop later if the results achieved differ substantially from the forecast. He should therefore arrange to have his work on the forecast, and possibly on the audit, reviewed by another partner.

The division of responsibility

The responsibility of the directors

The role of the accountants in making a forecast public cannot be considered without first defining the responsibility of the directors. The sole responsibility for forecasts rests with the directors. They cannot be relieved of their responsibility by accountants or financial advisers and these accountants or other advisers cannot in any way underwrite, guarantee or otherwise accept responsibility for the ultimate realisation of the forecasts. The directors must understand that there is no question of the profit forecasts being 'audited'.

The forecasts should represent the directors' best estimates of the results they reasonably and honestly believe can and will be achieved, as distinct from targets which they may have set as desirable. However, there may be a difference of emphasis between a profit forecast issued in a takeover situation, where speed may be imperative and an over-pessimistic approach may damage the legitimate interests of the company's shareholders, and a profit forecast issued for prospectus purposes, where speed is seldom so important but where over-optimistic forecasts, subsequently not achieved, may harm shareholders by damaging the company's market status.

The directors must also understand that in no circumstances can the accountants prepare the forecasts on their behalf. Preparation of forecasts involves a close working knowledge of all the factors affecting profitability of the business, including the future intentions of the board. The accountants do not have this knowledge and if, in exceptional circumstances, they find it necessary to assist in the preparation, they must make it clear that the responsibility remains with the directors alone.

The efficiency of the preparation of the forecast will be assessed by the accountants, who will require all management involved to explain the procedures adopted and the thinking behind any part of the forecasts. Directors may have to take part in the discussions and must be prepared to devote time to this. The accountants will need to know when top management and the board will be available during the period of the examination, so that they can arrange to discuss the forecast with them.

The board must be prepared to meet frequently, if necessary, for detailed discussion of the forecasts and to accept them formally by board minute before they are published.

The responsibility of the reporting accountants

A profit forecast cannot be confirmed and verified by accountants in the same way as financial statements which present the final results of completed periods, and there is no question of a forecast being audited even though the reporting accountants may be also the company's auditors.

The City Code requires that 'the acounting bases and calculations for the forecasts must be examined and reported on by the auditors or consultant accountants'. The Stock Exchange uses similar wording in its requirements. It is customary, therefore, for published reports to use this form of wording, which seems at first sight to be a rather narrow responsibility.

However, accountants regard the assumptions on which a forecast is based as being an integral part of the forecast. They satisfy themselves as informed persons rather than as experts that the assumptions are realistic in the circumstances; that they are clearly stated in or directly related to the forecast, that no assumptions of importance have been omitted, and that the forecast is reasonable and attainable.

The accountants will make every effort to ensure that the directors have prepared and presented the forecasts in an honest and responsible manner and have compiled the best estimates of the results they reasonably and honestly believe can and will be achieved. An important part of the accountants' work will comprise understanding the instructions which have been given, meeting the personnel involved and questioning them closely on their contributions to the forecasting exercise, and meeting with the directors to ensure that they fully understand and accept the forecasts.

Independent accountants are well qualified to satisfy themselves that the forecasts have been prepared carefully. Although many of the procedures and techniques are similar to those used on audit work, the accountants will place greater emphasis on assessing the degree of skill and care which has gone into the preparation of the forecasts and less emphasis on the examination of underlying evidence to support the explanations given.

In current year forecasts, part of the relevant accounting period will usually have expired, and its results will form a vital part of the calculations. The accountants will therefore assess the efficiency with which management or interim accounts are normally prepared. A review of monthly management accounts in previous financial periods and comparison with previous years' forecasts and the final results will indicate both the efficiency of internal accounting and the reliability of forecasting methods. Such a review forms an integral part of the accountants' work.

If the entire accounting period has expired, but the results have not yet been announced, the reporting accountants will press for the audit to be progressed speedily, and for attention to such critical areas as the evaluation of year-end stocktaking and debtors. In such circumstances the accountants will review the audit work as it proceeds and will take particular care that the figures are substantially finalised, leaving no room for material difference when the audit is complete.

The reporting accountants are 'required to give their consent to the issue of the document with the inclusion therein of their report in the form and context in which it is included.' This is interpreted by accountants as meaning that they are generally satisfied that the document in which their report is to be published is not in any way misleading. The accountants will therefore ask to see all proofs of any such document and to attend any drafting meetings thereon. Attendance at drafting meetings will help to satisfy them that the document has been considered in detail by all parties.

No restrictions on the scope of the work of the reporting accountants will normally be acceptable; but if they have to be accepted they will be described in their report in detail.

In no circumstances will reporting accountants issue an unqualified report if:

(a) they have reason to believe that any of the stated assumptions are invalid or misleading or if an assumption of material importance has been omitted from those listed in the document, or

(b) they are unable to satisfy themselves as to the amount of the forecast or the form of words used to describe it.

The reporting accountants' ultimate sanction is the requirement to give their consent to the issue of the documents. The right to withhold their consent should ensure that no document is issued if it contains anything of a material nature with which the reporting accountants are dissatisfied.

Relations with other financial advisers

The reporting accountants will liaise closely with financial advisers who will be of considerable assistance to them. In the case of profit forecasts made subject to the rules of the City Code or The Stock Exchange, the responsibilities of other financial advisers are laid down. They are required to report on the forecasts and their report must be included in the document and their consent given to publication.

In particular, The Stock Exchange requires the issuing house, or, in the absence of an issuing house, the sponsoring brokers, to report whether they have satisfied themselves that the forecast has been stated by the directors after due and careful enquiry.

In theory, it can be argued that the responsibility of the reporting accountants is more limited than that of financial advisers, as it is restricted to the accounting bases and calculations. In practice, it will be found that both the reporting accountants and financial advisers will wish to be satisfied that the forecasts are attainable.

Every effort will be made by the accountants and financial advisers to establish a close working relationship from the outset. The directors should ensure that copies of all forecasts and supporting documents are sent to both.

In practice, most of the detailed examination and questioning of officials will be carried out by the accountants, who will also advise on the statement of assumptions. In some cases the financial advisers may ask the accountants for a long-form report on the results of their examination. In other cases the financial advisers will seek a joint review of some aspects of the accountants' examination and conclusions. This may be done at a meeting with the directors before the respective reports are published.

As the responsibilities of both financial advisers and reporting accountants are common they are well placed to put any necessary pressure on the board if they think the forecasts are unduly optimistic or otherwise unfairly presented.

Organising the work

The initial approach

A request to act as reporting accountants in connection with profit forecasts to be used in a takeover or merger negotiation is inevitably unpredictable in its timing. Reporting accountants can therefore expect short notice of such an engagement. In addition, the time available to carry out the task will be short and they will be asked to start work almost immediately, especially if their client is defending itself against an unwelcome bid. One reason for such urgency is that under the City Code an offer does not have to be left open for more than twenty one days from the posting of the formal offer document. This posting will normally be preceded by the announcement of an intention to make a bid, but in any event it usually means that the defending side will want to issue its reply within, say ten to fourteen days after the offer has been posted and this reply may include a profit forecast.

On notification of an offer, a board of directors is required to obtain independent professional advice on the reasonableness of the offer and to include the substance of that advice in their reply. Inevitably, the financial advisers will wish to know how reliable the profit forecasts are before they can formulate their conclusions.

There may well be situations where reporting accountants will decline to act and time spent reviewing certain matters prior to settling the terms of the engagement will be time well spent. These matters and the circumstances in which reporting accountants may decline to act are dealt with below.

Initial information required

Reporting accountants will need to know:

    (a) The reason for the proposed publication of the forecast;
    (b) The period to be covered;
    (c) The date by which their report will be required;
    (d) The types of report required;
    (e) Whether the forecast incorporates changes in previous accounting policies;
    (f) The availability of directors and other key executives for discussion on particular aspects of the forecast.
    (g) The names of the financial advisers.

Furthermore, if the reporting accountants are not the auditors, or have no previous client relationship with the company, they will also need to know:

(a) The nature and background of the company's business;

(b) The structure of the group where there are subsidiaries or associated companies;

(c) The location of the accounting units;

(d) The accounting policies normally followed by the company and the consistency with which such policies are applied in subsidiaries and/or branches;

(e) The profit and cash flow forecasting procedures used by the company and the reliance which can be placed on interim accounts and costing records;

(f) Whether the auditors have qualified their reports in recent years.

The above list is not exhaustive and as information is made available other questions will invariably arise. In view of the degree of urgency which usually obtains, the reporting accountants need to have this information within a day or two of the approach being made. Having obtained this information the reporting accountants will consider whether they are willing to act.

Critical matters to be considered before an engagement is accepted

Before deciding whether to accept an engagement to report on profit forecasts, the reporting accountants will consider the critical matters, all of which are inter-related, which are set out in the following paragraphs.

First, the degree of sophistication of the company's forecasting procedures and the adequacy and reliability of interim accounts are clearly of fundamental importance when the forecast represents a projection for a substantial unexpired time or when it is required in a hurry. In the case of a prospectus, where speed is less likely to be crucial it is clearly in the long term interests of the company to rectify any deficiency in forecasting procedures. A reputable issuing house will not agree to sponsor an issue unless steps are taken to install and implement satisfactory procedures before compiling a forecast for publication. However, when timing is critical, as in a takeover situation, and the forecasting procedures and preparation of interim accounts are unsatisfactory, then, unless the company's structure and operations are of the simplest nature, the reporting accountants will probably decline to act, or will warn the directors that their report may have to be qualified as to the reliability of the forecasting procedures. This applies particularly when the reporting accountants are not the auditors and do not have detailed knowledge of the accounting procedures.

Secondly, the period to be covered by the forecasts may be critical. Reporting accountants will not normally undertake to report on forecasts for more than the current accounting period and, provided an adequate part of the current year has elapsed, the following accounting year. Definition of the proportion of the current year which can be accepted as adequate will depend on the whole client situation, but it is now generally agreed that accountants will only accept an engagement to report on a period other than the current one in exceptional circumstances. If they consider the period to be covered by the forecasts to be unreasonable they will decline to act or request the directors to shorten the period.

Thirdly, the nature of the business should not be such as to make it almost impossible for the directors to forecast the outcome with any degree of certainty. Examples of this are jobbing or dealing businesses where the profits may fluctuate so much in timing and volume that even when a substantial part of the forecasting period has elapsed the final result cannot be foreseen. In such circumstances reporting accountants will decline to act or indicate to the directors that their report will probably be qualified as to the acceptability of the assumptions on which the forecast is based.

Fourthly, the time within which the accountants' report is required should not be so severely restricted that it precludes them from obtaining sufficient information for a sound professional judgement. In practice, one of the major differences between a forecast required for a prospectus document and that required for a City Code document is the amount of time likely to be available to the reporting accountants to carry out their work. In the former case, a reasonable time will usually be allowed, but in a takeover situation the timing requirements of the City Code put the reporting accountants under pressure to report within two or three weeks. Reporting accountants must allow themselves sufficient time to carry out their work and if this is not forthcoming they will decline to act, or request that the issue of circulars be appropriately deferred.

The letter of engagement

It is important for the reporting accountants to confirm their understanding of their instructions in a letter of engagement which should be sent to the client at the earliest practicable time.

Controlling, staffing & completing the engagement

Controlling the engagement

Reporting accountants normally require their partner or manager controlling the engagement to be at the centre of the operation. It is that person's responsibility to ensure that the standard of judgement applied over the whole operation is as uniform as possible. It is his responsibility to instruct and brief those who do the detailed work; and all reporting back and all final reviews of working papers and findings should be made to, and done by, him.

The circumstances under which a report on profit forecast is made usually help in exercising this central control. The directors should be willing to arrange that much of the physical movement is of directors and officers coming to see those controlling the engagement at a central point — which is probably the client's head office.

At the outset reporting accountants will determine:

(a) The areas of the company's activities which are significant as regards their contribution to the forecast results and to previous audited results;
(b) The areas which are likely to give rise to difficulties by reason of the nature of the activities or the economic factors affecting the activities;
(c) The acceptability of the accounting policies previously followed or to be followed in the forecast if different from the previous policies;
(d) The reasonableness of the assumptions on which the forecast is based as set out in any instructions issued by the company to its accounting locations.

Once these matters have been determined then reporting accountants will prepare detailed instructions to their staff or other offices, or other firms who will carry out specific sections of the work.

These instructions will call for working papers or a report which may include:

(a) Various figures from the previous audited period, unaudited expired period, and forecast period;
(b) Experience of forecasts for previous periods and subsequent outturns;
(c) The assumptions used as a basis for the forecast figures and an opinion as to whether they are reasonable;

90

(d) The names and positions of the persons with whom the forecast has been discussed;

(e) Confirmation that the forecast has been formally adopted by the subsidiary company or divisional board;

(f) An opinion as to whether the forecast has been carefully prepared in accordance with the instructions issued by the company and represents management's best estimates of the results likely to be achieved on bases consistent with the accounting policies previously followed and on the basis of the assumptions made;

(g) An opinion as to whether the company's production resources, financial resources, and management resources appear to be adequate for the attainment of the forecast;

(h) Depending on the general cash resources available within the group the instructions may call for detailed information about the cash flow projections and working capital requirements;

(i) If inter group trading or charging is material, details may be needed to avoid duplication.

Many firms of reporting accountants have detailed check lists for the work to be done on the examination of profit forecasts.

Staffing the engagement

Work on profit forecasts involves an onerous degree of responsibility and the exercise of a great deal of judgement. It can be properly discharged only if the partners or managers concerned are ready and able to cooperate fully. If a proper relationship is established between the partner controlling the engagement, the company's directors, and the financial advisers, the two latter will be anxious to have the accountant's advice and help in the many meetings needed when profit forecasts are to be published.

When the auditors are appointed reporting accountants it is usually an advantage if the partners and managerial staff who handle the audit are also engaged on the profit forecasts. They must recognise, however, that reports on profit forecasts require a greater degree of partner or senior manager involvement than recurrent audit work. It will often be necessary for other partners and managerial staff to assist in examining the forecasts of operating units and subsidiaries.

The use of other offices and other firms

When reporting accountants are asked to report on the profit forecasts of a group, some subsidiaries of which are audited by other firms, the question will arise as to what use, if any, should be made of those other firms. The arguments in favour of using the auditors are fairly strong. On the other hand, in the case of a group forecast, it is only the reporting accountants whose name appears in the document and who take ultimate responsibility. As a result they will probably wish to use their own offices as far as possible.

If the client expresses the wish that other firms of auditors should be involved, the reporting accountants will weigh the reputation and standing of the other firms and the relative importance of the subsidiaries concerned, before deciding whether that engagement is acceptable to them. If it is, they must establish clearly at the outset that the other firm is to work on the engagement under their overall control and accept whatever instructions and supervision the reporting accountants impose.

Where the client has a wide geographical spread it will be necessary for the reporting accountants to use their own overseas offices and associates. They must give proper briefing and guidance to the other offices, who, in their turn, must respond by making partners and staff of sufficient calibre available to do the work and by accepting supervision of the partner in overall charge.

Completing the work

As the work nears completion the reporting accountants will collate the information and consolidate the figures emanating from other persons, firms or offices participating in the work. At the same time they will agree with the company the precise description of the assumptions on which the forecast is based and the amount of the forecast or the form of words to be used to describe it.

Time must also be allowed for meetings with the financial advisers and the directors at which all aspects of the forecasts will be reviewed. If the reporting accountants have material reservations they will inform the directors and financial advisers of their doubts in good time so that the forecast can be amended if necessary.

Before signing their report, the reporting accountants will ensure that the forecast is formally considered at a board meeting at which they are present. The financial advisers will also wish to attend. At this meeting the accountants may re-emphasise the directors' responsibility for the forecast. They will ensure that the directors confirm by minute that in their opinion:

(a) the forecast has been carefully compiled and is reasonably attainable; and
(b) the assumptions on which the forecast is based are reasonable and that none have been omitted.

The wording of the forecast and of the assumptions will be set out in the minute.

If the reporting accountants are also satisfied with the contents of the document in which the forecast and their report thereon is to be published, they will then sign their letter of consent.

Forms of report

Unpublished long-form accountants' report

It is now common practice for the merchant bankers, or other financial advisers, or the directors, to ask the reporting accountants to provide them with an additional long-form report on the profit forecasts.

Preparation of such a report is often difficult in the limited time available and also because the directors may revise their forecasts up to the last minute as further information becomes available. Nevertheless, writing such a report is a useful discipline for the reporting accountants, since it records the information on which they have formed their opinion.

While it is still in draft form, reporting accountants will discuss their report with the directors and with the financial advisers. This will ensure that there is no disagreement as to facts, and will give the directors and financial advisers the opportunity to examine with the reporting accountants any matters which may have been overlooked or misinterpreted.

The long-form report will indicate the nature and extent of the enquiries made by the reporting accountants and the replies received. As far as possible it will be confined to factual matters. Reporting accountants may summarise possible variations to the forecast which arise from their examination but they will avoid adjusting the amount of the forecast reported upon unless such variations are specifically agreed. Any expression of opinion by the reporting accountants on detailed matters will be clearly distinguished from matters of fact.

The report may contain:
  (a) A recital of the scope of the work;
  (b) A recital of the forecast figures;
  (c) A recital of the assumptions on which the forecast is based;
  (d) Information as to the accounting policies adopted by the directors;
  (e) Information as to the interim results included in the forecasts and the reliability shown in the past by interim accounts;
  (f) A recital of any recent forecasts made by the directors and the outcome;

(g) Comments on trends and on other significant amounts and ratios;

(h) Details of the methods used to compile the forecasts, and by whom;

(i) Explanations given to the reporting accountants and by whom.

For a large group similar information may have to be given for each constituent company or sub-group which is material to the compilation of the total forecast.

Published short-form accountants' report

Provided the reporting accountants have no material reservations about the accounting policies and calculations for the forecast and have no reason to think them inconsistent with the stated assumptions, their short-form report for publication will be on the following lines:

> 'We have reviewed the accounting policies and calculations for the profit forecast (for which the Directors are solely responsible) of [Blank Public Ltd. Co.] and its subsidiaries ('the Group') for the year ending [31st December 19. .] included in [the offer document] dated [30th September 19. .] addressed to [the shareholders of Target Public Ltd. Co.].
>
> In our opinion, the forecast, so far as the accounting policies and calculations are concerned, has been properly compiled on the basis of the assumptions made by the Board set out in [the offer document] and is presented on a basis consistent with the accounting policies normally adopted by the Group.'

If the reporting accountants have been unable to obtain all the information they require, or have serious reservations to their opinion, then they will set out the facts and the effect these facts have on their opinion.

Recent changes in the City Code require that any unaudited profits figures published during an offer period should also be reported on by the auditors or consultant accountants and any financial adviser.

Published financial advisers' reports

The financial advisers are not specifically required to report on the assumptions, although they sometimes do so. Generally they will refer to any report made by the reporting accountants and to discussions which they themselves have had with the directors. Their opinion is normally that the forecasts have been prepared with due care and consideration. It should be noted that The Stock Exchange requires the issuing house, or in the absence of an issuing house, the sponsoring brokers to report 'whether or not they have satisfied themselves that the forecast has been stated by the directors after due and careful enquiry'.

Consent to publish

The reporting accountants and the financial advisers have to give their consents to the issue of the document with the inclusion therein of their respective reports in the form and context in which those reports appear. This emphasises the need for the accountants to satisfy themselves that the presentation of the forecast and the other matters contained in the document are fair and reasonable. They can reasonably expect that their views on drafting and other points which arise will be given careful consideration. Their consent will be addressed to the people issuing the document, which may be either the directors or financial advisers.

Dating the report

Reporting accountants will date their report with the same date as that of the document in which it is published. They will consider it important to keep events constantly under review up to that date in order that anything which could materially affect the forecast profits, such as changes in interest rates, serious strikes, loss of valuable orders, or disasters, can be considered by the directors before the forecast is issued.

Extended use of the report

If the directors wish to use the forecast again either in a later document concerned with the same transaction or, within 60 days, in the context of a different transaction, the consent of the reporting accountants and financial advisers is required. Before giving their consent, reporting accountants will discuss the forecast and the assumptions on which it is based with the company's officials and obtain their oral confirmation that the assumptions are still valid and that nothing has come to light which could materially affect the outcome of the forecast results. The document should contain a statement by the directors that the forecast remains valid for the purposes of the offer and the directors, in approving the document, will be asked to pass a board minute to that effect.

8 The role of the merchant bank

R W Heley, Director, Hill Samuel & Co. Limited

Introduction

Profit forecasting for publication and, thus, public scrutiny, is highly demanding and also highly sensitive. It is not surprising that British listed companies seldom disclose their specific profit forecasts except in circumstances when shareholders need special guidance for their investment decisions, for example, when they are asked to subscribe further capital, to accept shares as takeover considerations or to accept or reject an offer for their shares.

By statute and by City self-regulation, there is a network of defences to protect the shareholder from basing his investment decision on an irresponsible forecast. One of the key components of the defensive network is the judgement of an independent financial adviser which must usually be published in the same document as the profit forecast in question.

This chapter reviews the present functions and responsibilities of the financial adviser or merchant bank, illustrates how these obligations are fulfilled and comments on areas in which further thought is required in the interests of improving the quality of published forecasts.

When should profit forecasts be made public?

As a rule, a company can choose whether to incorporate a profit forecast in a public document relating to a capital raising operation or a takeover. The company's financial adviser will be expected to provide guidance on the relevance of, and necessity for, a public forecast in any particular circumstances. The following section outlines some of the general rules that apply in common situations. References in this section to profit forecasts include profit estimates (i.e., in relation to financial periods already completed but not yet audited), although the question of reporting on estimates as opposed to forecasts is not within the terms of reference of this chapter.

Flotations

Profit forecasts are included in a very high proportion of prospectuses published by companies arranging listing on The Stock Exchange or quotations on the Unlisted Securities Market and inviting the public to subscribe for their shares.

Profit forecasts are incorporated in prospectus documents to satisfy two requirements:

(a) that potential subscribers should be provided with all information relevant to their decision whether or not to subscribe. The necessity to express the company's profit prospects in the form of a detailed forecast is normally avoided only when publicised financial information is fully up to date and it is too early in the financial year for a worthwhile forecast to be made. Prospectuses published at the time of the announcement of the previous year's results may fall into this category.

(b) that the company or vending shareholders should achieve the best possible price for their shares consistent with a successful issue; that is, fully subscribed by genuine investors. New issues are normally made when the issuer's profits are on a rising trend, but subscribers may be expected to place greater weight on prospective earnings where there is a formal forecast than where they must make their own judgement even of short term profit prospects.

In considering these requirements, it should be borne in mind that timing a flotation is under the control of the issuer and its advisers, subject only to market conditions at the date of launch. Such operations are planned months or even years in advance and timing will co-ordinate with the issuer's financial calendar and forecasting arrangements. In consultation with its advisers, the company will have every opportunity to develop forecasting systems capable of producing a forecast to publication standard at the time of issue of the prospectus.

The provisions of the Companies Act 1948 with regard to the standards of care that must be observed by directors in the compilation of a prospectus delineate responsibilities for conservative forecasting quite effectively.

Rights issues

Rights issues are usually made in rather different circumstances to flotations. The relatively short gestation period, more limited correlation between issue terms and forecast profits, and heavy dependence on prevailing market conditions tend to reduce the significance of a profit forecast so far as the issuing company is concerned. Nonetheless, a rights issue circular together with accompanying issue documents is a prospectus in the Companies Act sense and the standards of care in presenting information in such a circular are clearly defined.

As a matter of practice, a financial adviser would be reluctant to underwrite an issue based on a circular that did not incorporate a profits forecast unless very recent financial results were available. In many cases, companies timing rights issues to coincide with interim results would have made forecasts on an earlier occasion, such as a chairman's statement at an annual general meeting or in the latest annual report and accounts, which require formal reports from the auditors and financial advisers.

The relative infrequency of profit forecasts in rights issue documents reflects the choice of many companies to make such issues simultaneously with their preliminary announcements of results or publication of annual reports and accounts. The popularity of such timing reflects the relatively limited impact of profit forecasts on rights issue terms. The onus on a financial adviser to advise his client on the combination of timing and inclusion of a profit forecast in a rights issue circular is therefore particularly great.

Takeover offers and defences

The inclusion of profit forecasts in documents relating to takeovers is governed by the City Code on Takeovers and Mergers, popularly called 'the City Code'.

Profit forecasts are published in only a minority of takeover offers and defences. When so published however, they tend to be highly publicised and even more widely criticised if they are not subsequently achieved. For this reason and in view of the usual urgency of preparation of takeover documentation, companies avoid including such forecasts in takeover or defence circulars wherever possible.

Profit forecasts may form a major feature in a takeover battle when published by a bidder to support the price of its own shares offered as consideration, or by a bid target, to support rejection of an offer on the grounds that the terms are inadequate. In these cases, the tactical considerations relating to use of the forecast as a weapon will be critically assessed by the company's financial adviser. Before considering tactics, however, the financial adviser must have details of the forecast and the extent to which it meets publication standard. Despite the shortage of time in the context of a takeover, it is essential that a company be advised to prepare or update and improve its forecast to this standard, even if the revised figures are never published. Such forecasts must also be kept up-to-date throughout the currency of a bid.

Most of the forecasts published by either offeror or offeree in takeover documents result from the provisions of City Code Practice Note No. 6. This implies that any forecast made before the advent of a takeover is likely to be material in the context of that takeover and should be published. The City Code now insists also that figures already published in relation to a current financial period (usually interim results) be reported on in the same way as a profit forecast.

Whatever the circumstances that give rise to publication, there are particular hazards in publishing profit forecasts in offer or defence circulars. Takeovers almost invariably involve a restrictive timetable during which senior officers of offeror and offeree companies have many other problems upon their hands. In an offer or defence circular, as stated in Practice Note No. 7 of the present City Code, it may be a disservice to shareholders to err on the conservative side. Thus the usual defensive mechanism of including a reasonable margin for error in a forecast is usually curtailed or eliminated in this context as opposed to other instances where forecasts are published.

The principles involved in reviewing a forecast made in a takeover situation do not differ from those employed in other forecast contexts. The adviser does not confirm the figures in the forecast; but that the forecast has been made after due and careful enquiry by the directors of the company. The outturn of forecasts made in the context of takeovers tends, however, to receive wider and more documented scrutiny, largely as a result of the interest of the Takeover Panel. The Panel has published detailed reviews of individual forecasts which have not been met and general observations on forecasting practice in its annual reports and updating of the City Code. This is the major source of 'case law' on the way reporting accountants and financial advisers exercise their responsibility to report on profit forecasts.

The responsibility of the financial adviser

The City Code

The provisions of the City Code relating to publication of profit forecasts are set out in Rule 16 and Practice Notes 6 and 7 of the present edition. The important feature of these provisions is that they cover the requirements where a forecast is included in a document and detail the reporting requirements. Guidance on the standards whereby the financial adviser should review a forecast before providing its report is strictly limited.

Three points that are made in the City Code are of major significance to the fulfilment of the financial adviser's role:

(a) Any profit forecasts must be compiled with the greatest care by the directors whose sole responsibility they are;

(b) Any financial adviser mentioned in a document containing a profit forecast must report on that forecast;

(c) A duty is placed on the financial advisers to discuss the assumptions upon which a profit forecast is based (and which must be published in the document containing the forecast) with their client company and to satisfy themselves that the forecast has been made with due care and consideration. Financial advisers and accountants have substantial influence on the information given about assumptions and neither should allow an assumption to be published which appears to them to be unrealistic (or one to be omitted which appears to them to be important) without commenting on it in their reports.

The Stock Exchange

The publication of profit forecasts by listed companies in prospectuses or documents issued otherwise than in the context of takeovers, is subject to the requirements set out in Schedule II Parts A and B to The Stock Exchange 'Admission of Securities to Listing'. The Stock Exchange provides even less guidance than the City Code on the matter of forecasting standards and practices. The following are germane:

(a) Where a profit forecast appears, the principal assumptions upon which it is based must be stated;

(b) The issuing house involved must report, in addition to the reports of the auditors, whether or not it has satisfied itself that the forecast has been stated by the directors after making due and careful enquiry.

In practice the standards implied by the City Code for method of presentation and responsibility for profit forecasts are observed generally for documents subject to The Stock Exchange regulations.

Other

As stated above, there is little case law or practical definition of the concept of 'due and careful enquiry' or 'due care and consideration' and undoubtedly there is a wide range of interpretation among merchant banks. In reaching an acceptable definition, one must examine in a little more detail the responsibilities of the financial adviser when it provides a letter for publication in the terms required by The Stock Exchange or the Takeover Panel.

(a) *Contractual*
The financial adviser has a contractual duty to provide competent advice to its client. Usually it will have an existing relationship and knowledge of the client's financial systems and similar matters. Any failure to maintain reasonable standards of competence in the provision of advice, including the statement relating to 'due and careful enquiry', could *in extremis* be a breach of contract rendering the financial adviser liable to civil action for damages for any loss by the client arising from such breach.

(b) *Professional*
In addition to their contractual duty, financial advisers are subject to the doctrine of negligent mis-statement as clarified in the *Hedley Byrne* case. Thus, they can be held liable for mis-statements made negligently by them which are relied upon by those whom the merchant bank could reasonably have foreseen would rely upon them. In the context of reporting on profit forecasts, this liability is potentially extremely great. The common form of wording of a financial adviser's report on a profit forecast is that the directors are solely responsible for the forecast and the assumptions on which it is based. On the other hand the merchant bank goes on record as saying that a forecast has been made by the directors after due and careful enquiry or with due care and consideration. If, in the event, it becomes clear that this could not have been so, the merchant bank may be held liable. In addition, in the case of a document published by a merchant bank on behalf of a company, the merchant bank may be held responsible for any negligent statement throughout the document, which may include a profit forecast by the company. The merchant bank will always obtain warranties from the company and sometimes from the directors in relation to the completeness, fairness and accuracy of all information in the document. This, however, entitles it only to claim separately against the company and directors if it is sued itself by a person reasonably relying on that document.

(c) *Ethical*
Finally, merchant banks believe that they owe a duty to all users of the capital markets to maintain fair play and professional standards. This non-legal duty underlies the written rules of the

City Code and The Stock Exchange and both banking and institutional practice.

Responsibility in practice

Translation of these requirements and responsibilities into a code of practice by the financial advisers when publication of a profit forecast is required is still relatively crude. Some basic principles and observations are set out below. In essence, the financial adviser may normally be expected to concentrate on establishing the following:

(a) that the assumptions employed are reasonable and responsible in all the prevailing circumstances;

(b) that the directors have exercised adequate control over the employment of the economic and commercial assumptions in formulating all components of the forecast;

(c) that the resultant forecast is consistent with the assumptions;

(d) that the directors have been adequately involved in the preparation and review of the forecast;

(e) that the forecast has been fully and correctly maintained up to date and amended to reflect any changes in underlying assumptions, management accounting information and other changes in external factors since its original formulation;

(f) that the accounting bases, including consistency of practices and policies, and the calculations and compilation of the forecast are logical and accurate;

(g) that all forecasting systems in use are theoretically sound and have a reasonable historic record of accuracy.

The distinction between the responsibility of the financial adviser and the accountant reporting on a forecast is difficult to determine. I believe that, in the absence of the relevant professional skills and suitable labour force, the financial adviser cannot undertake fundamental investigation of items (e) and (f). He must rely on the reporting accountant to inspect the bases and compilation of the forecast both for individual units and upon consolidation. While the accountant is instructed by and reports formally to the company, it is accepted practice, usually written into letters of instruction, that the reporting accountant will discuss with the financial adviser any aspect of his investigations.

A financial adviser may reasonably accept the auditor's opinion as an independent verification of accounting bases and compilation of a forecast, but the remaining aspects of review must be considered with the directors separately. Again, however, it is usual practice to request that the reporting accountant be prepared to discuss the other aspects of any forecast with the directors in conjunction with the financial adviser. Extremely close co-operation between the two is, therefore, essential to ensure that no misunderstanding arises with regard to division of responsibility or areas of investigation which the financial adviser would wish to discuss with the directors and reporting accountants. As in so many aspects of professional and management life, clear and precise initial instructions and the fullest communication will obviate the vast majority of difficulties encountered in the conduct of a forecast review.

The conduct of profit forecast investigations

The timetable

Consequently, it should be invariable practice at the earliest possible stage for the financial adviser to prepare and circulate to all parties concerned a fully detailed and documented timetable covering all aspects of the operation in question. This alerts the company and reporting accountants to target dates for publication and to the way their respective responsibilities for the profit forecast fit into the many other features of the transaction. It is impracticable to generalise about the form that the timetable is likely to take. I would only emphasise the importance, in practice, of co-ordinating the programmes of the reporting accountants and the financial adviser and of the latter's initial impressions of procedures and practices with a company — this helps immensely to identify areas in which special attention and additional work may be required by the company. At the formal review, say, a few days before publication it is too late.

The formal instruction letter

The second key preliminary document is the letter of instruction to the reporting accountant from the company. The critical features from the financial adviser's point of view are the inclusion of the authority from the company to the accountant to discuss without restraint any aspect of his review with officers in the company and with the financial adviser. No accountant or financial adviser could produce an unqualified report on a profit forecast without full and free access to all information sources within a company and to each other's work.

The formal review

Formal review of a profit forecast is usually conducted by the financial adviser after the investigating accountant has completed his report in a final, if draft, form. By then, the financial adviser will have had detailed discussions with the key company executives involved and with the investigating accountant during his field work before preparing for the final review.

1. *Who should be present?*
    The persons who should normally attend the forecast review with financial adviser and reporting accountant will be:
    (a) all executive directors;
    (b) non-executive directors comprising the audit committee, if one exists;
    (c) other key executives involved in preparing the forecast — these may be line executives (say, managing directors of substantial divisions or subsidiaries) or staff executives (say, the corporate planning department responsible for forecasting systems and techniques).

Access may also be required by telephone or other means to overseas line executives or to directors of major associated companies.

2. *What material should be available?*
    Subject to modifications or additions to take into account special areas of concern identified at a preliminary review, the following will be the most important categories of information required:
    (a) the consolidated profit forecast identifying all significant profit and loss account items in a manner capable of direct comparison with published reports and accounts and with management accounts;
    (b) a statement of the bases upon which the forecast has been prepared including the forecasting systems, the review procedures and the underlying assumptions;
    (c) full supporting documentation in respect of each major reporting and forecasting unit indicating special additional bases or assumptions relevant to that unit, together with supporting information such as order book details, costing procedures etc.;
    (d) latest available management accounts plus a comparison with original forecast and an indication of how the original forecast for subsequent periods has been revised to take these into account;
    (e) full records of previous forecasts compared with actual results, including revised forecasts made at a comparable stage of earlier years;
    (f) the draft final report of the accountant, containing the results of his review of the compilation of the forecast;

(g) a cash flow projection for the profit forecast period, and, in the case of a review of a working capital statement, for at least the following financial year with supporting statements confirming indebtedness and facilities available.

The financial adviser's objectives

In carrying out the review, the financial adviser will have several objectives:

(a) to identify the manner in which the forecast has been formulated and to ensure that those elements of the forecast which are susceptible to the application of statistically sophisticated quantitative techniques have been so prepared and that the inevitable element of business judgement has been confined to areas capable of no other approach and that those judgements have been made on the basis of duly considered analysis, experience and are logical and consistent with all other aspects of the forecast;

(b) to identify all facts already known in relation to the profit forecast period including management accounting information for any part of the period already completed and background data such as order books etc.;

(c) to ensure that where subjective judgement has been employed it has been adequately monitored and controlled. In particular, no judgemental element contributed by a single executive should have been accepted without evaluation by a jury of others with relevant experience, including responsible main board directors;

(d) to assess the quality and sophistication of quantitative forecasting techniques employed;

(e) to identify and consider the reasonableness of the assumptions made and ensure that they are limited to basic economic predictions, the estimated effect of qualitative or non-quantifiable factors on the forecast, and the specification of critical aspects of prevailing uncertainty (such as date of completion of a factory unit, ending of industrial action, result of litigation or statutory investigation etc.).

Practical observations

The financial adviser must consider, in particular, the forecasting systems and the assumptions employed in formulation of any forecast. Few cases have arisen where failure to meet a profit forecast has been demonstrated to have resulted from errors in compilation. The reasons for failure are usually rooted in areas of judgement or of assumption, whether published in the relevant document or unpublished. Financial advisers are, therefore, paying increasing attention to the definition of 'unforeseen circumstances', (that is, any change in factors external to the forecast which could not reasonably be foreseen at the time of the forecast), to the reasonableness of the actual assumptions upon which the forecast is based, and to the assessment of the materiality of such assumptions and the selection of those to be published in the document containing the forecast.

When determining the structure of his review and the areas in which special scrutiny will be required the financial adviser will assess the nature of the company and its business. The nature of the adviser's approach will reflect his interpretation of the industry or industries in which the company operates and his knowledge of the company and its forecasting techniques. He will endeavour to isolate critical sensitivities, especially in the case of an industry involving high volatility and, thus, forecasting risk.

Factors normally regarded as implying high risk or volatility for a particular company or business sector are:

(a) dependence on small number of contracts, customers or suppliers;

(b) sensitivity to product mix in a volatile market;

(c) dependence on new products or product modifications;

(d) high overhead content and low marginal cost of sales;

(e) dependence on overseas sales with volatile exchange rates.

Forecasts and forecasting systems

From experience, I would suggest that there are two areas where profit forecasts tend to be weak. The first is the absence or weakness of the quantitative statistical techniques used in preparation of the forecast. The second is the failure of companies to define sufficiently rigorously the assumptions upon which their profit forecasts are prepared.

Inevitably, standards vary between companies. Predictably, larger companies tend to be more sophisticated. There are many cases, however, of smaller companies where the directors do not agree a common set of economic and commercial assumptions to be employed by all units in formulating their individual component of the forecast. In some cases, forecast procedures in units within the same company may differ or the underlying assumptions may be inconsistent between units. Such inconsistencies and variations must be eradicated or fully investigated and determined to be immaterial in the context of the forecast (which is likely, by definition, to be difficult to establish) before a financial adviser can give an unqualified report on the forecast.

The greatest difficulty encountered by the financial adviser in many smaller companies is that of identifying the actual forecasting methods in use. Most smaller companies rely almost entirely on subjective forecasting methods for which adequate tests are difficult to devise. Many also tend to use such projections as budgets or management targets; thus incorporating a potential element of distortion.

Examples of the various factors that may be used in varying degrees for a subjective sales forecast are:

(a) past sales trends of the unit;
(b) sales department estimates based on executive opinion, field sales force reports or customer enquiries;
(c) general economic or industry indicators;
(d) plans for new products; product promotion;
(e) competitor activity and production capacity;
(f) instinct or hunch, based on personal knowledge

The latter is often found to be the most powerful influence of all. To question it may create tension and conflict with the manager(s) involved. Nonetheless, this is frequently the weakest feature of a company's approach to profit forecasting.

Where essentially subjective techniques are being employed the financial adviser has particular difficulty in making a reasoned appraisal. Reference to the accuracy of previous forecasts by the same unit/individual, detailed investigations of the unit's business, and any relevant external data and forecasts available are the major tools in such a study. Even so, it may be difficult to ascertain essential factors such as the underlying reasoning for the forecast, reasons for departures from the forecast in the past, the impact of particular external factors on the forecast under review and the indentification of intrinsic assumptions which might in practice warrant publication. There is always room for talented and experienced subjectivity, but it is far more useful in the context of a professionally prepared forecast. The substantial development of forecasting techniques in academic circles, the professions and large companies should be reflected in improved technical quality of forecasting within companies generally. There is a substantial onus on merchant banks to introduce their clients to the best forecasting methodology.

In practice, the further detailed study that may be carried out by the financial adviser may also be limited by his own lack of industry knowledge. Normally he will have access only to published industry information, such as industry statistics from the Central Statistical Office, the Board of Trade or a Trade Association, to assess specific market trends related to the forecast or trends in raw material or other direct cost items.

Whatever verification procedures may be adopted, a key technique used in such cases by the financial adviser is the assessment of sensitivity of the resultant profit forecast to changes in the variable which has itself been forecast by questionable subjective procedure. High sensitivity will mean the final profit forecast is expressed either after an appropriately large contingency or in the form of a range of possible outcomes. In extreme cases, publication of a general assumption regarding the forecasting unit in question may be required, possibly indicating the scale of sensitivity of key variables in the forecast to different assumptions.

To place the magnitude of the problem in context, the only authoritative survey of business forecasting practices in the UK (Turner, 1974. Surrey University Press) established that twelve per cent of the 300 largest UK companies employed only subjective forecasting methods and thirty-four per cent relied on such methods for at least half of their forecasting efforts. Thus, only fifty-four per cent used formal systems for more than half of their forecasting activity.

Underlying assumptions

It is inevitable that consideration of any profit forecast by a financial adviser should involve close scrutiny of the assumptions upon which the forecast is based.

The financial adviser's primary concern will be to establish the exact nature of the assumptions employed in any forecast. The City Code suggests that as a result of their review, the reporting accountants will be in a position to advise the company on the assumptions that should be listed in the circular and the way in which they should be described. Often the financial adviser becomes heavily involved also in the process of identifying assumptions. This is an area where he may feel that, unlike the compilation of the forecast, he cannot rely solely on the reporting accountants.

Identification of assumptions is often a major problem especially in the case of unstructured and subjective forecasts, where many assumptions may have been made but not written down. The reporting accountant and financial adviser would then have to discuss the bases and make-up of the forecast with the executives responsible and translate them into a written set of assumptions.

The second practical difficulty is appraising the significance of an assumption and determining those that should be published. The City Code Practice Note 7 attempts to give some guidance in this field. In view of the unique nature of each individual profit forecast, it is beyond reasonable expectation that a code of conduct defining accurately the elements of the professional judgement involved could be drafted. There can be no substitute for judgement, nor is there an objective test that can be applied, especially in areas involving commercial interpretation in an industry in which the forecaster is, by definition, the expert.

Nonetheless, there are basic standards which any financial adviser will expect to be observed. In essence, he will be concerned that assumptions should be mutually consistent and consistently applied. Thus, they should reflect reasonable expectations based on historic trends and available factual evidence, unless an identifiable special factor has to be taken into account. All components of a forecast, and the forecasts of all subsidiaries or forecasting units, should use reconcilable assumptions. This may seem simplistic, but failure to observe these basic principles is probably the most common source of difficulty in forecast appraisal.

The following are general guidelines on assumptions based on practical experience. They are not based on the City Code or The Stock Exchange requirements and should not be regarded as definitive — only as a practitioner's view. Any finance director preparing a forecast to publication standard should consult the City Code and, in particular, Practice Note No. 7 on this subject.

1   *Assumptions relating to general economic conditions*
Few smaller companies believe themselves to be affected by trends in overall economic activity, but even the most subjective forecaster abstracts his view of such factors as personal disposable income and consumer expenditure, investment expenditure, government or public sector purchasing. While not advocating that each company should publish its view of the trend in GNP, I believe it is essential that the forecasting company should have adopted and circulated to forecasting units a set of assumptions about major economic aggregates. Where one or more of these assumptions has a material influence on an individual component of the detailed forecast, rather than acting as general background, it should be published.

Rates of inflation in wages and other elements of costs and companies' ability to match increased costs in their pricing are some of the most critical factors in profit achievement for any company. An overwhelming majority of UK companies has suffered a substantial decline in margins at the operating and pre-tax profit level during the last decade. Yet a very high proportion of companies that have published profit forecasts have avoided the determination of future inflation by means of a general assumption to the effect that gross margins will be unchanged. In many cases such an underlying assumption has not even been published. Wording on the following lines: 'it will be possible to increase selling prices approximately in proportion to increases in costs' is frequently encountered. This form of assumption requires substantial additional background analysis by the appraiser. The following factors must be considered:

(a) the time lag with which price increases may be effected after cost increases have been notified, taking into account commercial factors and applicable local legal regulations;

(b) the level of competition, including import penetration, and its impact on an individual supplier's ability to raise prices without affecting market share;

(c) in conjunction with exchange rates, effects of price changes on export market achievements;

(d) trends in productivity and the influences underlying the rate of improvement (or deterioration) built into the forecast.

A more specific assumption about inflation rates, even if only based on an external economic forecast and, say, the company's own known wage awards, should be a matter of general practice.

2   *Assumptions of a commercial nature relating to the specific company and its business*

Many items under this heading can only be incorporated by way of assumption as they are matters of purely subjective judgement. They might include, for example:

(a) the achievement of target levels of sales set in conjunction with an advertising campaign or other form of promotion;

(b) the achievement of targets for the introduction of new products or design modifications for existing products and the market's acceptance of them;

(c) the achievement of targets for completion and coming on-stream of new production facilities, conversion or moving of existing facilities;

(d) successful defence against attacks on patents, licence-protected technology, designs etc., or achievement of such protection for new products;

(e) that the rate and quality of production of a new product will be adequate to meet the market's requirements;

(f) that proposed revisions to work schedules will be accepted by employees.

This type of assumption can only be reviewed by reference to all factual evidence available. In most cases this will be given by historical correlation based on experiences of similar events in the company's history. Often, it will lend itself to sensitivity analysis. The financial adviser's views on whether such an assumption should be published and whether publication should include a sensitivity report will be based on such tests and judgement of materiality. A conflict between a desire to publish and the company's concern about giving away unnecessary commercial information may also arise from time to time. In the event of an extreme conflict it may be necessary for the financial adviser to seek Panel dispensation for a non-specific form of wording.

I also believe that for publication purposes, a financial adviser should persuade companies to accept the linking of assumptions of this nature to their own specific decisions. The reader should be greatly helped by wordings similar to the following examples:

'group resources devoted to leasing will not be increased from present levels/will be expanded to meet the anticipated level of demand'

'the X factory will switch from production of A to production of B in April and achieve fully operational output levels by June'

'the group's X subsidiary will promote its agency to distribute C in the UK by appropriate staff recruitment and training and the acquisition of appropriate new facilities by no later than June'

'the closure of X factory will be effected by September/the new Y facility will be fully on-stream at operational output levels by September'

'the strike affecting production at X factory or Y factory of customer X will cease in 0 weeks and normal working resume 0 days thereafter'.

Such assumptions can be supported by sensitivity analyses. The financial adviser should require these to be carried out, albeit in a relatively crude form if there are practical constraints on full analyses.

3   *Assumptions relating to external circumstances*
Specific external circumstances, such as governmental decisions, trade union action, international tariffs or trade pacts can seldom be forecast in the same manner as basic economic and commercial variables. Thus the essence of a financial adviser's appraisal is to determine whether it is reasonable to assume that such external factors will not arise. In other words, the financial adviser must establish whether any evidence suggests a materially above average likelihood of any particular type of event occurring; for example, a bill presented to Parliament; semi-official pronouncements on international treaties; other actions 'pending or threatened'. Many of these matters pre-suppose detailed

knowledge of the particular markets and legislative framework within which a company operates. The onus must be fully on the directors to satisfy the financial adviser that they have enquired into and satisfied themselves (or otherwise) with regard to all matters of this nature.

It has become popular, albeit unnecessary, for global assumptions of this type to be published. For example:

'there will be no major disruption to production arising from failure to obtain raw materials, plant breakdowns, or industrial disputes within the group or at its suppliers or customers'

'profit will not be affected by changes in legislation, government policies etc.'

'duties, quotas and exchange control regulations generally will be unchanged.'

I would argue that, if there is no evidence of such external changes pending, then these are unforeseen circumstances and no detailed assumption need be published. If there is, judgement is required as to the form of assumption and how best to express it. It should, however, be as definitive as possible with regard to the nature of the contingency and the impact it would have on the forecast profits.

Inevitably, the above resumé of the categories of assumption and financial adviser's approach toward their assessment is incomplete. It is impossible to deal with every type of assumption that arises in practice by virtue of the variations between companies and between industries. The summary seeks to give some direct guidance as to the basic principles whereby the financial adviser's judgement is formulated.

Review conclusions and final expression of the forecast

In studying the data upon which a forecast is based and the draft review of the reporting accountant, the financial adviser should be able to assess the potentially difficult or weak areas of the forecast. Examination of past performance and the structure of the industry will indicate probable levels of risk. In a formal review with the directors, the financial adviser must satisfy himself on all such aspects that special features of the forecast have been justified by the directors after full internal investigation.

The final area in which the financial adviser will wish to be satisfied is the contingency margin allowed in the figure to be published. The selection of margin will be determined by the volatility of the industry, the sophistication of the company's forecasting system and its complexity, the length of period forecast and standard of available historic figures, the number of subjective elements in the forecast and the sensitivity of the result to those elements and the degree to which the financial adviser is satisfied that the assumptions made are wholly realistic. Selection of this margin should emerge upon completion of the review. It is not acceptable for the directors to rely upon a substantial contingency provision to justify any lax or inadequate aspect of their forecasting procedures. Nor should individual margins be built into subsidiaries' forecasts. This is a function for the group directors.

In my view there is a strong argument in favour of the publication of forecasts framed as a range of possible outcomes. This gives the reader a better indication of the probabilities which attach inevitably to any forecast. The object of the forecast is, after all, to inform the shareholder and improve the basic information available to him in making an investment decision.

Conclusion

The standards of care which must be observed in the context of profit forecasts for publication represent a simple extension of the principles employed in relation to publication of factual information in a prospectus or similar document. This chapter is designed to relate these general principles to the codes of behaviour and approach which are sought by financial advisers when advising on preparation of forecasts and their subsequent review.

In the absence of statutory prohibition, UK shareholders or prospective shareholders regularly receive profit forecast information to assist in their investment decisions. On balance this is still believed to be an advantage to shareholders when compared, for example, with the absence of company forecasts in the US. Standards are rising continuously, as are forecasting techniques. The onus placed on financial advisers and reporting accountants is likewise increasing. Although there remain few cases where either has been sued or even severely criticised by The Stock Exchange or the Takeover Panel, reputations are crucial to financial advisers and can suffer greatly by virtue of association with a failed forecast. This effective check on the care with which the financial adviser or accountant will operate permits continuing flexibility in the UK approach. Provided the responsibilities of the accountant and adviser are not increased to the point where neither is prepared to report without major caveats and exclusions, this system can be retained to the advantage of shareholders and the companies in which they invest.

9　The role of The Stock Exchange

J R Knight, Chief Executive, The Stock Exchange

General considerations

Although profit forecasts are often included in documents issued by companies listed on The Stock Exchange, there is no stock exchange regulation requiring the publication of profit forecasts. Very occasionally The Stock Exchange will insist on a forecast being made to clarify a company's position in relation to an exceptional transaction or situation. But in principle The Stock Exchange would not favour any proposal that profit forecasts be made generally obligatory, for the following reasons. Reporting on forecasts may be expensive to the company and may cause delay. Compulsory forecasts would tend to be hedged with too many qualifications and might encourage companies to reserve the release of more precise information for dissemination through unofficial sources. It would be difficult, if not impossible, to hold companies accountable where unofficial forecasts proved misleading.

However, there is a stock exchange requirement that prospectus documents contain a statement as to the financial and trading prospects of the company including reference to relevant material information and special trade factors. The advantage of this approach is that it is flexible. A company is relatively free to describe its situation in terms appropriate to the circumstances and may consider factors which are relevant in a longer term context.

Reference will be made throughout this chapter to 'prospectus documents'. The words are used as defined in The Stock Exchange 'Yellow Book', *Admission of Securities to Listing*. In addition to prospectuses falling within the Companies Act definition, they include documents issued in relation to such matters as acquisitions and disposals, schemes of arrangement and reorganisation, rights issues, rejection of takeover offers, and general information circulars.

Profit forecasts are affected by The Stock Exchange's listing requirements in two ways. First, if there is a significant difference between the level of profit achieved and that forecast, an explanation is required by virtue of the Listing Agreement, the current LA/9 form of which states in paragraph 10(b) 'an explanation in the event of trading results shown by the accounts for the period under review differing materially from any published forecast made by the company.' This explanation is required in the company's annual report, and the company would be expected to consult the Quotations Department on the form of the explanations. The wording will therefore be screened. If this procedure did not take place, and no explanation was included in the annual report, the company would be asked to issue a statement at the AGM and that statement would be announced to The Stock Exchange and disseminated to the market and the public in the normal way. Secondly, where a forecast is included in a prospectus document, as defined, that forecast is subject to independent reporting. In such circumstances the auditors or reporting accountants would report on the bases and calculations, while a report by the issuing house or sponsoring broker would indicate that the forecast had been stated after due and careful enquiry.

Definition

In order to administer the regulations appertaining to profit forecasts it is necessary to decide what constitutes a forecast. A Stock Exchange Council Notice (No. 83/75) of 6 August 1975, stated that in determining whether a profit forecast has been made, The Stock Exchange would have regard 'to any words which may be used in commenting either upon future accounting periods, or on past accounting periods for which results have not been announced to the public. Whenever it becomes possible, by using such words in conjunction with published data, to arrive at an approximate figure for future profits by an arithmetical process, the Council will take the view that a forecast has been made and require it to be reported upon in accordance with Appendix 34'. In deciding whether a statement represented a forecast in terms of this definition, one of the more obvious considerations is whether a minimum level of anticipated profits had been suggested, either specifically or by implication.

Reporting on forecasts

The majority of forecast statements, or indications deemed to be forecasts within the above definition, are contained in half-yearly interim reports. Profit forecasts, or statements in the nature of forecasts, are also found in the chairman's statement in annual reports and may emerge in the course of annual general meetings. Forecasts made in these well defined circumstances, or even a forecast announced on some other occasion during the year, are not subject to the formal reporting procedure referred to above unless a company is subsequently obliged to issue a prospectus document. This fact has considerable practical significance as such reporting by the auditors or reporting accountants may be both expensive and time consuming from a company's standpoint. If, however, a company enters into a transaction or becomes involved in a situation which gives rise to the issue of a prospectus document, that document must include a report on any forecast then outstanding. For instance, a forecast made in an interim report would then, as it were, be formalised. The Council Notice referred to above states 'The Council have also decided that if there is in existence any profit forecast in respect of an unexpired accounting period, or period which has expired but for which the results have not been announced to the public, a statement should be made in any prospectus (as defined in Appendix 34) confirming, amending or withdrawing such forecast'. Many forecasts subject to reporting are made because a company elects to make a forecast in a particular situation. Examples of this are forecasts in offer or rejection circulars, schemes of arrangement and initial listing prospectuses.

These Stock Exchange regulations are not designed to discourage forecasts nor are they so applied. Indeed, The Stock Exchange would regard a soundly based forecast as price-sensitive information of particular relevance to the market in the realistic evaluation of a company's shares. However, because forecasts are so important as a determinant of share prices, a corresponding burden of responsibility must be ascribed to listed companies in making such statements. The one occasion when The Stock Exchange will not generally insist on a forecast being reported on is in the case of a Class 1 circular relating to a cash acquisition or disposal. There is a corresponding dispensation under the City Code in relation to an offeror making an acquisition solely for cash.

Perhaps understandably, listed companies are somewhat reluctant to make profit forecasts in case formal reporting might be required subsequently. Companies generally do not relish the expense and management time involved in formal forecast reporting. Various techniques are used to indicate profit expectation without making a statement which is sufficiently specific as to be regarded as a forecast. Considerable effort and ingenuity are often exercised in this connection.

Monitoring of forecasts

The Quotations Department of The Stock Exchange monitors the results of all forecasts, whether subject to formal reporting or otherwise, and requires an explanation to be published in the case of any significant variation. This would generally take the form of a statement as to the basic assumptions and change in circumstances. It would be set out in the directors' report section of the annual report. An explanation would tend to be examined more critically where the forecast had been reported upon. This is because a company may have facilitated a specific transaction by reference to anticipated profits which appeared to have been formally endorsed because they had been reported upon.

Since The Stock Exchange does not wish to discourage the release of profit forecasts, an explanation for a failed forecast need not generally be expressed in such terms as to imply that the company is seriously at fault. The Panel on Takeovers and Mergers also investigates failed forecasts made, confirmed or amended in connection with takeover offers. The Stock Exchange's approach in the case of failed forecasts is very similar to that of the Panel as described in the Panel's report for the year to 31 March 1978. Like the Panel, The Stock Exchange does not endeavour to conduct a witch hunt when profit forecasts are not achieved. It attempts to put itself in the position of the directors when the forecast was made and to establish the reasons for the subsequent discrepancy from that standpoint. In determining whether a forecast had failed, The Stock Exchange would tend to regard a variation of 10 per cent or more above or below the forecast level as significant.

The incidence of unsatisfactory forecasts is very low. It is noticeable that companies are often not prepared to commit themselves in reasonably specific terms. It would appear from available statistics[1] that more than half of all interim reports published by UK listed companies in 1977 and 1978 included reference to the profit expectation for the full year, although generally in a veiled and oblique manner.

Notes

Text of The Stock Exchange requirement specifying that profit forecasts appearing in a prospectus document should be reported upon:

> 'Where a profit forecast appears in any prospectus the principal assumptions, including commercial assumptions, upon which the directors have based their profit forecast, must be stated. The accounting bases and calculations for the forecast must be examined and reported on by the auditors to the company, or any reporting accountants, and such report must be set out. The

issuing house, or, in the absence of an issuing house, the sponsoring brokers must report in addition whether or not they have satisfied themselves that the forecast has been stated by the directors after due and careful enquiry and such report must be set out'.

Reference

[1] *Survey of Published Accounts* published annually by the Institute of Chartered Accountants in England and Wales.

10 The role of the City Panel

R A Wade, Coopers & Lybrand, Zambia

Introduction

This chapter is not intended as a history of the events that led to the creation of the Panel on Takeovers and Mergers ('the Panel' or 'the City Panel') as we know it today. To those who are interested in exploring that subject in more depth, I recommend *Accounting Principles and the City Code* by Professor Edward Stamp and Christopher Marley, published by Butterworths, and *The City Takeover Code* by Sir Alexander Johnston, published by the Clarendon Press.

Prior to 1968 the City Working Party, a body set up by the Governor of the Bank of England, published 'Notes on the Amalgamation of British Businesses' which were intended as voluntary guidelines for those involved in takeovers and mergers. There were, however, no procedures for administering or enforcing the recommendations and the view was often expressed that this form of voluntary regulation was ineffective. This view gained ground in 1966 and 1967 when a series of widely publicised offers appeared to flout the spirit, if not the letter, of the guidelines. As a result, the City Working Party was reconvened and in 1968 published the first edition of the City Code on Takeovers and Mergers ("the Code"). At the same time, the Governor of the Bank of England set up the Panel to interpret and enforce the Code.

During its first year the Panel, acting under its chairman, Sir Humphrey Mynors, deputy Governor of the Bank of England, met as frequently as was necessary to deal with the matters put before it. This proved an unworkable method of operating and in 1969 a Director General and a full time executive were recruited to deal with interpretation and enforcement on a day to day basis. This *modus operandi* broadly continues today: the executive makes decisions on the basis of established precedent, referring difficult or unusual cases to the full Panel for decision. Companies that are involved in takeover or merger transactions may appeal to the Panel against an interpretation made by the executive, as may shareholders of those companies.

A recent development that had no practical effect on the role of the Panel, but which changed its position within the regulatory framework, was the creation of the Council for the Securities Industry ('CSI'). The CSI was set up by the Governor in March 1978 to assume responsibility for all aspects of the voluntary regulation of the securities markets. The Markets Committee of the CSI took over the responsibilities of the City Working Party in relation to drafting takeover codes, and the membership of the Panel was increased by the addition of the chairman of the CSI. There were, however, no alterations in the procedures or authority of the Panel which remained the final authority on the interpretation of the Code: there was no right of appeal to the CSI against decisions of the Panel. During the same year accountants were formally represented on the Panel for the first time when the chairman of the Consultative Committee of Accounting Bodies became a member of the Panel.

Requirements of the Code

The provisions of the Code fall into two categories:

(a) general principles of conduct to be observed in takeover and merger transactions; and
(b) rules, some of which are examples of the application of the general principles, while others are rules of procedure to govern specific situations.

In addition to these, the Code contains practice notes which are intended to serve as a guide to the interpretation that the Panel normally places on the various rules and general principles.

The 1981 edition of the Code provides a framework representing best practice for the publication of profit forecasts in bid situations. This framework is essentially the same as that set out in the first edition published in March 1968. The only changes of any substance in the intervening period are as follows:

(a) reports by accountants and financial advisers, which in the March 1968 edition were required to be addressed to the directors and were not published have, since April 1969, been required to be published in the offer document or defence circular;
(b) any unaudited profits figure published during an offer period must, since February 1981, be reported on in accordance with Rule 16. Before 1981 such unaudited figures escaped the require-

ments of Rule 16 if they were 'up to publication standard, i.e. they have received the same degree of examination and carry the same degree of authority as normally apply to published but unaudited interim or preliminary final results of the company in question'. (Paragraph 3 of Practice Note No. 3 of the 1976 edition of the Code.)

Rule 16 of the February 1981 edition of the Code contains the present requirements in relation to profit forecasts:

(a) Directors must exercise the 'greatest possible care'.

(b) A profit forecast is the 'sole responsibility' of the directors.

(c) The assumptions on which the forecast is based must be stated in the document.

(d) The company's auditors or consultant accountants must examine and report on the accounting policies and calculations.

(e) The financial adviser, if any, must report on the forecast.

(f) The reports required under (d) and (e) must appear in the document together with statements of consent from the writers.

(g) In relation to forecast periods where trading has commenced any previously published profit figures which are available in respect of any expired portion of that trading period together with comparable figures for the preceding year must be stated.

The requirements of Rule 16 are the result of the application to the specific problem of profit forecasts of two of the Code's general principles, namely General Principle 3:

'Shareholders shall have in their possession sufficient evidence, facts and opinions upon which an adequate judgement and decision can be reached and shall have sufficient time to make an assessment and decision. No relevant information shall be withheld from them'.

and General Principle 12:

'Any document or advertisement addressed to shareholders containing information, opinions or recommendations from the board of an offeror or offeree company or their respective advisers shall be treated with the same standards of care as if it were a prospectus within the meaning of the Companies Act 1948. Especial care shall be taken over profit forecasts'.

Although General Principle 3 requires that no relevant information shall be withheld from shareholders, neither the Code nor the Panel, with one exception (referred to later) attempts to decree when a forecast is relevant and does not compel directors to make forecasts. These decisions are left to the directors who must balance the shareholders' needs for information with the requirement that information provided must be of a high standard.

Practice Note No. 6 contains guidance on the interpretation of Rule 16 and its application to specific situations, while Practice Note No. 7, written after consultation with the Consultative Committee of Accountancy Bodies, contains suggestions and guidance on framing assumptions so that they are of maximum assistance to the reader.

Although Practice Note No. 6 contains two new introductory paragraphs inserted in 1981 and its wording differs significantly from that of Practice Note No. 3 (1976) which it replaces, the only major change is that in paragraph 3 referred to above. Paragraph 3 says:

> 'An estimate of profits for a period which has already expired should be treated as a profit forecast within this Rule. Except with the consent of the Panel, any unaudited profits figure published during an offer period should be reported on in accordance with this Rule'.

Only the second sentence of this paragraph, introduced in February 1981, represents a new requirement. Before February 1981 there was a possibility that unaudited interim or preliminary profit figures would, in the heat of a takeover bid, be published more hastily and with less care than normal: this new requirement is designed to prevent that. It is a logical extension of Rule 16, but it remains to be seen what effect this change will have on the conduct of takeovers and mergers, and in what circumstances the Panel will exercise its discretion to waive the requirement. In one respect, however, this change favours the offeror who can safely announce his bid after publishing unaudited profit figures. The offeree, whose own timetable is largely determined by the date the bid is announced, may not have that opportunity.

Of the comments and interpretations in Practice Note No. 6 the most significant for offerors and offerees, and the most demanding from the Panel's point of view is contained in paragraph 4:

> 'Except with the consent of the Panel, any forecast which has been made before the commencement of the offer period must be repeated in the document and examined and reported on in accordance with this Rule. This provision does not, however, apply to unaudited statements of annual or interim results which have already been published.

At the outset an adviser should invariably check whether or not his client has a forecast on the record, so that the reporting procedures can be set in train with a minimum of delay.

Very occasionally representations may be made to the Panel to the effect that, because of the uncertainties involved, it is not possible for a forecast previously made to be reported on in accordance with this Rule nor for a revised forecast to be made. In these circumstances the Panel would insist on shareholders being given a full explanation as to why the requirements of the Code were not capable of being met'.

Sections 2 and 3 of this paragraph were added in 1981 and the wording of section 1 differs significantly from that of paragraph 2 of Practice Note No. 3 (1976) which it replaces. It is unlikely however, that any real change in the Panel's interpretation of the Rule is intended. This point is discussed in more detail in a later section.

Two other paragraphs of Practice Note No. 6 merit comment. Paragraph 6 recognises that after publication of a forecast, circumstances may change so as to invalidate the assumptions on which it was based. Subsequent circulars must therefore contain a reaffirmation of the forecast by the directors and a statement that the accountants and advisers have consented to the extended use of their reports.

Paragraph 8 of the Practice Note sets out certain additional information that should normally be given, but forecast earnings per share are, since 1981, no longer required. This represents a retrograde step since shareholders are interested in the measurement of earnings per share on a comparable basis rather than in the actual level of profits earned by the company.

Requirements of The Stock Exchange

In addition to the Rules of the Code, circulars issued in connection with takeovers may, where they involve listed companies, be subject to the requirements of The Stock Exchange, as set out in Admission of Securities to Listing, 'the Yellow Book'. No conflict arises, however, since the requirements of the Code and the Yellow Book in relation to profit forecasts are essentially the same.

Application of the Code

Although drafted with listed companies particularly in mind, the Code also applies to takeovers of unlisted public companies. Takeovers of private companies are not caught, however. A private company is one that does not qualify as a public company under section 1 of the Companies Act 1980.

The Code does not apply to offers for companies that are non-resident in the United Kingdom, including the Channel Islands or the Isle of Man. A non-resident company is normally regarded as one incorporated outside the United Kingdom or one whose head office and place of central management and control is situated outside the United Kingdom. However, such offers will fall within the jurisdiction of the Yellow Book if the offeror company is listed on The Stock Exchange. The Code does, however, apply to offers for companies resident in the Irish Republic and listed on The Stock Exchange or traded on its Unlisted Securities Market.

Certain situations arise under Rule 34 of the Code where no bid is in contemplation but the requirements of the Code apply. Where, for example, an asset is to be acquired in exchange for shares that would result in the vendor of the asset acquiring 30 per cent or more of the voting rights attributable to the issued share capital of the purchasing company, the shareholders of that company might be asked to approve the waiving of the mandatory bid that would normally result. In these circumstances, if the circular sent to shareholders contained a profit forecast, the requirements of Rule 16 would apply (see Practice Note No. 15 — second part of paragraph 9 — Independent vote of shareholders on the issue of new securities).

Administration of the Code

It will be apparent from the outline above that the framework laid down by the Code for publication of profit forecasts should require little administration by the Panel: within certain guidelines matters are left to the judgement of the directors and professional advisers concerned, and the shareholders' protection lies in the assurance that responsible individuals with their own good names to safeguard have followed certain procedures prior to publication of the forecast. This is broadly true, and the Panel's only role in respect of many forecasts is to examine published documents to determine whether the Code's requirements have been met. However, companies and their advisers are urged to consult the Panel in advance of and during takeover transactions and it is in the interpretation of the Code's application to specific situations that the Panel's main role lies.

Interpretation of the Code

Since a forecast can be made in words, the most common question the Panel is asked is whether a form of words constitutes a profit forecast. The request may come either from companies who wish to avoid making forecasts or from opposing sides alleging that a form of words already used constitutes a forecast. The question is asked most frequently by those who are advising chairmen on the form of words to be used in describing future prospects in the annual report or interim statement: their concern stems from the comment in paragraph 4 of Practice Note No. 6 that

> 'except with the consent of the Panel, any forecast which has been made before the commencement of the offer period must be repeated in the document and examined and reported on in accordance with this Rule'.

This is by no means a new requirement, although the wording of this paragraph is stronger than that of its predecessor (paragraph 2 of Practice Note No. 3-1976) where there appeared to be some room for debate as to whether any particular forecast on the record should be repeated and reported on. The Panel has power to grant exemption from this requirement but this power is unlikely to be used frequently, as a recent case demonstrates. The case concerned was the bid by Vantona Group Limited ('Vantona') for J. Compton Sons & Webb (Holdings) Limited ('Compton') and the circumstances were described in a statement published by the Panel on 1 November 1978. Vantona had made a forecast in its interim statement but the board of Compton and Hill Samuel, their advisers, maintained that the forecast was no longer of material importance to the shareholders of Compton in considering the share offer. In arriving at this view they took into consideration the fact that ten months' trading results of Vantona were published in the offer document. (Publication of such unaudited results would not be allowed under the 1981 version of the Code.) While accepting the representations of Compton in this instance the Panel said that the circumstances were unusual and it would 'find it extremely difficult in future to accept that forecasts that are on the public record and have influenced the market have no material importance in relation to subsequently announced takeover transactions'.

In the same statement, though not strictly related to the Vantona case, the Panel commented on the withdrawal of forecasts. It pointed out that a withdrawal of a forecast could only be effective if the forecast were replaced with an up-to-date commentary which itself would probably constitute a forecast. In very rare circumstances the Panel might accept that a forecast on the record could not be reported on or replaced by an up-to-date statement. In such situations a genuine withdrawal would be allowed but such a course of action must, as the Panel pointed out, 'seriously bring into question whether there was a sufficient basis for making the prediction in the first instance'. In the February 1981 version of the Code the Panel's views on withdrawal of forecasts were incorporated in paragraph 4 of Practice Note No. 6 for the first time.

In summary, therefore, where a forecast is on the record the Panel will, in most cases, require that it should be repeated or updated. In rare cases forecasts may be withdrawn but with the likely admission that they should not have been made in the first place.

Enforcement of the Code

Once a bid is announced, and in many cases even before it is publicised, the Panel plays a watching role to see that the Code is observed. In relation to profit forecasts, there are two chief dangers to guard against; first, there is the possibility that, inadvertently or otherwise, spokesmen for companies involved in takeover transactions may make remarks in public that amount to profit forecasts and that are subsequently reported in the press. In these circumstances, the Panel will require from the parties concerned an immediate confirmation or denial of the remarks attributed. If the reports were accurate then the remarks are treated as a forecast on the record that must be dealt with in the manner described above.

Secondly, there is a possibility that defending companies may delay their formal forecasts, while urging shareholders not to take action until they have seen them. This is contrary to General Principle 3, which requires that shareholders should have information in good time. Where the Panel considers that this principle is being infringed, it may extend some of the time limits imposed on the offeror, thus removing any tactical advantage that the defending company hoped to gain.

The situations in which the Panel is required to intervene vary enormously and are seldom as clear cut as the examples quoted above. However, they are not significant in number since the existence of the established framework and the fact that the Panel is known to be monitoring all bids act as a check on excesses. However, talk of enforcement of the Code in relation to profit forecasts leads inevitably to a consideration of failed forecasts.

Failed profit forecasts

It is impossible to set down an adequate yardstick for measuring the outcome of profit forecasts since it is in the nature of forecasting that the actual results may differ significantly from the prediction. Such a situation would not automatically lead to the conclusion that the forecast was irresponsible or 'bad', nor would the achievement of the forecast results confirm that the forecasting had been responsibly carried out. Nevertheless, an important part of the Panel's role is to monitor the outcome of forecasts and its object in doing so is to determine whether the standards of conduct and disclosure laid down by the Code appear to have been followed.

For approximately two and a half years up to 31 March 1972 the Panel enquired into the outcome of every single forecast made in a bid situation and reported the results of its enquiries in its annual reports. Since then it has monitored the outcome of forecasts on a sample basis.

The volume of forecasting in takeovers and mergers can be gauged from the following table:

Table 10.1
Forecasting in bids and mergers

| | Year ended 31 March | |
	1980	1981
Number of bids for which documents were published	141	134
Forecasts by offeror	15	13
Forecasts by offeree	45	28
Total	60	41

Although the total number of forecasts was not large, the majority were offeree forecasts where there is a greater risk that directors, in defending against an unwanted bid, will overstep the bounds of objectivity.

In view of these statistics it is significant that the Panel has never published a statement critical of the work of directors, advisers or accountants in relation to forecasting and only in one instance has the Panel published its findings. This was the case of the forecast made by Dunford & Elliott Limited in the context of the Lonrho offer early in 1977. The Panel, in a statement dated 20 May 1980, described the detailed investigation it had carried out with the assistance of a firm of accountants. It concluded that 'the directors of Dunford & Elliott and their advisers acted in good faith and with appropriate care in the preparation of the forecast'.

The Panel offers no redress for those who may feel that they have suffered financial loss as a result of a reckless forecast. Legal remedies are available in such cases but where they are pursued the Panel encounters possible conflicts between its own role and that of the law. If parties to a bid consider they have grounds for legal action then the Panel will normally suspend its own enquiries until the litigation has run its course. Were it to proceed with its enquiries there would be a possibility that one of the parties to the litigation might seek an injunction restraining the Panel from proceeding or from publishing a statement on the ground that such conduct might prejudice the outcome of the litigation. At the very least the Panel might be faced with a lack of co-operation from the parties involved in the litigation. This approach, understandable though it is, has the disadvantage of delaying any enquiry by the Panel with a possible reduction in its effectiveness.

Sanctions available to the Panel

The Panel's authority is based primarily on the fact that nearly all takeover bids in the United Kingdom involve a member of one or other of the bodies represented on the Panel. These bodies have undertaken to support the Panel and require a similar commitment from their members. Disciplinary measures can therefore be taken against firms and individuals who are represented on the Panel, and pressure can be brought to bear on companies and individuals who, though not represented on the Panel, wish to continue to use the services offered by members of the Panel. Against such organisations and individuals, which have a reputation or a business to protect, the threat of publication of a critical statement by the Panel can be a potent weapon.

The Panel experiences greatest difficulty in enforcing its views with those who either fall outside the influence of its member bodies or have no wish to protect their reputation or livelihood (for example, some companies based outside the United Kingdom, small unlisted companies or private individuals). Sanctions that are available to the Panel in these circumstances are limited, although the Department of Trade and Industry has indicated that it will give serious consideration to representations by the Panel with regard to the appointment of inspectors or the continuation of a dealing licence. In addition there have been instances of owners of shares being restrained from voting them until Panel rulings have been complied with.

Notwithstanding the obvious difficulties and weaknesses referred to above, the Panel has enjoyed considerable success in imposing its rulings. The removal of United Kingdom exchange controls may, however, restrict the influence that the Panel can bring to bear in future on overseas companies.

Conclusions and comments

Although constant vigilance is needed in this area, the established framework is sound and works well. This is borne out by the fact that only two relatively minor changes have been necessary since the first edition of the Code was published in 1968. Furthermore, no significant or dramatic changes are likely in the future. Despite the success of the framework laid down by the Code, however, the Panel, and those engaged in forecasting and reporting on forecasts, are faced with a public relations problem. The investing public does not understand the nature of forecasting and its place in takeovers and mergers. To a large degree the process of education must be undertaken by financial commentators, but the Panel could also be more active in this respect, in particular by being more forthcoming about the results of its enquiries into the outcome of forecasts. A general commentary in its annual report on the lessons to be learnt and areas in which improvements could be made would assist in this respect.

PART THREE

USING PROFIT FORECASTS

Overview

Many companies do not publish forecasts, so stockbrokers, and others, have to compile their own. Martin Gibbs and Bill Seward of Phillips & Drew, one of London's largest stockbrokers, describe in fascinating detail and with several actual examples, how, from outside the company, they build up a forecast of its likely performance and decide whether to recommend their clients to buy or sell the shares.

So far in this book most of the authors have described how they make or review forecasts, but how accurate are they? This is the question I have tried to answer by reviewing the published research on the subject (mainly from the USA; some, including my own, from the UK). As you will see the answer is, as Professor Joad used to say, 'it all depends'. Forecasts should never be taken as gospel — accuracy depends on how far ahead they are made, the industry of the company, the state of the economy, and many other things, not forgetting the skill, motivation and knowledge of the forecaster. Forecasts are valuable to the investor and no business can be managed successfully without them but they should never be treated as a guarantee of what will happen.

C.A.W.

11   How an investment analyst uses a profit forecast and makes his own

P M D Gibbs and W T Seward, Phillips & Drew

The investment analyst's principal task is to identify those shares likely to outperform (or underperform) the market as a whole. Because movements in a company's share price essentially reflect changes in profits, the analyst's success in predicting share price movements arguably rests on his ability to forecast profits more accurately than the rest of the stock market. This chapter explains how analysts use profit forecasts to help form their investment recommendations. Since published profit forecasts are available only infrequently, and then are usually deficient for his purposes, the analyst usually has to generate his own estimates of profits. In the second part of this chapter we explain how the analyst undertakes this process.

The work of the investment analyst

Investment analysts are employed by most major institutional investors (insurance companies, pension funds, unit trusts, and others) in order to help their fund managers make correct investment decisions. Similarly, most larger firms of stockbrokers (including our own firm) have teams of analysts whose advice is available to the firm's clients. Stockbrokers receive their remuneration via a commission or brokerage on the value of shares bought or sold by their investing clients; hence the quality of the investment advice given by a stockbroking firm's in-house analysts helps to determine the volume of business given to that particular broker. It is usual for individual analysts to specialise in one or two related sectors of the market only — for example, one analyst may be responsible for covering shares in both brewery and wine and spirit companies. Typically each analyst may advise on the relative merits of the shares of perhaps twenty to thirty companies.

Why the analyst needs forecasts

In theory, a company's share price should tend towards the discounted value of the future dividends which the shareholder can expect to receive from his investment. However, since different companies adopt widely different payout policies, most institutional investors regard it as sounder to value shares on the basis of earnings (the post-tax profits attributable to each share) rather than dividends. To arrive at an informed judgement on the appropriate price for a share, analysts generally estimate the future level of earnings and then decide the rate at which these earnings should be capitalised.

We shall return to a closer examination of these two aspects of the decision-making process later, but in the meantime, it will be clear that where the analyst's conclusions indicate a higher share price than that at which the company's shares are currently quoted in the stock market, he will recommend his clients to buy the share – and vice versa. If the share price of a company differs from the value which the analyst feels should be attributed to it, this is usually because his perception of the outlook for its profits, either on a short or a longer term view, differs significantly from the consensus view of the rest of the stock market.

As a rule, the larger and therefore more important a company is, the more highly researched it will be, and the more the market price is likely to reflect a consensus view. This is not to say that the consensus view is necessarily correct, as even the best informed analysts can reach the wrong conclusion. As might be expected, however, the share prices of smaller companies, whose shares are much less carefully followed, often drift furthest from their true value, since there is usually a steady stream of small selling from deceased estates and other sources, which may not be matched by new buying. In the case of both large, well researched companies and smaller, less closely followed ones, however, the 'proof of the pudding' lies in the publication of the company's profits – or, more rarely, an official profits forecast. When either appears, the share price will adjust to the results unless the figures are close to the consensus of expectations.

Making forecasts

The ways in which an analyst produces his own profits forecast are discussed in more detail in a later section. Two general points concerning their application can be made immediately, however:

1   Time horizon:

Logically it might be argued that a company's profits should be forecast from the current year to infinity; it would clearly be impossible to do this with any accuracy, however. Typically, an analyst will aim to produce a forecast of profits for each of the next two years, together with a considered view of the likely average growth rate over the subsequent five year period.

2   *Reacting to events:*

It is not enough for an analyst merely to sit down once a year and produce a set of profits forecasts. New information of varying relevance is constantly made available, and he will need to incorporate the latest intelligence into his forecasts. This will often result in a change in his profit forecasts. Because there is inevitably a time lag while the analyst estimates the impact on profits of a change in background factors, one of the most useful services an analyst can perform is to provide his clients with some 'sensitivity analysis' – that is to answer the question 'what will be the effect on profits of a given change in (say) foreign exchange rates or interest rates or selling prices?' The provision of such a 'ready reckoner' allows clients to adjust the analyst's forecast to allow for such changes as soon as they occur, and to assess the vulnerability of profits to the changes in background factors which he, personally, considers likely. Clearly, the client's view of the outlook for these factors may not be the same as the analyst's.

Relating forecasts to share prices

Once a set of forecasts has been generated, the analyst must consider whether this prospect is correctly reflected in the share price. This is normally achieved by the use of the Price/Earnings Ratio (often shortened to P/E).

The P/E is defined as the share price divided by the earnings attributable to each issued ordinary share in the company. When calculating earnings per share, most analysts exclude non-trading gains and losses and deduct a full deferred tax charge from the historic cost profits. Largely because of this different treatment of deferred tax, the analyst may arrive at a substantially different earnings per share figure from that shown by the company in its published accounts. Perhaps it is worth noting at this stage that most investors still regard the historic cost figures as the prime measure of earnings, although this situation may change in the next few years as more current cost figures become available. Estimates of current cost earnings have proved to be remarkably good indicators of individual share price movements in the last few years. (See, for instance, *SSAP16 – the Standard on Current Cost Accounting,* Phillips & Drew, April 1980.)

The P/E for a given company will depend upon a number of factors of which the most important is the overall level of P/Es of shares generally, that is, the market average P/E. For this reason, individual company P/Es are often expressed as percentages of the market average P/E, the resultant percentages being known as price earnings relatives, or P/E relatives. In our firm we operate a computer programme covering about 200 leading UK equities. The analysts have to input two-year forecasts of profits, earnings, dividends, and dividend cover for each of their companies. Current share prices are fed in each day and the computer then prints out data for each share, including its P/E relatives for last year and for each of the two forecast years. To do so, the computer has to calculate future market average P/Es for each time period by aggregating our forecasts for individual companies and relating them to the appropriate financial years.

Some of the figures relating to Marks and Spencer and Vickers, as shown in a recent print-out (April 1982) are reproduced below:

Table 11.1
Price relatives, actual and forecast

	1981 (Actual)	1982 (Forecast)	1983 (Forecast)
Marks and Spencer @ 146p			
Year to 31 March			
Earnings (p)	6.5	7.5	8.3
P/E	22.4	19.5	17.6
P/E relative	165	159	171
Dividend yield %	3.7	4.2	4.8
Vickers @ 159p			
Year to 31 December			
Earnings (p)	14.7	18.0	22.0
P/E	10.8	8.8	7.2
P/E relative	86	83	82
Dividend yield %	10.3	10.8	10.8

The fact that Marks and Spencer's first year forecast P/E relative is 159 per cent of the market average, whereas Vickers' equivalent figure is only about 83 per cent, does not necessarily mean that Marks and Spencer's shares are relatively dear or that Vickers' shares are relatively cheap. Some shares tend to stand on higher P/E relatives than others. The future P/E relative of a particular company will depend upon such factors as the likely subsequent growth in earnings (the higher the expected growth rate, the higher the P/E relative is likely to be), the variability of earnings (the market prefers steady growth to cyclical growth); the degree of risk attaching to the company and the business

137

in which it operates; its policy with regard to <u>dividends</u> (within reason, the market likes to see a fairly generous proportion of the earnings paid out as dividends); and the general image of the company and its management.

One of the key jobs of the analyst is therefore to determine the appropriate future P/E relative for each of the companies that he follows. The decision is principally on two comparisons – first the level of P/E relative offered by shares in other companies in the same or comparable industries, and secondly, perhaps most important, the level of P/E relative upon which shares in the company under review have been valued historically. Where the nature of a company changes, however, so that future earnings are thought likely to grow at a far different rate than they have in the past, then the historic P/E relative loses its relevance. The identification of such 'status changes', through a close examination of the nature of the business and the way in which it may be altering, is a particularly important part of an analyst's work. When, for example, a company's long term rate of earnings growth increases, its P/E relative is likely to increase as well. The resulting movement in the company's share price following the market's general acceptance of such a status change can be very substantial.

Relative profits graphs

Another technique which we adopt for forecasting the direction of short term movements in share prices is illustrated in the graph on page 139. This shows the six-year movements in the rate of growth of Johnson Matthey's profits relative to the growth of aggregate company profits, plotted against movements in the relative price of the ordinary shares. The profits histogram is plotted quarterly and represents the percentage increase in Johnson Matthey's profits, compared with the same quarter of the previous year, relative to the rate of growth of aggregate company profits during the same period. The share price curve is plotted monthly and shows the price of Johnson Matthey's shares relative to the level of the Financial Times-Actuaries All-Share index.

It will be seen that there has been no significant 'status change' in Johnson Matthey's business during the six years and hence the relative share price has reflected the relative profits trend. Consequently, an analyst who managed to forecast Johnson Matthey's relative profits correctly would have been able to predict the direction of short term movements in its share price relative to the market. We maintain similar graphs for about 150 companies but they do not all show such good correlations as the one we have chosen as an illustration of the

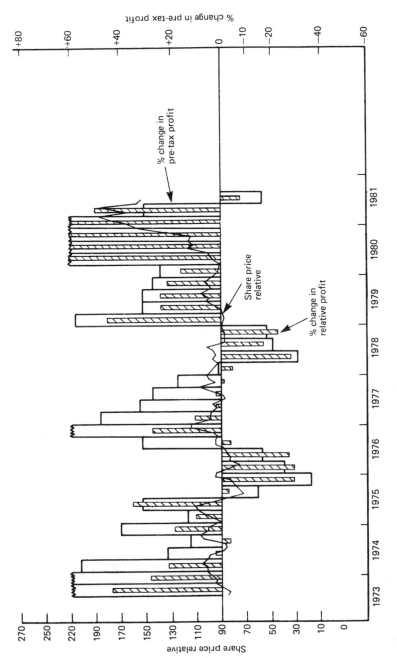

Figure 11.1 Johnson Matthey — share price relative

method since, in the short term, share prices can be affected by many factors other than the rate of growth of reported profits.

Deficiencies of published profit forecasts

As a rule UK companies tend not to make profit forecasts except in general terms, for example: 'Your directors expect another satisfactory year's trading'. The most common exceptions are when new shares are to be issued by way of rights issues, or when an acquisition is either being contemplated, or, more often, where the company is the target in a takeover bid.

Hence the most obvious deficiency of published profits forecasts from the viewpoint of the investment analyst is their rarity. Even when they are available, they may be based on assumptions which the analyst regards as either too pessimistic or too optimistic. Profit forecasts made with rights issues understandably lean to the cautious side – the company does not wish to be accused of asking shareholders for new money on the basis of expectations which may be disappointed. On the other tack, there have been occasions when forecasts made by unwilling victims in a takeover battle seem to have taken too rosy a view of the future. In either event, the analyst must make his own assessment, based on his view of the environment, of the most likely outcome. The other deficiency of published profit forecasts is that they usually cover too short a period – often well under a year. As we have seen, a rather longer horizon than this is required, as a rule.

How analysts make their own forecasts

The prevalence and magnitude of these deficiencies forces the analyst to produce his own profits forecasts. In order to ensure consistency and to make best use of the lessons of the past, the analyst will normally try to construct a model which can be used to generate forecasts. This model is simply a means of using past experience to establish relationships between relevant and regularly-updated industry statistics on the one hand, and the level of profitability of the company under study, on the other. A wide range of industry statistics is available from various government bodies and from trade associations; the most useful relate to deliveries and to order levels, but valuable information is also sometimes published on price and cost levels. The model can vary in complexity from a straightforward correlation between total industry delivery levels and the level of the company's profits, to highly sophisticated models which incorporate several sets of input information. The most sophisticated and complex models are often run on a computer in order to speed the calculation process, particularly where it is necessary to examine the impact on profits of possible changes in some of the input factors. The framework of two such models — the first very simple, the second much more complex — is described in a later section. For all profit forecasting models, however, the process is essentially the same. The principal steps are listed below.

1   *Identify the company's products and customers, in order that relevant industry statistics can be found*

In essence, what the analyst seeks to do is to divide the business into segments, the profits of each of which, with the help of relevant industry statistics, will be more easily forecast than would the results of the business in its totality. For example, if the company under study was a building materials producer, the analyst would try to quantify the contribution from each product area — where background influences were likely to differ — as well as treating any overseas contribution separately. Thus he would want, say, to show profits from brick-making separately from, say, ready mixed concrete manufacture, since the former is used mainly in house building whereas the latter has much wider applications and rather better growth prospects. Similarly, the factors that influence demand in both the UK brick and concrete markets would not apply to our mythical company's Australian subsidiary.

It is surprising how many apparently familiar companies earn large percentages of their profits either from products quite different from those with which they are normally associated, or from overseas. A vital part of the analyst's job, therefore, is to try to break down a company's total profits so as to show the contribution of each geographical area, and if possible within that, the contribution of each product group. Often, the profits breakdown shown in the report and accounts is inadequate (sometimes for reasons of trade secrecy) and a further refinement must be attempted.

In most cases, the analyst will try to arrange a meeting with senior management of the company concerned in order to find out more about the group's activities and its place in the industry. A similar purpose is served by the regular meetings organised by the Society of Investment Analysts between company representatives and investment analysts. Such meetings are usually welcomed by both sides, since mutual understanding between investers and the company can only be beneficial. It should be noted, however, that both sides are careful not to request (or to divulge) information which is not, or could not be made, generally available to shareholders. The Companies Act 1980 has made it a criminal offence to deal, or advise someone else to deal, on the basis of unpublished price-sensitive information. (See *Guidelines to Insider Dealing*, the Society of Investment Analysts, May 1981.)

Other sources of information which the analyst will use include the annual returns filed with the Registrar of Companies in the case of UK subsidiaries, or the results of quoted overseas subsidiaries where these are available. If all else fails, the analyst can only use intelligent guesses based on the chairman's comments on divisional performances in the report and accounts.

2   Establish relationships between industry statistics and profits

Once the business has been sub-divided into its constituent parts as far as is necessary or possible, the analyst can then proceed to search for useful correlations between the level of profits in each segment, and the chosen industry statistics. The normal method is to express profits and the industry statistic as percentage changes compared with the previous year and to plot the resulting figures over a reasonably long period of time — say ten years — to assess the degree of correlation. More formal statistical methods are sometimes used, of course.

It is rare to find that movements in the chosen industry statistics faithfully mirror those in profits. To return to the example of our building materials producer, the level of new house building starts might not correlate with movements in profits from brick-making because in certain years, profits may have been depressed by strikes or by other outside forces such as the activities of the Price Commission. This is not a major problem, provided that the reasons for the divergence can be identified and assessed.

3   Forecast the industry statistics

Most companies announce their profits at six-monthly intervals, whereas industry statistics are published monthly or even weekly. Generally, therefore, the analyst will have some idea of likely developments in the company under study before profit figures are released. However, as we have seen, it is normally necessary to forecast profits up to two years ahead, and hence the industry statistics themselves must be forecast. This must be done within the context of an overall forecast of UK and overseas economies, if different analysts within the same organisation are not to make inconsistent assumptions. In our own firm, our economics team produces, on a monthly basis, framework forecasts which include the main elements of consumption and investment, interest rates and exchange rates, and so on, for all the main economies. These overall guidelines are then used by the analysts when making their own assumptions about individual industries.

4   Deriving the profits forecast

Once the forecast of the relevant industry statistics has been made, the model can be used to generate profits forecasts. The basic output of the model will, of course, be modified by the analysts' judgement of other factors which are difficult to incorporate in a model; for example, the effect of strikes. It will be clear that a good deal of skill is involved in this process of interpretation and modification of the model's results. In particular, the analyst must ensure that he takes full account of any indication as to future prospects which the company has made in its published accounts or at the AGM.

Two typical models

1   Motor distribution profits

A typical quoted motor distributor probably draws around half of its profits from the sale of new cars, and to a much lesser extent commercial vehicles with the remainder coming from parts and service, car hire, etc. New car sales have shown marked cyclical fluctuations in recent years and profits from this source have shown similarly large swings. As profits from the motor distributors' other activities tend to be reasonably stable, it is possible to forecast overall profits quite successfully on the basis of new car sales alone. The chart on page 144 shows how profits earned by a sample of four companies have tended to reflect the level of new car sales quite closely.

2   A Scotch whisky company

The rather more sophisticated model of a whisky company summarised on pages 146 and 147 incorporates parameters for sales volume, costs, prices and finance charges. In the interest of clarity some of the less important inter-relationships have been omitted. The structure of the model is straightforward, however, and the model can be studied most conveniently in terms of each of these main sectors.

Sales Volume   It is necessary to consider domestic and export sales separately, as different price levels pertain in each market. Statistics on total UK shipments to the home and export markets are forecast, and the company's estimated market share applied to give sales volume in each market.

Costs   The finished product is, typically, a blend of malt and grain whiskies made some years before and allowed to mature. The original

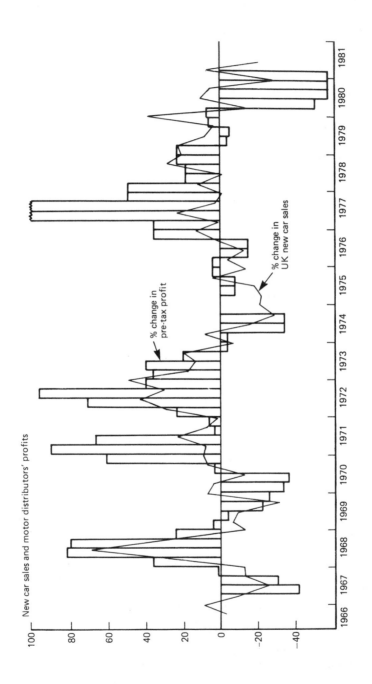

Figure 11.2   Motor distributors' profits and new car sales

cost for each input is obtained from published statistics, and the overall historic cost of the 'fillings' obtained. Most whisky companies do their own product advertising in the UK, so the cost per case is higher for home sales than for exports. (In export markets local agents normally have responsibility for advertising.)

Prices   Price levels in both UK and export markets must be forecast; the latter will usually involve a view on the outlook for sterling, since this will affect the company's pricing policy in export markets.

Profits   Profits from home and export sales can then be estimated and added together to give profits before interest charges.

Interest Charges   To calculate interest charges, a view of both the future level of interest rates and the level of working capital is required. The latter can be sub-divided into the expected increase in debtors — which in practice tends to be the duty element in domestic sales made within eight weeks of the year end — and the increase in stocks. The increase in stocks, which mainly consist of whisky being laid down that year to mature, can, in turn, be estimated from industry statistics for the distillation of new whisky that year.

Pre-tax Profits are then arrived at by deducting interest charges from group profits before interest.

Conclusions

To recapitulate, the principal task of the investment analyst is to identify shares which are likely to outperform or underperform the stockmarket as a whole. Most analysts attempt to do this by deciding an appropriate P/E at which to capitalise the expected future level of earnings per share. Since few companies publish profit forecasts while those that do so seldom give forecasts for more than one year ahead, the analyst usually has to make his own forecasts. In doing so, he is pitting his judgement, and that of the other members of the team with whom he works, against the consensus view of the market. This is a task in which there can be no guarantee of success. The analyst who beats the consensus view of future profits significantly more than half the time will provide a very valuable service to his clients.

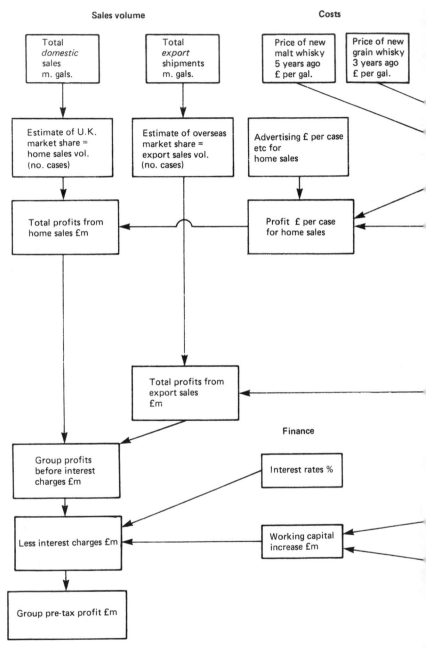

Figure 11.3   Scotch whisky companies' model

146

Prices

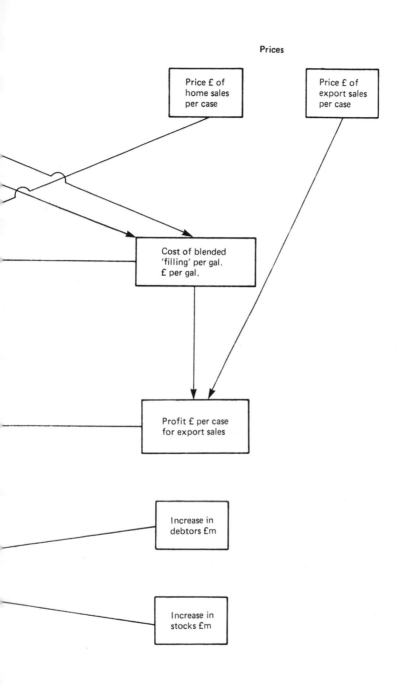

12 How accurate are profit forecasts?

C A Westwick, Arthur Andersen & Co.

Introduction

A reasonable amount of research has been carried out, mainly in the USA and to a lesser extent in the UK, into the question 'How accurate are profit forecasts?' This chapter summarises thirty-four of the more recent research findings and endeavours to draw some conclusions. The research is classified primarily according to who made the forecast and the situation in which it was made or published, as follows:

Management forecasts

(a) Internal forecasts
(b) Forecasts published with annual or interim accounts or on occasions other than prospectuses or takeover bids
(c) Forecasts in prospectuses
(d) Forecasts during a takeover bid
(e) Comparisons of forecasts made by companies with those made by investment analysts.

Analysts' forecasts

(f) Forecasts produced by analysts
(g) Forecasts produced from statistical models
(h) Comparison of analysts forecasts with those produced from statistical models.

But before we look at the results it is desirable to consider some of the problems in measuring forecast accuracy.

Problems in measuring the accuracy of forecasts

It might be thought that the accuracy of a profit forecast could be measured simply by comparing the result with the forecast, but in practice several problems arise.

Dev (1973) points out from her experience of analysing UK prospectus forecasts that it was not always clear whether the forecast profit was

(a) 'normal trading profit' or net profit before tax
(b) before or after deducting minority shareholders' interests
(c) before or after extraordinary items.

Ferris (1975) studied thirty-one firms publishing prospectuses in 1973. Twenty-one (68 per cent) of the firms stated that the published forecast was less than the internal estimate by a 'contingency factor' of 2.5 per cent to 20 per cent of the original estimate, with a mean discount of 8.2 per cent. Ten of the companies admitted to having undertaken, or avoided, accounting adjustments in order to help make the reported figures closer to the forecast. Twenty-six of the firms consciously allowed operating decisions to be influenced by the desire to achieve the forecast. Examples included:

1   The decision was made not to sell a building that they had planned to sell.
2   Large repairs to a factory roof were deferred.
3   Revenue was recognised in one accounting period rather than another.
4   The company declined to take on risky business that it would have accepted as a rule.
5   The company deferred a decision on the acquisition of loss making companies which would have been included in consolidated results.

On the other hand Morris and Breakwell (1975) found no evidence from their study of 300 large British companies of 'widespread doctoring of earnings figures' though they do not 'rule out the possibility that a very small minority may have resorted to such tactics to boost their results when profits were falling.'

The combined effect of these two pieces of research suggests that the publication of a prospectus forecast increases the pressure on management to achieve desirable published results by 'creative accounting'.

Internal forecasts

Vancil (1970) obtained information from corporate planners in some sixty US companies about their forecasts for sales in 1969, made in each of the years 1964 to 1968. Not surprisingly, the nearer the forecast was made to 1969 the more accurate it became.

Table 12.1
Ratio of planned to actual sales for 1969

Year plan was prepared	No. of companies	Mean	Standard deviation
1964	16	0.841	0.278
1965	19	0.849	0.223
1966	21	0.951	0.187
1967	27	0.972	0.148
1968	39	0.986	0.075

The earlier a forecast was made the more conservative it tended to be. Vancil conjectured that this might be the result of either revenue from unexpected acquisitions made during the five year period, and/or the effects of inflation over the five year period. Vancil found no significant correlations between planning accuracy and such factors as capital intensity, organisation structure, rate of return on investment, or the impact of technological change on product obsolescence.

Vancil summarised his main findings as follows:

'1   In terms of planning 'bias' (the tendency of plans to be consistently high or low), companies with a low rate of profit growth were inclined to be relatively more optimistic than high growth companies.

2   In terms of absolute 'accuracy' (ignoring whether the planning deviation is higher or lower than actual, companies with a high rate of profit growth were very accurate in forecasting for one or two years ahead relative to other companies, but not so accurate for the fourth or fifth year out.

3   Large companies do more accurate planning than smaller ones, and accuracy is lower among companies in highly competitive industries.

4   Accuracy is greater in those companies which asserted that an important purpose of planning is 'to provide a frame of reference for the operating budget.'

5   The old cliché that 'the top executive must be involved in planning' apparently has a pay-off in terms of accuracy; the greater his involvement, the more accurate the plans tend to be.

6   On the other hand, the familiar 'top-down versus bottom-up'

dichotomy of the way goals and objectives are set showed a surprising result. The more 'top-down' the process, the more likely the plans will be inaccurate (either too high or too low). To put it another way, when subordinates have helped set their own goals, they tend to deliver what they promised.

7 Rigorous discipline in 'linking' the plan to the budget, either by permitting no variation or requiring a complete explanation of any change, helps to improve accuracy.

8 Optimistic plans tend to be supported with more detailed financial documentation than are pessimistic plans.'

Buckley (1973) selected a random sample of a hundred medium sized quoted UK companies 'covering the whole spectrum of industry and commerce', which returned profits between £1million and £5million in 1970 and had made no substantial acquisitions in the previous three years. He obtained thirty usable replies which he acknowledges may well be biased towards the more successful forecasters. His principal results are set out below.

Table 12.2
Ratio of actual to planned turnover for 1970

Year plan was prepared	Mean Incl. acquisitions	Mean Ex. acquisitions	Standard deviation
1967	1.068	0.935	0.140
1968	1.044	0.964	0.122
1969	1.030	0.969	0.083

Table 12.3
Ratio of actual to planned net profit before interest and taxation for 1970

Year plan was prepared	Mean Incl. acquisitions	Mean Ex. acquisitions	Standard deviation
1967	0.796	0.705	0.244
1968	0.853	0.779	0.258
1969	0.933	0.875	0.244

It will be seen that turnover was estimated more accurately than profit and that accuracy improved nearer the event. Buckley also found (but provided no data to support) that:

(a) low growth companies tended to overestimate;
(b) high growth companies tended to underestimate;
(c) cyclical companies tended to overestimate on the downside of the cycle and underestimate on the up;
(d) companies rarely forecast a drop in profit or turnover;
(e) larger companies are less vulnerable to missing their forecasts than small ones.

The USA's Financial Executive Research Foundation (1972) commissioned management consultants A. T. Kearney Inc. to study internal forecasts. Ninety-five per cent of the 338 companies responding to the questionnaire used in the study prepared forecasts of corporate earnings, expenses and sales. The accuracy of these forecasts is shown in the following tables.

Table 12.4
Quarterly variance

Rank (1)	Type of forecast	5%	Cumulative per cent variance (2)			
			10%	15%	20%	21+%
1	Corporate expenses	80%	97%	99%	100%	0%
2	Corporate sales	72%	94%	96%	98%	2%
3	Expenses by division	74%	93%	97%	99%	1%
4	Expenses by corporate chart of accounts	72%	92%	95%	99%	1%
5	Changes in capital structure	71%	90%	91%	96%	4%
6	Changes in productivity	69%	87%	92%	98%	2%
7	Sales by division	55%	87%	95%	98%	2%
8	Corporate earnings	58%	85%	90%	93%	7%
9	Earnings by division	43%	76%	87%	92%	8%

(1) Based upon cumulative variance at 10%
(2) Per cent variances represent plus or minus differences

Table 12.5
Yearly variance

Rank (1)	Type of forecast	5%	Cumulative per cent variance (2)			21+%
			10%	15%	20%	
1	Corporate expenses	65%	90%	97%	98%	2%
2	Expenses by corporate chart of accounts	55%	84%	92%	98%	2%
3	Corporate sales	53%	84%	93%	95%	5%
4	Changes in capital structure	53%	84%	92%	95%	5%
5	Expenses by division	53%	82%	95%	97%	2%
6	Changes in productivity	47%	77%	92%	97%	3%
7	Sales by division	36%	74%	88%	94%	6%
8	Corporate earnings	37%	70%	80%	87%	13%
9	Earnings by division	22%	58%	73%	82%	18%

(1)   Based upon cumulative variance at 10%
(2)   Per cent variances represent plus or minus differences

If plus or minus 10 per cent is allowed as an acceptable level of error, then 85 per cent of companies achieved their quarterly forecast, and 70 per cent their annual forecast, of corporate earnings. Corporate expenses were more accurately forecast than sales and, not surprisingly as they are the residue from sales and expenses, earnings forecasts were significantly less accurate than both sales and expenses forecasts.

Kearney's analysis of the variances showed no significant differences based on the following factors:

1   The industry classification of the respondent,
2   The existence of written assumptions,
3   The length of the written assumptions,
4   The use of a range format of presentation.

The only relationships discovered in the research were as follows:

1   The yearly variance of a forecast is greater than the quarterly variance,
2   Smaller companies experienced a greater variance in their yearly sales forecasts than did larger companies.

Daily (1971) had conducted a much smaller, but more in-depth, study of twelve to eighteen firms' experience over 'as many years as was practicable, usually five years'. He concluded that (a) differences exceeding 15 per cent between forecast and actual net income were present in one-third of the observations, (b) forecasts of net income were less reliable than those of revenue, (c) size did not seem to affect accuracy but (d) 'industry' did (the three banks' forecasts were more accurate because they were able to pass the effects of changes in interest rates on to their customers; two textile firms and one truck transportation firm were reasonably accurate but the remaining firms, in packaging and fabricated metals, were highly erratic), (e) the firms which devoted limited resources to forecasting activities and as a result used less sophisticated forecasting methods produced the least accurate results.

Forecasts published with annual accounts or on occasions other than prospectuses or takeover bids

Copeland and Marioni (1972) extracted fifty predictions made by management of earnings per share (EPS) from the Wall Street Journal for early 1968 which were (a) point or range estimates and (b) from companies which published quarterly EPS figures. The forecasts were made when between 3 per cent and 99 per cent of the year had elapsed. The average relative error $(F-A)/A$ (%)) was 20.1 per cent, with a marked tendency for companies to overestimate earnings.

The authors compared these forecasts with those produced from six 'naive' models using various combinations of EPS data from the past two years and the first quarter of the year being forecast. The average relative error of the six models ranged from 26.5 per cent to 98.9 per cent. (See Table 12.6.)

Another method used by the authors for evaluating the performance of the models and the executives was a numerical ranking system based upon the absolute amount of the error. Under this procedure, the model which produces the value closest to the actual result receives a rank of 1, the next most accurate forecast is given a rank of 2, and so on until the least accurate prediction is given a rank of 7. In cases where a model is unable to generate a forecast, that model is automatically given a rank of 7. Thus, a model receives a rank varying from 1 to 7 for each company in the sample, based on the accuracy of the model's forecast of each company's earnings. In this way, the forecasts are evaluated solely on how close they come to the result in relation to all other forecasts, and no penalty is imposed for the size of the error.

The rankings of the six models and executive forecasts are summarised in Table 12.7. Note that the predictions of the executives are still the superior ones; that is, on average, their forecasts are closer to actual EPS more often than any of the models. Executive forecasts

Table 12.6

Summary measures of forecasting errors, company executives versus the models

Type of error	Company executives N = 50	Model 1 N = 50	Model 2 N = 50	Model 3 N = 49	Model 4 N = 50	Model 5 N = 50	Model 6 N = 50
Total of absolute errors, ignoring sign	$18.48	$33.25	$47.68	$37.49	$27.61	$84.13	$28.53
Average of absolute errors, ignoring sign	0.37	0.67	0.95	0.77	0.55	1.68	0.57
	N = 49	N = 49	N = 50	N = 49	N = 50	N = 50	N = 50
Total of relative errors, ignoring sign	983.6%	1,336.1%	2,016.8%	1,945.2%	1,327.1%	4,945.9%	1,351.1%
Average of relative errors, ignoring sign	20.1	27.9	40.3	39.7	26.5	98.9	27.0

Model 1: EPS this year = EPS last year
Model 2: EPS this year = EPS last year plus (EPS last year – EPS year before)
Model 3: EPS this year = EPS last year times (EPS last year ÷ EPS year before)
Model 4: EPS this year = 4 times the first quarter's EPS of this year
Model 5: EPS this year = EPS last year times (First quarter's EPS this year ÷ first quarter's EPS last year)
Model 6: EPS this year = First quarter's EPS this year plus EPS last year – EPS first quarter last year.

achieve a higher rank than that expected by chance (14 per cent) on a significant number of occasions.

Table 12.7
Ranking of executives' forecasts compared with forecasts made by six naive models (1968)

Rank	Observations	Percentage
1	15	30
2	10	20
3	6	12
4	6	12
5	3	6
6	2	4
7	8	16
Total	50	100

Surprisingly, the authors made no attempt to assess the influences of either the date when the forecast was made (although they measured it), or the industry of the forecast company, on the accuracy of the forecasts by executives or by the naive models. The authors did, however, replicate their studies on data for 1964 and 1965. They concluded that executive forecasts were more accurate than those from any of their naive models.

McDonald (1973) studied news articles, mainly about the annual shareholders' meeting, in the Wall Street Journal. He limited himself to those predictions which (a) were published within a short enough time period to be included in the annual report, (b) were for net income and not operating earnings, and (c) were point estimates and not range or open ended estimates.

The study covered the period 1966 to 1970 during which the level of profits varied significantly. For the years 1966, 1968 and 1969 corporate profits increased 10 per cent, 9 per cent and 3 per cent respectively; in 1967 and 1970 corporate profits decreased by 1 per cent and 7 per cent, respectively. The differing economic conditions within the study period helped to make the results of the study more general.

McDonald warns against generalising from his study and points out that the firms voluntarily made their predictions public. It is therefore possible that only those firms with an above average ability to predict earnings chose to publicise their forecasts, thus biasing the results of the study. He also notes that fewer observations were found in 1967 and 1970; the two years when profits declined. It seems that companies are understandably more reluctant to forecast a drop in earnings than a rise.

The 201 predictions were made up of 152 firms which made one prediction in the five years covered, 23 making two forecasts and 1 making three. The industries and years concerned are shown in the following table.

Table 12.8
Firms whose predictions compose the subpopulation classified into general industry groupings

Year	Industrials	Utilities	Finance Banking and Insurance	Transportation	Other	Total
1966	27	4	2	7	5	45
1967	19	4	7	1	2	33
1968	29	7	3	2	2	43
1969	28	8	–	3	5	44
1970	22	8	3	1	2	36
Totals	125	31	15	14	16	201
%	62.2	15.4	7.4	7.0	8.0	100.0

McDonald measured accuracy by Relative Prediction Error =

$$\frac{\text{Actual earnings} - \text{predicted earnings}}{\text{Predicted earnings}}$$

Overpredictions therefore have a negative sign and underpredictions a positive one.

McDonald's results are summarised in the following tables.

Table 12.9

Statistical Summary of Relative Prediction Errors for the Five-Year Study

Year	Number of Observations	Range %	Mean %	Standard Deviation %	Coefficient of Skewness
1966	45	− 57.0 to 30.7	− 1.7	17.8	−1.0
1967	33	− 81.3 to 33.5	−15.6	26.4	−0.7
1968	43	− 80.2 to 55.0	−10.6	25.7	−0.7
1969	44	− 52.2 to 11.8	−12.1	16.7	−0.9
1970	36	−395.6 to 108.5	−32.1	83.5	−2.8
5 years	201	−395.6 to 108.5	−13.6	41.6	−5.1

Table 12.10

Findings of the study by general industry groupings for the five years

Classification	Number	Range %	Mean %	Standard Deviation %	Coefficient of Skewness
Industrials	125	−395.6 to 108.5	−17.2	50.5	−4.4
Utilities	31	− 15.3 to 18.7	− 0.6	6.7	0.3
Finance, Banking and Insurance	15	− 81.3 to 4.2	−12.2	20.7	−2.5
Transportation	14	− 55.3 to 13.3	−16.7	20.7	−0.6
Others	16	− 57.0 to 28.0	− 8.9	23.4	−0.8

Table 12.11

Distribution of overpredictions, underpredictions and exact predictions by years

Year	Number of Overpredictions	Number of Underpredictions	Exact Predictions	Total
1966	22	22	1	45
1967	25	7	1	33
1968	28	15	0	43
1969	29	12	3	44
1970	24	12	0	36
Total	128	68	5	201

He concludes that:

    (a) 35 per cent of forecasts were within 5 per cent of actual, and 49 per cent within 10 per cent, but 40 per cent were more than 15 per cent from actual;

(b) the worst years for accuracy were 1967 and 1970 when profits fell;

(c) overpredictions significantly outnumber underpredictions and exact predictions combined;

(d) earnings predictions for utilities were most accurate (not surprisingly because their revenue is subject to regulation).

Dev (1974) studied the information on future prospects contained in the annual report and accounts of 424 companies quoted on the UK Stock Exchange. 212 of these companies were newly quoted in 1968 or 1969 and the reports relate to the periods covered by the profit forecast in the prospectus. The other 212 were the 1972 reports of the largest UK industrial quoted companies.

Her main findings are given below.

Table 12.12
Comments on prospects for all 424 companies

Longer term prospects	8 No mention	9 Conditional	10 Good/poor	Total (profits for current year)
Profits for current year				
1 No mention	33	9	6	48
2 Too difficult to forecast	66	8	14	88
3 Much higher/ lower	19		10	29
4 Higher/lower	105	6	56	167
5 A little higher/ lower	35	6	9	50
6 Similar to last year	18	4	2	24
7 Not less than £x	15		3	18
Total (longer-term prospects)	291	33	100	424

She comments that the above analysis is highly subjective because the comments made by companies tended to be imprecise. 'In particular the differences between categories 3, 4, 5 and 6 are not as clean cut as the tables imply.'

Dev went on to examine the annual reports of the 15 newly quoted companies that made specific forecasts (i.e. not less than £x) in the year of study. Her results are as follows:

Table 12.13
Ratios of actual to forecast profits before corporation tax for 15
newly-quoted companies (a)

Year of forecast	1	2	3	4	5	6
Company ref. No.						
1	1.94	1.20	*	*	*	*
2	1.50	0.84	*	*	*	
3	1.44	(b)				
4	1.39	1.37	*	*	*	
5	1.36	1.07	*	*	*	
6	1.16	0.71	*	*	*	*
7	1.11	1.44	*	*	*	*
8	1.10	1.03	*	*	(c)	
9	1.09	1.38	*	*	*	*
10	1.08	1.11	*	*	*	(c)
11	1.08	1.06	*	*	*	*
12	1.04	1.02	*	1.25	1.20	*
13	1.04	0.63	*	*	*	*
14	1.03	1.10	1.15	1.12	1.31	*
15	1.00	0.57	*	*	*	*

(a) These companies made prospectus forecasts in either 1968 or 1969 (year 1) and forecasts in the year of study (year 2).
(b) Forecast published but company taken over and separate results not disclosed.
(c) Taken over, or merged with another company, in this year, and no forecast published in the annual report.
* No forecast included in the annual report.

There is a wide variation in accuracy in both year 1 and year 2. Moreover, the variability between the ratios for years 1 and 2 is slight for some companies but quite substantial for others.

Lorek, McDonald and Patz (1976) took a sample of 40 management forecasts from the 201 predictions used by McDonald (1973) in the research described earlier in this section. They compared these forecasts with those that they had prepared themselves using the Box-Jenkins methodology on the reported quarterly earnings of each of the firms concerned for between 32 and 52 quarters prior to the year being forecast. The Box-Jenkins (B-J) forecasts were more accurate than management's on 27 out of 40 possible occasions.

Of the 13 firms whose management forecasts were superior to the B-J forecast, seven had published their forecasts after the publication of their first quarter's results. When these first quarter's results were utilised in the B-J formula three additional B-J forecasts surpassed their respective management forecast making the adjusted 'score' 30 out of 40 in favour of B-J.

Hagerman and Ruland (1979) compared the accuracy of management forecasts which appeared in the Wall Street Journal for December, January and February in the five years from 1968, with forecasts from four relatively simple models which an investor could use relatively cheaply by inputting past earnings data for the company and publicly available forecasts for the corporate sector as a whole (from the *Wharton Quarterly*). They found that management forecasts were more accurate than each of the models tested for the five year period as a whole and for four of the five individual years. The accuracy of management forecasts declined, the longer the period being forecast. Larger firms' forecasts were more accurate than smaller ones. In one subgroup out of four (small companies forecasting further ahead) the models were more accurate than those of management but the difference was not statistically significant. The authors examined the firms tested to see if they differed from COMPUSTAT firms as a whole. No significant difference was found for the proportion of new equity issues made, or whether the company was rate regulated or not, but the firms tested were significantly larger than average.

Platt (1979) examined between 81 and 298 interim and annual reports published between 1973 and 1976 by a number of the larger listed industrial companies included in the annual survey of published accounts published by the Institute of Chartered Accountants in England and Wales. He does not say how these reports were selected from the total number of companies (usually 300) in the survey.

Table 12.14
Proportion of companies making forecasts

Year of publication	Annual reports		Interim reports		
	1973-74	1974-75	1973-74	1974-75	1975-76
Number of reports examined	298	118	221	191	81
	%	%	%	%	%
Profit forecast made	39	34	72	62	67
Comment on short-term prospects	30	43	6	10	9
Forecast not considered possible	24	14	2	10	4
No forecast or reference to prospects	7	9	20	18	20
	100%	100%	100%	100%	100%

Many of the 1973-74 annual reports and 1974-75 interim reports were issued at the time of the miners' strike and energy crisis of December 1973 to March 1974 with the result that the proportion of cases in which no forecast was considered possible was probably higher than normal.

Platt makes a similar comment to Dev when he says 'in many cases it is necessary for the purpose of analysis to make assumptions as to the meaning to be attributed to rather vague statements.' With that caveat he presents the following comparison of results (usually net profit after tax and before extraordinary items) with forecasts.

Table 12.15
Forecasts and 1974-75 results

Forecasts	Results			
		Percentages of forecasts on line		
		Improvement	Similarity	Deterioration
Percentages of total forecasts	%	%	%	%
Annual accounts 1973-4				
Improvement	42	56	9	35
Similarity	9	26	26	48
Deterioration	6	25	8	67
Approximate profit/loss				
figure	—	—	—	—
Optimistic outlook	36	45	14	41
Pessimistic outlook	7	7	26	67
(Total number of forecasts: 206)	100			
Interim accounts 1974-75				
Improvement	47	80	11	9
Similarity	16	45	23	32
Deterioration	19	12	4	84
Approximate profit/loss				
figure	4	—	100	—
Optimistic outlook	10	39	38	23
Pessimistic outlook	4	50	—	50
(Total number of forecasts: 136)	100			

Forecasts tend to be more often 'right' than 'wrong' — although they are wrong with disturbing frequency. Platt says, however, that 'the forecasts of 1973-74 results had a higher rate of correctness than those of 1974-75 and 1975-76 which were made at a more unsettled period when forecasting was correspondingly more difficult.' Forecasts made at the interim state are more accurate than those made with the report for the previous year.

As most forecasts are not couched in exact terms the degree of accuracy can only be assessed imperfectly. Of the forecasts examined, only 95 stated or implied a specific figure. The variance of the results from those forecasts is given below.

Table 12.16
Variances of results from profit forecasts

| | Number of instances | | | |
	Interim Reports	Annual Reports	Total	Percentages
Forecasts of specific profit figures				
Variances of results:				
up to 5%	13	1	14	44
over 5% up to 20%	13	–	13	41
over 20%	4	1	5	15
	30	2	32	100%
Forecasts of profit similar to previous year				
Variances of results:				
up to 5%	6	7	13	21
over 5% up to 20%	21	7	28	45
over 20%	12	10	22	34
	39	24	63	100%
Totals				
Variances of results:				
up to 5%	19	8	27	28½
over 5% up to 20%	34	7	41	43
over 20%	16	11	27	28½
	69	26	95	100%

Unfortunately, the ranges chosen are perhaps too broad. It would have been interesting to see how many of the forecasts were within plus or minus 10 per cent. However 1 in 3 forecasts are within 5 per cent and 7 out of 10 are within 20 per cent.

Forecasts in prospectuses

Dev and Webb (1972) studied the accuracy of 212 forecasts of net profit before tax made in prospectuses issued in 1968 or 1969 in the UK. Accuracy was measured by the ratio of reported to forecast profit. The authors quote Sir Timothy Harford, a merchant banker, as saying that 'Having arrived at a forecast that is as realistic as possible and that is approved by all concerned, a contingency discount is then applied to this realistic forecast to produce the figure that will actually be used in the prospectus. The size of the discount will be governed by how much uncertainty there is over the achievement of the profit forecast (which in turn is primarily determined by the nature of the company's business and how much of the financial year has elapsed by the time of the flotation) and by the caution of the directors and the sponsors of the issue; the normal range is 7½-10 per cent'.*

This means that, to the extent that this practice is followed, the expected ratio of reported to forecast profit would be 1.08 to 1.11 had the forecast been accurate in the first place. The observed ratios ranged from 0.466 to 1.964 with a mean of 1.12. The mean (of 1.12) was then taken as the target to which companies had been aiming and errors were measured from this target and not from unity (1.00). Overall, a fairly high degree of 'accuracy' was found. 136 of the 212 results (64 per cent) were within plus or minus 10 per cent of the 'target' forecast (i.e. the ratio of results to forecast was within the range 1.02 to 1.22).

Share issues may be made at any time during the year, so the period being forecast in this study ranged between 1 week and 14 months with an average of 5.65 months. A small but significant correlation (0.316) was found between the error and the length of time being forecast. Some evidence was also found that forecasting accuracy was more consistent (as indicated by a smaller standard deviation for the ratio of reported to forecast profit) in some 'industries' (building, timber and roads, and foods, groceries etc.) than in the sample as a whole.

Ferris and Hayes (1977) examined by means of a statistical technique called 'path analysis' the effects of (a) the size of the company, (b) the length of time being forecast and (c) general economic conditions, on the accuracy of forecasts published in 279 prospectuses by UK companies between 1970 and 1973.

They concluded that, of the factors measured:

> (a) the length of period forecast had the greatest effect on accuracy (9 per cent) but, contrary to expectation, the longer the period the more accurate the forecast (perhaps because manage-

---

* *Journal of Business Finance,* Vol 1, No. 1, 1969, p. 17

ment has longer in which to exercise discretion in deferrable expenditure decisions to bring actual close to forecast?);

(b) the size of the firm provided 6 per cent of the effect on accuracy but, again contrary to expectation, the smaller firms were more accurate;

(c) general economic conditions (measured by the average size of the Financial Times All-Share Index for the 200 days immediately preceding the issue of the prospectus) provided only a maximum of 4 per cent of the explanation and suggested that forecasts were more accurate in a downturn.

Forecasts made during a takeover bid

Westwick (1972) examined 210 forecasts made in bid situations in the UK. The forecasts were made since 1 May 1969 and related to periods ending on or before 30 September 1970. He suggests that the economic climate was such that 'It would not appear . . . that there were any unusual difficulties in forecasting during this period.'

Overall, accuracy was high: 170 (81 per cent) of the forecasts were achieved within a margin of ±10 per cent. However, many of the forecasts were made towards the end of (or even after) the year to which they related and accuracy (i.e. within ±10 per cent) dropped as low as 50 per cent when the whole year was being forecast. As there were few forecasts in this category, the generalisation should be treated with caution, not surprisingly. Nevertheless, the length of the period being forecast appears, not surprisingly, to have a significant effect on the accuracy of the forecast.

1   (a) 23 per cent of forecasts were 'spot on' (±2 per cent)
    (b) more forecasts were exceeded by results (53 per cent) than vice versa (24 per cent), but
    (c) there is a greater likelihood of results falling far short of forecast than vice versa (7 per cent of results were more than 28 per cent below forecast, but only 2 per cent were more than 28 per cent above forecast).

2   (a) offerors whose bids succeed have significantly fewer results which fall short of forecast and significantly more results which exceed forecast by between 3 per cent and 12 per cent
    (b) offerees who failed to fight off the bid made for them are in exactly the reverse position: in other words, the higher failure rate by offerees is largely made up of results falling short of forecast rather than of results exceeding forecast.

Possible explanations for this difference include: (a) the offeror has more time in which to prepare his forecast; (b) offerees who fail to fight off bids may have poorer management; (c) the post bid results of offerees who succumb to a takeover may be depressed by a 'deck clearing' exercise by the successful offeror.

3   (a) both offerors' and offerees' results will tend to exceed forecast (P = 0.6 and 0.4)* or be met (P = 0.3 and 0.2), but
(b) there is a much stronger possibility that offerees' results will fall far short (more than 22 per cent) of forecast (P = 0.16) than offerors' (P = 0.01).

4   the nature of the bid (e.g. agreed or opposed) does not seem to affect the accuracy of the forecast.

The nature of the data supplied to the author by the Panel on Takeovers and Mergers did not permit him to assess the effects of the size of the company or the industry in which it was engaged, on the accuracy of the forecasts.

Comparison of forecasts made by companies with those made by investment analysts

Basi, Carey and Twark (BCT) (1976) examined 88 forecasts of earnings per share made by companies and published in the Wall Street Journal during 1970 and 1971 which were either point or range forecasts (open ended forecasts were ignored). They also examined forecasts made by investment analysts for the same companies published in Standard and Poors' Earnings Forecasts on or before the company published its forecast. Errors were measured by subtracting the actual results from the forecast and expressing this difference as a percentage of the actual result. Thus, positive figures represent overestimates.

On average, analysts overestimated by nearly 9 per cent while corporate forecasts averaged a 6 per cent overestimate. The actual range was from −37.5 per cent to + 126.4 per cent for company forecasts and −25.0 per cent to + 150.0 per cent for analysts' forecasts.

The accuracy of the forecasts examined is difficult to classify as clearly good or bad. On the one hand, more than 70 per cent of the estimates by both analysts and executives were within 10 per cent of actual figures, which appears highly commendable. On the other hand,

---

*   P = Probability, measured on a range 0 to 1, where 0 = certainly will not happen, and 1 = certainly will happen.

roughly 5 per cent of the company and 7 per cent of the analysts' forecasts represented errors greater than 50 per cent. For the American Stock Exchange (AMEX) firms, more than 5 per cent of the company forecasts and 10 per cent of the analysts' forecasts showed errors greater than 100 per cent. Forecasts made during 1971 were more accurate that those released in 1970, probably as a result of changes in the economic climate. There was some evidence that forecasts improved in accuracy as the release date for the results approached. Company estimates tended to be better than those of investment analysts but not enough so to be statistically significant.

Both companies and analysts were better at forecasting the results of utilities than non-utilities, and those on the New York Stock Exchange (NYSE) list than on the AMEX list. Utilities, as regulated firms, are subject to less risk and their results should therefore be easier to forecast. NYSE listed firms tend to be larger, more mature firms; AMEX listed firms tend to be newer, smaller, riskier firms.

The authors' caution against assuming that the forecasts surveyed would be typical of all forecasts made by companies. They suggest that only those with a high degree of confidence in their forecasts choose to publish them.

BCT's paper was criticised by Albrecht, Johnson, Lookabill and Watson (AJLW) (1977) but BCT responded (1977) and rebutted vigorously most of AJLW's points.

Ruland (1978) obtained management forecasts by searching the December, January and February issues of the Wall Street Journal from December 1969 to 1973. Only point estimates and closed end ranges (of which the midpoint was taken) were used. To permit comparison of these forecasts with others developed from extrapolating past data, only companies with at least six years' data available on COMPUSTAT were used, thus restricting the sample to more established and larger companies. These restrictions meant that only 79 forecasts were available.

These management forecasts were matched with analysts' forecasts issued within two months of the management forecast and published in Standard and Poor's Earnings Forecaster. Because of the absence of suitable analysts' forecasts the sample was further reduced to 65.

The problem of comparing management and analyst accuracy is that their forecasts are rarely issued on the same day. To take analysts' forecasts published earlier than management's would bias the results in favour of management and vice versa. The author therefore divided the forecasts into two groups (see table).

Results suggest that management forecasts are more accurate than analysts' but the difference is not statistically significant.

Table 12.17
Relative accuracy of the management and analyst forecasts

| | Percentage of Observations | |
| | Analyst forecasts issued prior to the | Analyst forecasts issued after the |
Outcome	Management Forecasts	Management Forecasts
Analyst forecast more accurate than management	38%	32%
Analyst forecast less accurate	51%	47%
Analyst forecast same accuracy	11%	21%
Total	100%	100%

Both the management and the analysts' forecasts were compared with a 'naive model' (based on the results of earlier unpublished research by Hagerman & Ruland) which uses a regression of earnings over the past six years, with the following results:

Table 12.18
Management and analyst forecasts compared to those of the simple extrapolative model

| | | Percentage of Observations | |
| | Management | Analyst forecasts issued prior to the | Analyst forecasts issued after the |
Outcome	Forecasts	Management forecasts	Management forecasts
Forecast more accurate than Naive Model	68%	55%	66%
Forecast less accurate than Naive Model	32%	45%	34%
Total	100%	100%	100%

Management forecasts, and analysts' forecasts made after the management's forecasts, were statistically significantly more accurate that the naive model, but analysts' forecasts made before the management forecasts were not.

Imhoff (1978) examined whether companies which published forecasts are representative of all companies and concluded that probably they were not. He found that companies which publish forecasts have a lower earnings variability, and a higher systematic risk, than those which do not. He also found that analysts' forecasts of companies which do not publish forecasts are less accurate than analysts' forecasts for companies which do. He suggests that analysts' and management's forecasts may not be independent: analysts may receive information from management; management may be influenced by analysts' forecasts.

Jaggi (1978) studied management forecasts published in the Wall Street Journal in the first four calendar months of each of the years 1971 to 1974. Only forecasts made at least eight months before the company's year end were used so as to restrict the sample to those forecasts which could have been included in the company's annual report. Only point and range forecasts were used. This resulted in 156 forecasts for 141 firms. Analysts' forecasts for the same firms were obtained from *Value Line Service*.

His main results were as follows:

Table 12.19

Year	N	Average percentage error		Number of forecasts within ± 10% of actual	
		Management	Analyst	Management	Analyst
1971	23	37.1	47.8	9	8
2	23	13.9	15.5	16	12
3	64	21.5	23.0	34	31
4	46	35.3	34.3	16	12
1971-74	156	26.7	28.3	75	63

As a result of statistical tests he concludes that the management forecasts in the sample are comparatively more accurate than the analysts'. Analysts' forecasts made before management's were published were less accurate than management's; there was no significant difference in the accuracy of analysts' forecasts made after management's were published and management's forecasts.

Forecasts made by management in companies in the chemicals and service industries were significantly more accurate that those of analysts. There were no significant differences for utilities and banking.

No trend was found between differences in management and analyst accuracy and the size of the company.

Forecasts produced by analysts

Stewart (1973), as part of a larger study for the USA Financial Analysts Federation, examined two unpublished studies prepared by large banks and two computer based statistical services. He concluded:

'1   An earnings forecast for the 'average' firm made twelve months prior to the year end tends to deviate from actual year end results by about 10 per cent – 15 per cent. However, the range of accuracy is from average errors of nearly 50 per cent to average errors of about 3 per cent.

2   There seems to be a slightly optimistic bias to most forecasts.

3   There is some slight evidence that the optimism of forecasts is related to the strength of the stock market.

4   Among the analytical groups included in the study, no substantial differences in forecast accuracy were discovered.

5   The relative accuracy of analysts' forecasts is often not much better than the accuracy of forecasts based on simple, extrapolative models; however, analysts are consistently superior to models at turning points and in difficult to forecast industries.

6   Forecasts tend to be less accurate at turning points.

7   The accuracy of a forecast is quite dependent upon its futurity; the shorter the prediction period, the more accurate the forecast in most cases.

8   The accuracy of forecasting is strongly influenced by the nature of the industry to which the firm whose results are being forecasted belongs. Certain industries such as automotive, aerospace, and steel are much more difficult to forecast than other industries such as food, oil, and drugs. There is some evidence indicating that volatility of a company's earnings, the difficulty of forecasting such earnings, and the market volatility of the stock are interrelated.'

Richards (1976) studied forecasts of 1972 earnings for 93 companies listed on the New York Stock Exchange made by 5 firms of analysts during the period December 1971 to February 1972. He concluded that accuracy was affected by the company being forecast and the industry in which it operated, but that there was no significant difference between the accuracy of the 5 analysts studied even though the cost of using them differed significantly.

Richards and Fraser (1977) collected forecasts of earnings for the calendar year 1973 for 213 companies (most of which are listed on the New York Stock Exchange) made by 9 investment analysts during January and February 1973. They found that 'analysts are generally in agreement in their predictions such that differences in forecast errors are not significant among analysts' even though the cost of using different analysts varied significantly.

They also noted that the effect of averaging all the analysts' forecasts may be to reduce forecast error, which suggests that research based on the use of such averages may be unduly favourable to analysts.

Fraser and Richards (1978) studied forecasts made by investment analysts and published in Standard and Poor's Earnings Forecaster for 35 public utilities (20 electricity companies, 9 gas and 6 telephone) for the years 1975, 1976 and 1977. They found, contrary to the generally held belief, that rate regulated industries' profits are easier to forecast than those for the rest of industry, that errors were as high or higher than those for other industries and varied between subgroups of utilities and over time.

Table 12.20
Distribution of earnings forecast errors

| | Number of Firms | | |
	1975	1976	1977
10 per cent or less	20	17	12
10-25 per cent	10	12	13
25-50 per cent	4	4	4
50 per cent and over	1	2	3
Mean Relative Error	9.1%	9.9%	14.4%
Mean Absolute Relative Error	14.3%	16.3%	23.4%

Note: Information for three firms in 1977 was unavailable at the time of the analysis.

Table 12.21
Forecast errors classified by nature of public utility

Subgroup	Mean Absolute Relative Error		
	1975	1976	1977
Telephone	9.4%	7.5%	4.7%
Gas	6.2%	22.8%	21.8%
Electric	19.5%	16.0%	29.1%

Table 12.22
Forecast errors for industry classifications, 1976

	MRE %	MARE %
Public utilities	9.9	16.3
Banking	−3.6	3.7
Building	16.0	28.1
Chemical	14.2	14.5
Drugs	1.1	8.6
Electrical equipment	−8.4	8.4
Office equipment and computers	−3.4	8.1
Paper	2.1	10.0
Petroleum	4.6	10.7
Retail stores	−6.8	10.2

Notes: MRE and MARE computations for the public utility industry were made by the authors. All other MRE's and MARE's are from: 'An Examination of the Accuracy of Earnings Forecasts', by R. Malcolm Richards, James J. Benjamin, and Robert H. Strawser, *Financial Management,* Fall 1977.

Richards and Fraser (1978) identified 24 variables believed to affect the degree of difficulty of forecasting earnings for various corporations. These variables then were used in an effort to explain the errors associated with 1973 earnings forecasts for 100 corporations. The variables related to the financial structure of the firm, the operating leverage, the growth of the firm, the size of the firm, the relationship between the firm and the overall market, and other factors deemed to be directly related to earnings. The average forecast error for all forecasts was found to be 22.3 per cent.

Examination of the correlation among the variables revealed a substantial lack of relationship between errors in the earnings forecasts and the firms' financial variables. No one variable or group of variables stood out as being highly correlated with the errors in analysts' forecasts of corporate earnings. A multilinear regression model was employed in an effort to explain the errors. The authors concluded that 'knowledge of the financial characteristics of the firm does not provide much information in explaining the forecast errors.' The variables included in the study could account for less than 20 per cent of the forecast error, leading to the conclusion that the 'errors appear to be random in nature and not readily explainable by characteristics of the firm.'

Forecasts produced from statistical models

Kinney (1971) predicted the earnings for 24 companies for 1968 and 19 for 1969 by means of 4 relatively simple models using predictions of the growth of GNP, the trend of past consolidated earnings, subentity sales and earnings data, predictions of industry sales, etc. He concluded that 'predictions based on segment sales and earnings data and industry predictions were on the average more accurate than predictions based on models using consolidated performance data alone.'

Emmanuel and Pick (1980) conducted similar research on 39 UK companies and made predictions for 1973 to 1977. They comment on the paucity of UK industry forecast data compared with the USA but generally came to a similar conclusion to Kinney.

Carey (1978) examined the accuracy of forecasts produced by several simple models utilising past data about the earnings of the firm, e.g. postulating no growth, equal percentage growth, geometric growth. The data related to 517 firms for the period 1963 to 1972. He concluded that:

1   Errors can be reduced by matching the model to the industry of the firm using the 'life-cycle' concept of 'pioneering, investment maturity, and stabilization'.

2   When using growth models, use of results for 2 to 3 years gave more accurate results than the last year alone, but going beyond 3 years did not improve accuracy.

Comparison of analysts' forecasts with those produced from statistical models

Richards, Benjamin and Strawser (1977) compared analysts' forecasts published in Standard and Poor's Earnings Forecaster for 92 companies listed on the New York Stock Exchange for 1972 to 1976 with forecasts generated from 3 simple statistical models. They concluded:

1   Analysts were more accurate than the naive models.

2   There were significant differences in the forecast errors for different industries.

Brown and Rozeff (1978) randomly selected 50 firms for which quarterly earnings data and Value Line forecasts were available. They compared the Value Line forecasts with those produced by statistical methods for the period 1972 to 1975. They concluded that:

1   Value Line Investment Survey consistently made more accurate forecasts than those from Box-Jenkins* models.

2   B-J models were more accurate than martingale and submartingale models.

Crichfield, Dyckman and Lakonishok (1978) compared forecasts made by investment analysts for a non-random sample of 46 firms during the period 1967 to 1976 and published in Standard and Poor's Earnings Forecaster with 5 simple statistical models. They concluded that:

1   Analyst forecast accuracy improves the nearer the forecast is made to the earnings announcement.

2   There was no systematic bias in the errors in analysts' forecasts.

They had expected to find that the variability of analysts' forecasts would decline as the end of the forecast year approached, but this was not so. Collins and Hopwood (1980) suggest that this was due to a small number of outliers.

Collins and Hopwood (1980) compared the accuracy of forecasts from models identified by previous researchers as likely to be accurate, with those from analysts. They used a sample of 50 firms and quarterly data from 1951 to 1974. They concluded that:

1   Financial analysts provide forecasts more accurate than the statistical models studied.

---

*   For a clear and simple description of Box-Jenkins' techniques see M. Firth, *Forecasting methods in business management,* Arnold, 1977.

2   Premier models are a viable alternative to individual identification of models on a firm-by-firm basis, since they provide forecasts which are at least as accurate.

3   In the event of a premier model being used, it should contain a seasonal parameter.

4   For all methods, forecast accuracy increases in a linear fashion as the end of the year approaches.

5   Financial analysts are able to respond to situations such as strikes or sudden swings in earnings, whereas statistical models are either unable to respond or are slow to do so.

6   Differences in accuracy between the different forecast methods tend to decrease as the end of the year approaches.

Conclusions

Any conclusions drawn from the above survey must necessarily be tentative, especially as there is some evidence that companies which publish forecasts differ from those which do not (Hagerman and Ruland, Imhoff, Penman) and many researchers caution that their results relate only to the companies studied and may not apply to other companies and/or other periods and/or other investment analysts.

Problems arise in measuring accuracy. In some cases it is not clear which figure of profit is being forecast. The published forecast may differ from the internal forecast (especially for UK prospectuses). Management may take operating decisions or make changes in their accounting methods in the published results to minimise any deviation from the published forecast (Dev, Ferris, Morris and Breakwell, Platt).

Many factors may affect the accuracy of forecasts, but it is difficult to establish whether they do or not, and if so, how relatively important they are. Moreover, there is disagreement on which statistical techniques should be used to discover the relative importance of the various factors and to test the significance of any differences found. See Appendix on page 179 for a statistical critique of the following conclusions.

To some extent the more researchers support a conclusion the more valid it may be, but the converse is not necessarily true. The fact that only one, or a few, researchers support a conclusion may mean no more than that he or they are the only ones to have examined the point. Alternatively, it may mean that others have examined the point, and not come to a conclusion and not reported that fact.

With these caveats the following tentative conclusions emerge:

1   Accuracy declines with the length of time being forecast (Vancil, Kearney, Hagerman and Ruland, Platt, Dev and Webb, Westwick; Basi, Carey and Twark; Collins and Hopwood; Crichfield, Dyckman and Lakonishok; Stewart).
The opposite conclusion was reached by Ferris and Hayes.

2   Larger companies' forecasts are likely to be more accurate than smaller ones (Vancil, Buckley, Kearney, Hagerman and Ruland; Basi, Carey and Twark). The opposite conclusion was however reached by Daily, Ferris and Hayes, and Jaggi.

3   The industry of the forecasting company affects the accuracy of the forecast (Daily, McDonald, Dev and Webb; Basi, Carey and Twark; Fraser and Richards; Jaggi; Richards; Richards, Benjamin and Strawser; Stewart). The opposite conclusion was reached by Kearney.

4   Cyclical companies tend to overestimate on the downside of the cycle and underestimate on the up (Buckley). McDonald found that forecast accuracy was worst when profits fell. Ferris & Hayes suggest, however, that forecasts are more accurate in a downturn.

5   Forecast accuracy is influenced by the stability of the economy (Platt; Basi, Carey and Twark).

6   Accuracy is improved the more that the subordinates who will have to implement the plan are involved in preparing it, and the greater the involvement of the top executive the more accurate the plans tend to be (Vancil).

7   Low growth companies tend to overestimate (Buckley).

8   High growth companies tend to underestimate (Buckley).

9   Corporate expenses are more accurately forecast than sales, and earnings forecasts are less accurate than both sales and expenses forecasts (Kearney, Buckley, Daily).

10   Companies rarely forecast a drop in profit or turnover (Buckley). Whilst this was no doubt true at the time of Buckley's work, more recently companies seem to have become less inhibited about forecasting poorer results.

11   Management forecasts tend to be overoptimistic (McDonald; Basi, Carey and Twark).
      The opposite conclusion was reached by Westwick.

12   Forecast accuracy by a company in one year is no guarantee of forecast accuracy in subsequent years (Dev).

13   Offerors whose bids succeed have fewer results which fall short of forecast and more results which exceed forecast. Offerees who failed to fight off the bid made for them are in exactly the reverse position: in other words, the higher failure rate by offerees is largely made up of results falling short of forecast rather than of results exceeding forecast (Westwick).

14   Management forecasts are more accurate than those from 'naive' models (Copeland and Marioni, Hagerman and Ruland, Ruland).

15   Management forecasts tend to be less accurate than those derived from the use of Box-Jenkins techniques (Lorek, McDonald and Patz).

16   Management forecasts are more accurate than investment analysts (Basi, Carey and Twark; Ruland, Jaggi).

17   Analysts' forecasts made after the management's forecasts are more accurate than those from a naive model, but analysts' forecasts made before the management forecast are not (Ruland).

18   Analysts' forecasts are more accurate than those from statistical models (Brown and Rozeff, Collins and Hopwood; Richards, Benjamin and Strawser).

19   Box-Jenkins models are more accurate than simpler models (Brown and Rozeff).

20   Errors in the use of simple statistical models can be reduced by matching the model to the stage of growth of the industry of the firm (Carey). This conclusion was not supported by Collins and Hopwood.

21   Growth models are more accurate if they use two to three years of past data (Carey).

22   There is no systematic bias in the errors in analysts' forecasts (Crichfield, Dyckman and Lakonishok).

23   Statistical models using segment data are more accurate than those using consolidated data (Kinney, Emmanuel and Pick).

24   The accuracy of (some) analysts' forecasts does not differ significantly even though the cost of using them does (Richards, Richards and Fraser, Stewart).

25   Analysts' forecasts tend to be overoptimistic, especially when the stock market is strong (Stewart).

26   Analysts' forecasts tend to be better than those from statistical models at turning points and in 'difficult to forecast' industries (Stewart).

Appendix: Statistical critique of conclusions

I am grateful to Ralph Cantelow of Arthur Andersen & Co. for the following statistical critique of the conclusions summarised at the end of the chapter. The numbers refer to the number in the 'Conclusions' section.

Introduction

The following evaluation of the statistical support obtained by the authors for each conclusion is intended to give those without detailed statistical knowledge some idea of the reliance that may be placed on each conclusion. Because of this objective, judgements have been made without always providing statistical arguments for them. Those well versed in statistical theory are urged to refer to the articles should they require more information to form their own opinion.

The fact that an author has not used a statistical test does not mean that a conclusion is wrong but only that it has not been shown to be right. Even when there is some statistical support for a conclusion, the sample may be such that its application to a more general situation may not necessarily be justified.

1   Vancil, Platt, Stewart and Westwick appear not to have used any tests of significance and Kearney gives no real details of how he tested his results.

    Hagerman & Ruland did not actually test this conclusion and Crichfield, Dyckman and Lakonishok could not show that their result was statistically significant. Dev & Webb were unable to test the significance of their conclusion convincingly; however both Basi, Carey & Twark, and Collins & Hopwood adequately supported their conclusion.

    Ferris and Hayes reached a different conclusion but only achieved significant results for two of the four years they tested. Their conclusion may still be valid, though it should be noted that they were using forecasts in prospectuses, (as were Dev & Webb), whereas the others were dealing with forecasts made in other situations.

2   Vancil and Buckley do not appear to have performed any statistical tests and Kearney does not give specific details of any performed. Hagerman & Ruland did not actually test this conclusion. Basi, Carey & Twark, however, did perform adequate tests to support the conclusion.

Ferris & Hayes reached the opposite conclusion but could not prove it statistically and Jaggi only showed that there appeared to be no trend towards management forecasts being significantly better than analysts' forecasts as firms' size varied, not that forecast accuracy was independent of size.

3   McDonald, Fraser & Richards, and Stewart do not appear to have used any tests and Richards, Benjamin and Strawser say their result is significant but do not specify how it was tested. Dev & Webb did not test their conclusion convincingly and Jaggi only showed that management forecasts were significantly better than analysts' forecasts for some industries. Basi, Carey & Twark adequately tested their conclusion.

4   Buckley did not conduct any tests.

5   Platt did not test the significance of his results and Basi, Carey & Twark were comparing only two consecutive years which is not sufficient to support such a general statement.

6   Vancil does not prove this statistically.

7   Buckley did not conduct any tests.

8   Buckley did not conduct any tests.

9   Buckley does not appear to have used any tests of significance, Kearney does not detail any tests performed and Daily obtained no statistically significant conclusions.

10   Buckley did not use any statistical tests.

11   Basi, Carey & Twark did not test this conclusion statistically but McDonald tested it adequately for his sample.

The opposite conclusion reached by Westwick was not tested statistically; however, it should be noted that his sample was of forecasts in takeover bids rather than in a more general situation.

12   This was more of an observation rather than a conclusion and

was, therefore, not tested statistically, though the sample would not have provided an adequate basis for a definite conclusion.

13 Westwick did not perform any specific statistical tests in connection with this conclusion.

14 All three conducted reasonable tests and supported the conclusion well, though, of course, it is only relevant to the models they used.

15 They tested this conclusion adequately for their sample firms.

16 Basi, Carey & Twark's sample was biased against analysts, the management forecast having been made after the analysts', so devaluing their result. Ruland did not find the difference significant but Jaggi's analysis was adequate.

17 The first part was well tested. However, the second part of the conclusion came by implication rather than by statistical proof.

18 Collins & Hopwood did not test this statistically and Richards, Benjamin & Strawser did not specify how they tested their conclusion. Brown & Rozeff performed adequate tests to support their conclusion.

19 This was well supported by their statistical analysis.

20 Carey did not perform adequate statistical tests to support this.

21 This was adequately tested but, of course, only applies to the models used.

22 This was tested adequately though the sample is probably biased towards more stable firms.

23 Kinney did not apply a vigorous test to support this conclusion. However, Emmanuel & Pick performed adequate tests on the models they tested.

24 Stewart did not perform any statistical test but both Richards and Richards & Fraser performed adequate tests.

25 Stewart did not perform any statistical tests.

26 Stewart did not perform any statistical tests.

References

W.S. Albrecht & others, 'Comparison of the accuracy of corporate and security analysts' forecasts of earnings: a comment,' *Accounting Review*, July 1977, p 736.

B.A. Basi, K.J. Carey & R.D. Twark, 'Comparison of the accuracy of corporate and security analysts' forecasts of earnings,' *Accounting Review,* April 1976, p 244.

B.A. Basi, H.J. Carey & R.D. Twark, 'Comparison of the accuracy of corporate and security analysts' forecasts of earnings: a reply,' *Accounting Review,* July 1977, p 741.

A.D. Brown & M.S. Rozeff, 'Superiority of analyst forecasts as measures of expectations: evidence from earnings,' *Journal of Finance,* March 1978, p 1

A. Buckley, 'Planning estimates — a summary of their accuracy.' *Accountancy,* June 1973, p 56.

K.J. Carey, 'Accuracy of estimates of earnings from naive models,' *Journal of Economics and Business,* Spring/Summer 1978, p 182.

W.A. Collins and W.S. Hopwood, 'Multivariate analysis of annual earnings forecasts generated from quarterly forecasts of financial analysts and univariate time series models,' *Journal of Accounting Research,* Autumn 1980, p 390.

R.M. Copeland and R.L. Marioni, 'Executives' forecasts of earnings per share versus forecasts of naive models,' *Journal of Business,* University of Chicago, October 1972, p.497.

T. Crichfield, T. Dyckman, and J. Lakonishok, 'Evaluation of security analysts' forecasts,' *Accounting Review,* July 1978, p 651.

R.A. Daily, 'The feasibility of reporting forecasted information,' *Accounting Review,* October 1971, p 686.

S. Dev, 'Problems in interpreting prospectus profit forecasts,' *Accounting & Business Research,* Spring 1973, p 110.

S. Dev, 'Statements of company prospects,' *Accounting and Business Research,* Autumn 1974, p 270.

S. Dev & M. Webb, 'The accuracy of company profit forecasts,' *Journal of Business Finance,* Autumn 1972, p 26.

C.R. Emmanuel and R.H. Pick, 'The predictive ability of UK segment reports,' *Journal of Business Finance and Accounting,* Vol 7 No. 2, 1980, p 201.

K. R. Ferris, 'Profit forecast disclosure: the effect on managerial behaviour,' *Accounting and Business Research,* Spring 1975, p 133.

K.R. Ferris and D.C. Hayes, 'Some evidence on the determinants of profit forecast accuracy in the UK,' *International Journal of Accounting,* Spring 1977, p 27.

Financial Executives Research Foundation, *'Public Disclosure of*

Business Forecasts' FERF, New York, 1972.

D.R. Fraser and R.M. Richards, 'Accuracy of earnings forecasts for public utilities,' *Public Utilities Fortnightly*, November 23 1978, p 27.

R.J. Hagerman & W. Ruland, 'Accuracy of management forecasts and forecasts of simple alternative models,' *Journal of Economics & Business,* Spring 1979, p 172.

E.A. Imhoff, 'Representativeness of management earnings forecasts,' *Accounting Review,* October 1978, p 836.

B. Jaggi, 'Comparative accuracy of management's annual earnings forecasts,' *Financial Management*, Winter 1978, p 24.

W.R. Kinney, Jr., 'Predicting earnings: entity versus subentity data,' *Journal of Accounting Research*, Spring 1971, p 127.

K.S. Lorek, C.L. McDonald & D.H. Patz, 'Comparative examination of management forecasts and Box-Jenkins forecasts of earnings,' *Accounting Review,* April 1976, p 321.

C.L. McDonald, 'An empirical examination of the reliability of published predictions of future earnings,' *Accounting Review*, July 1973, p 502.

R.C. Morris & G.H. Breakwell, 'Manipulation of earnings figures in the UK,' *Accounting & Business Research*, Summer 1975, p 177.

S.H. Penman, 'Empirical investigation of the voluntary disclosure of corporate earnings forecasts,' *Journal of Accounting Research*, Spring 1980, p 132.

C.J. Platt, 'How reliable are profit forecasts,' *Accountancy*, April 1979, p 95.

R.M. Richards, 'Analysts' performance and the accuracy of corporate earnings forecasts,' *Journal of Business*, July 1976, p 350.

R.M. Richards, J.J. Benjamin and R.H. Strawser, 'Examination of the accuracy of earnings forecasts,' *Financial Management,* Fall 1977, p 78.

R.M. Richards and D.R. Fraser, 'Further evidence on the accuracy of analysts' earnings forecasts: a comparison among analysts,' *Journal of Economics and Business,* Spring/Summer 1977, p 193.

R.M. Richards and D.R. Fraser, 'Predictability of corporate earnings,' *Atlanta Economic Review,* March-April 1978, p 43.

W. Ruland, 'Accuracy of forecasts by management and financial analysts,' *Accounting Review,* April 1978, p 439.

S.S. Stewart, 'Research report on corporate forecasts, part III of Disclosure of Corporate Forecasts to the Investor,' *Financial Analysts Federation*, New York, 1973.

R.F. Vancil, 'The accuracy of long-range planning,' *Harvard Business Review,* September-October 1970, p 98.

C.A. Westwick, 'Profit forecasts in bid situations,' *Accountancy,* July 1972, p 10.

PART FOUR

PROFIT FORECASTS OUTSIDE THE U K

Overview

The first three parts of the book are mainly (with the exception of the chapter on accuracy) about the UK or UK based international businesses. In Part Four we go overseas.

Carol Schaller of Ernst and Whinney, New York and Ray Whittington of the American Institute of Certified Public Accountants summarise the USA's regulations and practice. Prior to 1973 the Securities and Exchange Commission prohibited the filing of profit forecasts. Since then it has encouraged public disclosure of forecasts and has provided a 'safe harbour' rule to protect companies if a properly prepared forecast is not achieved. The American Institute of Certified Public Accountants has published guidance since 1973 on the preparation, review and publication of forecasts. A contrast to the UK position is that the US auditor publicly acknowledges he has reviewed the assumptions underlying the forecast whereas the UK auditor does not.

The US investor appears to be better supplied with forecasts than his UK counterpart through management releases published in the Wall Street Journal and such services as Standard and Poor's Earnings Forecaster.

Gertrude Mulcahy of the Canadian Institute of Chartered Accountants describes the developing situation in her country. Canadian companies usually comment on their prospects in a narrative form without giving specific figures. Investment dealers and brokers publish their forecasts of companies' results and some regulatory bodies require companies under their jurisdiction to publish estimates of their future financial expectations. Earnings forecasts in prospectuses have generally been discouraged but, as a result of the experience gained in the UK and USA, this subject is currently under review by the Ontario Securities Commission (which has published draft regulations on the matter) and the Canadian Institute of Chartered Accountants.

Finally, Michael Renshall of Peat, Marwick, Mitchell gives a comprehensive review of forecasting regulations and practices in France, Germany, the Netherlands, Belgium and Luxembourg. He also describes how the EEC's programme of harmonisation of company law is likely to influence developments in this area in future years.

C.A.W.

187

13 Profit forecasts in the USA

C A Schaller, Ernst and Whinney, New York, and R Whittington, Academic Fellow, American Institute of Certified Public Accountants

Preparation of financial forecasts, projections and budgets is not new to the United States. Prospective data have played a major role in effective management of both profit and not-for-profit enterprises. In addition, informal forecasts and projections have been used widely to obtain debt financing. As a rule however, public companies have not elected to disclose their projected financial results to the general public. Despite the efforts of the Securities and Exchange Commission (SEC) to encourage public disclosure of financial projections, only a handful of public companies have presented financial forecasts or projections in SEC filings or annual reports. This chapter summarizes the major types of prospective information prepared in the United States and reviews the pertinent SEC regulations and guidance by the American Institute of Certified Public Accountants (AICPA).

Prospective information in the United States

Financial feasibility studies represent a major portion of the formal prospective information currently prepared in the United States. Many of these studies are used for the issuance of revenue bonds, especially in the health care industry. Other feasibility studies are prepared to assess the consequences of investment alternatives. For example, assessment of the cash flow and tax consequences to real estate investments are often prepared to market the investments; some states require these projections in certain offering circulars. Requests for governmental approval of proposed projects are also often supported by feasibility studies. For example, Certificates of Need from regulatory agencies are required by many organizations in order to undertake large capital expenditures.

Certified Public Accountants often assist in preparing prospective information and may review and report on it. Reports by CPAs on certain prospective information are even required by some state regulatory authorities. These requirements generally concern prospective information designed to promote debt or equity offerings.

Another important part of practice in the United States is the preparation of prospective information for loans from financial institutions. Cash flow projections are often requested to support loan applications, particularly by smaller, privately held companies. These companies often engage CPAs to help prepare the projections.

External financial analysts prepare earning forecasts for public companies. Some of these forecasts are compiled for use by the analysts' clients and others for publication in financial reporting services. The well-known Standard and Poor's Earnings Forecaster publishes annual earnings per share projections for several hundred public companies. The forecasts are prepared by a group of about fifty investment firms and the service publishes a single net income figure for each company covered, based on forecasts from one to ten or more analysts.

Most public companies do not present financial forecasts or projections in formal financial reports, but many of them disclose management's earnings forecasts by press releases that are published in the *Wall Street Journal*. These releases vary from a general indication that future earnings will show a favourable trend to quantitative statements of projected future results expressed as single amounts. Some reports merely comment on the reasonableness of forecasts that have been prepared independently by financial analysts.

Definitions

Common usage has not developed a consensus on the definition of the terms 'financial forecast' and 'financial projection' in the United States. However, the terms have been stated precisely in authoritative literature and the AICPA has adopted the two following definitions. 'A financial forecast for an entity is an estimate of the most probable financial position, results of operations, and changes in financial position for one or more future periods'. [1]. In this context 'most probable' means that the assumptions are considered by management to be the most likely set of conditions and management's most likely course of action. All other predictions of an entity's future financial results are considered projections, which are 'estimates of financial results based upon assumptions that are not necessarily the most likely. Financial projections are often developed as a response to such questions as; 'what would happen if. . .?' [2]

The SEC, on the other hand, uses the term 'financial projections' more broadly to refer to any statement made by a company regarding its future revenues, sales, net income, or earnings per share, expressed as a specific amount, range of amounts or percentage variation from a specific amount. [3] In the interest of clarity the AICPA definitions are used in this chapter, and prospective financial information is used to refer to both financial forecasts and projections.

SEC Rules

In an effort to attain equitable dissemination of prospective information, the SEC in a 1973 release [4], withdrew its long standing prohibition of prospective information in SEC filings. Since 1973, other releases have been issued that were designed to encourage the public disclosure of forecasts. The releases, issued in 1978 and 1979, [5] provide guidance for the disclosure of prospective financial information and a 'safe harbour' rule for issuers of such details.

General requirements

Under the SEC rules, the disclosure of prospective financial information is generally voluntary; companies are required to file the information only if it has been disclosed to selected outside parties, such as financial analysts or institutional investors. However, the SEC was concerned that investors might be misled if disclosure of forecasts was limited to periods in which favourable results were expected. Therefore, once a company has elected to file prospective information it must give a good reason for any decision to discontinue the practice, or else must resume disclosure of projections or forecasts.

The 1973 SEC release required that a company have a history of reporting with the SEC and prior budgeting experience before disclosing prospective information. These requirements were repealed in the 1978 release. However, a company's history of operations and budgeting experience should be considered in evaluating whether the financial forecast or projection is soundly based. Without a reasonable basis, prospective information should not be disclosed.

Presentation

The SEC rules do not establish minimum disclosure requirements, but suggest that announcements should generally consist of: sales or revenue, net income, and earnings per share. Other information may also be presented but the rules caution against disclosure of only the favourable elements of predicted results. The information may be presented as a specific amount, a reasonable variation from a specific amount, or a reasonable range of amounts.

Disclosure of assumptions

The SEC has indicated that investor understanding of the basis and limitations of prospective information would be enhanced by disclosure of the assumptions which, in management's opinion, influence the predictions, or which are the key factors on which the financial results of the enterprise depend. However, disclosure of underlying assumptions is required only when needed for proper understanding of projected results.

Period covered by a forecast or projection

The period to be covered by the forecast or projection depends on the company's circumstances. The SEC recognises that for some industries forecasts or projections for more than one year may be reasonable. For companies in other industries a reasonable basis may only exist for prospective information covering the current year.

Updating of forecasts or projections

The SEC has rules that require the full and prompt disclosure of material facts regarding financial position of public companies. This responsibility may extend to situations where management knows that a previously disclosed forecast of projection no longer applies. However, the SEC has no specific requirements to update predictions of future results.

Review

The SEC believes that additional support may be provided for forecasts or projections through an outside review, but specific requirements exist concerning the reviewer's qualifications. Instead, the qualifications of the reviewer must be disclosed, along with the reviewer's relationship with the company and the extent of the review. A person who actively participates in the preparation of the forecast or projection may not be named as a reviewer.

Safe harbour

A 'safe harbour' rule was adopted by the SEC to minimize the concern for legal liability under the securities laws arising from prospective information. The fact that predicted results are not attained does not, in itself, provide a basis for legal action against the company or the reviewer. The 'safe harbour' rule provides that the issuer is not liable unless the plaintiff can establish that the forecast or projection was prepared without a reasonable basis or was not disclosed in good faith.

AICPA Pronouncements

The AICPA has published three documents on financial forecasts:

1   Guidelines for Systems for the Preparation of Financial Forecasts (Guidelines), issued in March, 1975.

2   Statement of Position of Presentation and Disclosure of Financial Forecasts (Statement of Position 75-4) issued in August, 1975.

3   Guide for a Review of a Financial Forecast, issued in October, 1980.

All three of these pronouncements related to financial forecasts, as defined by the AICPA. That is, the pronouncements concern estimates of the 'most probably financial position and results of operations' for one or more future periods. The AICPA is currently developing guidelines concerning other prospective information.

Preparation guidelines

The quality of a financial forecast can be directly related to the attributes of the forecasting system which generated the information. The AICPA has issued broad principles for the preparation of financial forecasts in Guidelines. These principles include: [6]

1   *Single most probable result.* A financial forecasting system should provide a means for management to determine what it considers to be the single most probable forecasted result. In addition, determination of the single most probable result generally should be supplemented by the development of ranges or probabilistic statements.

2   *Accounting principles used.* The financial forecasting system should provide management with the means to prepare financial forecasts using the accounting principles that are expected to be used when the events and transactions envisioned in the forecast occur.

3   *Appropriate care and qualified personnel.* Financial forecasts should be prepared with appropriate care by qualified personnel.

4 *Best information available.* A financial forecasting system should provide for seeking out the best information, from whatever source, reasonably available at the time.

5 *Reflection of plans.* The information used in preparing a financial forecast should reflect the plans of the enterprise.

6 *Reasonable assumptions suitably supported.* The assumptions used in preparing a financial forecast should be reasonable and appropriate and should be suitably supported.

7 *Relative effect of variations.* The financial forecasting system should provide the means to determine the relative effect of in the major underlying assumptions.

8 *Adequate documentation.* A financial forecasting system should provide adequate documentation of both the forecast and the forecasting process.

9 *Regular comparison with attained results.* A financial forecasting system should include the regular comparison of the forecast with attained results.

10 *Adequate review and approval.* The preparation of a financial forecast should include adequate review and approval by management at the appropriate levels.

Presentation

The AICPA's *Statement of Position 75-4* suggests that financial forecasts should be presented in the form of the historical financial statements expected to be issued, but, at a minimum, the company should present: sales or gross revenues; gross profit; provision for income taxes; net income; gains or losses from disposal of a segment of a business and extraordinary, unusual or infrequently occurring items; primary and fully diluted earnings per share; and significant anticipated changes in financial position. The accounting principles used for the forecast should be those that are expected to be used in the period covered by the forecast. This expectation and a summary of significant accounting policies, should be disclosed with the forecast.

Unlike the SEC rules, the AICPA provides that 'financial forecasts should be expressed in specific monetary amounts representing the single most probable forecast result'.[7] However, supplemental disclosure of ranges or probabilistic statements is encouraged, since this information emphasises the tentative nature of a financial forecast. This recommendation is supported by the following rationale: [8]

> While a range informs the user of the probabilistic nature of the forecast, expressing a financial forecast *solely* in terms of ranges could result in the user's attributing an unwarranted degree of

reliability to the forecast ranges, because many users might assume (a) that a range represented the spread between the best possible result and the worst possible result or (b) that the range was based on a scientifically determined interval. Management should be in the best position to determine the single most probable result, and this burden should not be placed on outsiders. Also, single point estimates are necessary to aggregate the forecasts of an enterprise's individual operations, as well as to facilitate comparison between the forecast and later historical results.

Disclosure of assumptions

Management should disclose those assumptions that it believes are most significant to the forecast or are key factors on which the financial results of the enterprise depend. Also, disclosure of the basis or rationale for assumptions, and the relative impact of a variation in significant assumptions are desirable. Basic assumptions — even those with an enormous potential effect on earnings forecast (e.g. conditions of peace, absence of natural disasters) need not be disclosed unless there is reasonable likelihood that current conditions will not prevail. To emphasise the uncertainty related to predictions of future financial results, *Statement of Position 75-4* suggests that the summary of assumptions be preceded by an introduction, such as the following: [9]

> This financial forecast is based on management's assumptions concerning future events and circumstances. The assumptions disclosed herein are those which management believes are significant to the forecast or are key factors upon which the financial results of the enterprise depend. Some assumptions inevitably will not materialise and unanticipated events and circumstances may occur subsequent to   (date), the date of this forecast. Therefore, the actual results achieved during the forecast period will vary from the forecast and the variations may be material.

Period covered by the forecast

Neither the AICPA *Statement of Position 75-4* nor *Guidelines* provide specific requirements concerning the period to be covered by a forecast. *Statement of Position 75-4* indicates that management should consider the needs of the users and management's ability to forecast in determining the forecast period.

Updating a financial forecast

Statement of Position 75-4 indicates that financial forecasts should be updated to reflect significant changes in assumptions, actual results, or unanticipated events unless the original forecast included a statement that it was not intended to be updated or the issuance of historical financial statements covering the period is imminent. If material changes in a forecast cannot be quantified so as to permit an updating of the forecast, appropriate disclosure should be made. *Statement of Position 75-4* also provides that management may withdraw a previously issued forecast if it discloses the decision and the reasons for withdrawal.

Review

Currently, independent accountants may be associated with prospective information, provided that they do 'not permit their names to be used . . . in a manner which may lead to the belief the accountant vouches for the achievability of the forecast'.[10] However, when an accountant's name is associated with prospective information, full disclosure must be made of the sources of the information and the major assumptions used to prepare the information. Also, the accountant must include a report which specifies the character of the work performed by him and the degree of responsibility assumed.[11] Though accountants may be associated with various types of projections, specific guidance exists concerning only one type of prospective information—financial forecasts—and only one type of service—independent review and reporting.[12] These guidelines are contained in *Guide for a Review of a Financial Forecast (Forecast Guide)*.

Objectives and guidelines for a review of a financial forecast. The independent objective in a review of a financial forecast is to provide a basis for reporting whether, with respect to the forecast taken as a whole—

> The forecast was properly prepared based on the stated assumptions, and the presentation conforms with the recommendations in Statement of Position 75-4 (appropriately adapted when a comprehensive basis of accounting other than generally accepted accounting principles is used), and
> The underlying assumptions provide a reasonable basis for management's forecast.[13]

That a review of a financial forecast may be performed as a basis for reporting on the reasonableness of the underlying assumptions is particularly important. Many accountants have been concerned that reporting on the reasonableness of the assumptions might result in users placing undue reliance on the forecast information. Others were concerned that accountants were not sufficiently qualified to form a judgement on the reasonableness of the assumptions. However, the *Forecast Guide* concludes that a reasonable basis for a report on a financial forecast can be obtained through a review made in accordance with the following guidelines: [14]

1 The review should be performed by a person or persons with adequate technical training and proficiency to review a financial forecast.

2 In all matters relating to the engagement, the accountant should maintain an independence in mental attitude. [15]

3 Due professional care should be exercised in the performance of the review and the preparation of the report.

4 The work should be adequately planned and assistants, if any, should be properly supervised.

5 The accountant should obtain an understanding of the forecasting process as a basis for determining the scope of the review.

6 Suitable support should be obtained to provide a reasonable basis for the accountant's report on the financial forecast.

7 The report based on the accountant's review should contain a statement regarding whether the accountant believes the financial forecast is presented in conformity with applicable AICPA guidelines for presentation of a financial forecast and has been prepared using assumptions that provide a reasonable basis for management's forecast.

Scope of a review of a financial forecast. The scope of the accountant's review is affected by such factors as knowledge of the business, management's forecasting experience, the forecast period, and the forecasting process. Knowledge of the entity's business is essential to evaluate whether management's assumptions relate to all key factors that bear on the financial results. The accountant may have obtained certain knowledge through prior association with the entity. This knowledge may be augmented by inquiry of entity personnel, reference to published literature on the relevant industry, experience with other firms in that industry, and consultation with industry specialists.

The other factors — management's forecasting experiences, the forecast period, and the forecasting process — may bear on the quality of the forecast and the reliability of management's support for the assumptions. Therefore, an understanding of these factors also is important in determining the scope of the review.

Procedures for a review of a financial forecast. Review procedures can be classified as procedures to evaluate the reasonableness of the assumptions and procedures to evaluate the preparation and presentation of the forecast. To achieve the first of these objectives, the accountant should conclude: [16]

(a) that management has explicitly identified the factors expected to materially affect the operations of the entity during the forecast period and has developed appropriate assumptions with respect to such factors; and
(b) that the assumptions are suitably supported.

The accountant's knowledge of the business should provide a basis for deciding whether management's assumptions consider all key factors on which the entity's financial results depend. In evaluating whether the assumptions are suitably supported, the accountant should perform procedures to determine: [17]

1 Whether sufficient pertinent sources of information about the assumptions have been considered. (Examples of external sources the accountant might consider are government publications, industry publications, economic forecasts, existing or proposed legislation, and reports of changing technology. Examples of internal sources are budgets, labour agreements, patents, royalty agreements, engineering studies, historical financial statements and records, sales backlog records, debt agreements, and board of directors' actions involving entity plans.)
2 Whether the assumptions are consistent with the sources from which they are derived.
3 Whether the assumptions are consistent with each other.
4 Whether the historical financial information and other data used in developing the assumptions are sufficiently reliable for that purpose. (Reliability can be assessed by inquiry or by analytical or other procedures, some of which may have been completed in past audits or reviews of the historical financial statements.)
5 Whether the historical financial information and data used in developing the assumptions are comparable over the periods specified or whether the effects of any lack of comparability were considered in developing the assumptions.
6 Whether the rationale of the assumptions, considered with the supporting data, is reasonable.

In evaluating the preparation and presentation of the forecast, the accountant should perform procedures that provide reasonable assurance of the following: [18]

1 The forecast reflects the identified assumptions.
2 The computations made to translate the assumptions into forecasted amounts are mathematically accurate.
3 The assumptions are internally consistent.
4 Accounting principles used in the forecast are consistent with the generally accepted accounting principles (or other comprehensive basis of accounting) expected to be used in the historical financial statements covering the forecast period(s), and those used in the most recent historical financial statements, if any.
5 The presentation of the forecast follows the guidelines in *Statement of Position 75-4.*

After his review, the accountant should consider whether the forecast, including related disclosures, should be revised because of (a) mathematical errors, (b) unreasonable assumptions, (c) inappropriate or incomplete presentation, or (d) inadequate disclosure.

The report on a financial forecast. The suggested report on the review of a financial forecast is: [19]

> The accompanying forecasted balance sheet, statements of income, retained earnings, and changes in financial position, and summary of significant forecast assumptions of XYZ Company as of December 31, 19XX, and for the year then ending, is management's estimate of the most probable financial position, results of operations, and changes in financial position for the forecast period. Accordingly, the forecast reflects managment's judgement, based on present circumstances, of the most likely set of conditions and its most likely course of action.
>
> We have made a review of the financial forecast in accordance with applicable guidelines for a review of a financial forecast established by the American Institute of Certified Public Accountants. Our review included procedures to evaluate both the assumptions used by management and the preparation and presentation of the forecast. We have no responsibility to update this report for events and circumstances occurring after the date of this report.
>
> Based on our review, we believe that the accompanying financial

forecast is presented in conformity with applicable guidelines for presentation of a financial forecast established by the American Institute of Certified Public Accountants. We believe that the underlying assumptions provide a reasonable basis for management's forecast. However, some assumptions inevitably will not materialise and unanticipated events and circumstances may occur; therefore, the actual results achieved during the forecast period will vary from the forecast, and the variations may be material.

As illustrated, the report emphasises that the forecast, including the underlying assumptions, is management's responsibility. The accountant may assist management in the preparation of the forecast, but management must evaluate the assumptions and accept them as its own. The accountant provides 'positive assurance' concerning the reasonableness of the assumption and the conformity of the presentation with AICPA guidelines, but does not vouch for the achievability of the forecast or assume responsibility for updating the report.

Summary

Interest in prospective information has heightened in the United States. The SEC has issued rules which encourage the issuance of prospective information by public companies. Forecast information is presented as a matter of routine in offering circulars for various investment, such as revenue bonds. Guidelines for reviewing and reporting on financial forecasts have been issued by the AICPA, and the AICPA is currently studying standards for an accountant's association with other prospective information. Other types of prospective information services by CPAs, such as compilation of the prospective information, are also under consideration.

References

[1] Included in Management Advisory Services Executive Committee, *Guidelines Series No. 3*, 'Guidelines for Systems for the Preparation of Financial Forecasts', AICPA, March 1975, Accounting Standards Division, *Statement of Position 75-4,* 'Presentation and Disclosure of Financial Forecasts', AICPA, August 1975, and The Financial Forecasts and Projections Task Force, 'Guide for a Review of a Financial Forecast', AICPA, October, 1980.

[2] Ibid.

[3] *Securities Act of 1933 Release* No. 33-5581, April 1975, p. 24.

[4] *Securities Act of 1933 Release* No. 33-5362, February 1973.

[5] *Securities Act of 1933 Release* No. 5992, November, 1978; *Securities Exchange Act of 1934 Release* No. 15305, November 1978; *Securities Act of 1933 Release* No. 6084, June 1979; and *Securities Exchange Act of 1934 Release* No. 15944, June 1979.

[6] *Guideline Series No. 3,* 'Guidelines for Systems for the Preparation of Financial Forecasts', p. 3.

[7] *Statement on Position 75-4*, 'Presentation and Disclosure of Financial Forecasts', p. 4.

[8] Ibid., p. 4.

[9] Ibid., p. 6.

[10] *Code of Professional Ethics,* AICPA, Rule 201-E.

[11] Ibid., Interpretation 201-2.

[12] *Guide for a Review of a Financial Forecast,* p. v.

[13] *Guide for a Review of a Financial Forecast*, p. 5.

[14] Ibid., pp. 5-6.

[15] Independence is defined and interpreted by the *Code of Professional Ethics.* AICPA.

[16] *Guide for a Review of a Financial Forecast,* p. 10.

[17] Ibid., p. 10.

[18] Ibid., pp. 11-12.

[19] Ibid., p. 22.

14 Profit forecasts in Canada

Gertrude Mulcahy, Accounting Research Director, Canadian Institute of Chartered Accountants

The publication of earnings forecasts by public companies in Canada generally has occurred in an informal manner and without perceptible control by the securities authorities so far.

Inclusion of future-oriented comments in reports to shareholders, press releases and public announcements has been common practice among Canadian companies for many years. These statements of future expectations are usually in narrative form and on a general basis, without specific figures; nonetheless, they are a form of forecasting. The methods of disclosure and types of data provided, however, vary and are not subject to scrutiny by the securities authorities.

A number of regulatory bodies in Canada, such as the National Energy Board, the Canadian Radio-Television and Telecommunications Commission and the Canadian Transportation Commission, require companies under their jurisdiction to prepare estimates of their future financial expectations which, in some cases, become a matter of public record, once filed. Although such estimates are often referred to as forecasts, they are more properly regarded by the companies concerned as estimates reflecting specific assumptions or requirements of the particular regulatory body. *

---

* The following are examples of companies operating under the jurisdiction of the above-mentioned Canadian regulatory bodies:

National Energy Board:	Alberta Natural Gas Co. Ltd.
	Amoco Canada Petroleum Co. Ltd.
	Trans Canada Pipelines Ltd.
	Westcoast Transmission Co. Ltd.
Canadian Radio-Television and Telecommunications Commission:	Bell Canada
	British Columbia Telephone Company
	CNCP Telecommunications
	Rogers Cablesystems Inc.
The Canadian Transportation Commission	Air Canada
	Canadian Pacific Airlines Ltd.
	Canadian National Railways

The managements of some Canadian companies voluntarily provide information about their likely earnings to investment advisers and financial analysts. In contrast, earnings forecasts are not provided in the traditional investor documents — prospectuses, takeover circulars and information circulars for shareholders, as a general rule.

Disclosure of earnings forecasts made by third parties — brokers, investment analysts, market advisers, etc. — is accepted in practice in Canada. These disclosures are designed to assist the public to make investment decisions and are usually included in sales literature, market commentaries, periodic newsletters and company prospect analyses. The forecasts may be based on information obtained from the management of the company concerned or they may be based primarily on the analyst's knowledge of the economic environment and the industry, without acquaintance with management's plans.

Developments in Canada, the experience in the United Kingdom and the action by the Securities and Exchange Commission in the United States with regard to the inclusion of prospective financial information in the prospectuses and reports filed with it, have all served to focus attention on the critical issue of the public disclosure of earnings forecasts. As a result, there has been considerable discussion on this topic in recent years within the Canadian business community and, in particular, the securities commissions and the accounting profession.

For the most part, these discussions have concentrated on three basic questions: whether earnings forecasts should be disclosed publicly, and, if so, whether they should be prepared and presented in accordance with specific rules and whether they should be subject to some sort of third party review. Understandably, these questions elicited strongly-held differing opinions. Some progress has been made, in that the issues have been aired and debated and a proposal has been put forward for the voluntary inclusion of earnings forecasts in prospectuses, but there is no evidence of a consensus developing. The question of public disclosure of earnings forecasts remains far from being resolved in Canada.

Traditional restrictions on earnings forecasts

Before going into the details of developments in recent years and the current status of earnings forecasts in Canada, it will be helpful to provide a very brief explanation of the Canadian environment and the legislation relevant to the possible integration of earnings forecasts with the Canadian financial disclosure system.

In Canada, companies are incorporated under either federal or provincial legislation. Securities legislation has been enacted by provincial governments; the federal government has not enacted national securities legislation. Under the corporations and securities legislation, Canadian public companies are required to place on public file, transmit to shareholders, and disclose to the public, historical financial information relating to their operations and activities. Such historical cost data are provided in annual financial statements, interim reports, information circulars for annual meetings, insider trading reports, prospectuses, takeover circulars and press releases.

Except for specific sections of provincial securities legislation relating to prospectuses, corporate and securities legislation in Canada is silent with respect to the public disclosure of earnings forecasts *per se* and the administrative authorities have not officially interpreted any particular statutory provisions as either requiring or prohibiting the publication of such forecasts.

The inclusion of earnings forecasts in prospectuses has been effectively discouraged by the Canadian securities commissions. Securities legislation in Alberta, British Columbia, Manitoba, Ontario and Saskatchewan stipulates that estimates of future earnings are to be included in a prospectus only with the permission of the director/ chairman of the provincial securities commission. In addition, except in Ontario, if an estimate of future earnings is included in the prospectus, an auditor's or accountant's name is not to be associated with the estimate. Similarly, the Auditing Standards Committee of the Canadian Institute of Chartered Accountants has ruled that:

'The auditor should not express an opinion on any forecast earnings figures which might be contained in a prospectus'. [1]

It is not entirely clear whether the prospectus prohibition against the inclusion and attestation of earnings forecasts also applies to takeover bid circulars. However, this matter does not appear to be a major issue since the practice in Canada, unlike that in the United Kingdom, has been not to provide earnings forecasts, even in narrative form, in take-over documents.

It is interesting to note that, while the official position of the securities commissions over the years has been to discourage the inclusion of earnings forecasts in prospectuses, provisions have been made for requiring or allowing certain information relating to the future to be included in specific circumstances. For example, where the proceeds of the securities offered by a prospectus are to be applied in whole or in part, directly or indirectly, to finance the acquisition of a business by a purchase of assets or shares, the inclusion of *pro forma* financial statements, combining the assets, liabilities, income, etc., of the issuer and the business being acquired, as shown by their respective financial statements, may be permitted or required. Whether *pro forma* financial statements are permitted or required to be included in a prospectus is at the discretion of the director of the provincial securities commissions concerned.

Another example of a situation where information relating to the future has been allowed is where the prospectus covers securities with an interest in multiple unit residential buildings ('MURB') or real estate syndicates. In such circumstances, the inclusion of cash flow projections in prescribed form has been permitted in certain jurisdictions. With the reintroduction of the tax incentives for MURB's in the October 1980 federal government budget, (the original legislation having expired on December 31, 1979), the provincial securities commissions are considering the development of a national policy on the inclusion of such projections. This matter is expected to be discussed at the next semi annual meeting of the Canadian Securities Administrators scheduled for September, 1982. It should be noted, however, that the proposed projections cover a ten year period which is much longer than that appropriate for forecast data.

Although there has been no official interpretation in Canada of what constitutes an earnings forecast, the term has generally been accepted to mean an estimate of the most probable results of operations of an enterprise for one or two future periods. The phrase 'most probable' is fundamental and distinguishes forecasts from other types of prediction and projection.

Report of the Select Committee on Company Law, 1973

The growing interest in earnings forecasts in Canada over the past decade has been influenced and stimulated by several significant events and undertakings. The first of these occurred in 1973, when a provincial government committee in Ontario went on record as favouring the public disclosure of financial forecasts in specific circumstances and the review of such forecasts by the auditors.

The Select Committee on Company Law, in its *1973 Report on Mergers, Amalgamations and Certain Related Matters,* expressed the view that, in the case of a takeover bid, information on the short term prospects of the target corporation at least, and possibly also on the offeror corporation, would help shareholders to decide whether to accept or reject the bid, and urged that such information be made available to them.

The Committee also considered the desirability of more general use of financial forecasting to facilitate investor disclosure. It recognised that various informal and unofficial forecasts were in fact being publicised at that time but advocated that financial forecasting should be put on a more formal basis. The Committee also concluded that, if financial forecasts were published, they should be independently reviewed by public accountants.

Having regard to its view of the desirability of financial forecasts, the Committee recommended:

'. . . the Ontario Securities Commission institute a study of the matter with the accounting profession and members of the financial community with a view to developing necessary guidelines and regulations which will require financial forecasts reported on by the auditors of a company.'[2]

CICA research study 'Earnings Forecasts', 1976

The next major development was the release of the Research Study, *Earnings Forecasts,* in 1976. This study, under the authorship of Mr. Robert H. Kidd, CA, Thorne Riddell & Co., Toronto, was commissioned by the Research Department of the Canadian Institute of Chartered Accountants.

'The terms of reference of this project deliberately precluded the author from reaching a conclusion as to the desirability of publishing earnings forecasts. The aim was that all the pros and cons of publishing earnings forecasts should be set out so as to facilitate discussion of this vital issue by interested parties. The terms of reference also excluded the study of forecasts prepared for internal purposes and detailed consideration of forecasting techniques. The focus was intended to be on the publication of earnings forecasts.' [3]

The study provided an excellent overview of the issues involved in the disclosure of earnings forecasts and of the practices in this area in Canada, the United Kingdom and the United States at that time. Based on the assumptions that the disclosure of earnings forecasts would be allowed and would be subjected to independent third party review by public accountants, the author developed and presented standards that a public accountant might follow in reviewing an earnings forecast and commenting thereon.

The author's suggested disclosure standards encompassed the basic standards both for issuing earnings forecasts — the financial data, assumptions and other information they should include and the form of disclosure — and for keeping them up to date. They also covered the issue of earnings forecasts during periods of active corporate solicitations, the issue of such data in a condensed form and the disclosure of information on a company's future prospects orally or in a press release.

With respect to the third party review, the suggested standards restricted the review to consideration of the way in which the earnings forecast was prepared and the adequacy of its disclosure.

In concluding his study, R. H. Kidd included the following personal opinions and cautions:

> 'Earnings forecasts are not a panacea. They will not provide the users of financial reports with all of the information they want or that they require. The public disclosure of earnings forecasts would likely go a long way towards filling currently perceived information needs. However, financial reporting is an evolutionary process and the disclosure standard set, for example, in 1980 will not meet the desires and demands for financial information in 2000, just as those set in 1950 were inadequate in 1970.
>
> I hope that this Study will help coalesce opinion to the extent that the commencement of the disclosure of earnings forecasts will be on a timely basis. However, I hope as well that the disclosure of earnings forecasts, if introduced, will be introduced slowly – and not with a bang where it becomes mandatory for a great number of companies. Experience is an important teacher; if the disclosure of earnings forecasts is to be an effective vehicle for the communication of useful corporate information to the public – as I think it can be – the system for its disclosure should evolve gradually and be appropriately modified with experience.' [4]

Draft regulations: Earnings forecasts in prospectuses, 1980

In the discussions following the release of these two major studies, it quickly became clear that corporate management in Canada was reluctant to become involved in the publication of earnings forecasts. It became equally obvious that corporate management was inexorably opposed to the inclusion of such data in annual or interim reports and would resist any move to make such disclosures mandatory. Coupled with this was the obvious apprehension among professional accountants of any extension of audit responsibilities to future-oriented data and a concern that the auditor's association may lend undue credibility to the forecast results.

As a result of these reactions, the area of discussion narrowed and gradually centred on disclosure in prospectuses, with particular emphasis on modifying the securities authorities' long standing policy of restricting the inclusion of forecast data in such documents. As indicated previously, the disclosure of earnings forecasts made by third parties, such as investment dealers and brokers, is accepted practice in Canada. However, in recent years, the Canadian securities commissions have become increasingly concerned about the use of third party forecasts to facilitate the sale of securities. Consequently, this matter featured prominently in the ongoing discussions relative to prospectuses.

In July, 1980, the Ontario Securities Commission released for comment proposed amendments to the Regulations under the Ontario Securities Act, 1978, which would permit earnings forecasts in prospectuses.[5] The text of the draft Regulations is set out in the Appendix to this chapter.

The proposed Regulations would:

(a) allow a securities issuer to include a forecast in the offering prospectus subject to the directors' approval and provided the forecast was accompanied by an accountant's comments;

(b) prohibit circulation of any forecast outside the prospectus during the primary distribution unless the forecast was included in the prospectus.

It is worth emphasising that the inclusion of the forecasts is on a *voluntary basis*. Based on its discussion with interested parties over the years and taking into account the very little practical experience in the use of published forecasts in Canada, the Commission concluded that a voluntary forecast system was more appropriate than a mandatory one, at this time.

Unfortunately, the proposed regulations did not attract the attention deserved by such an important proposal – the introduction of forecasting into Canadian financial reporting. Only ten responses were received to the Commission's request for comments on its proposed regulations. Among the respondents there seemed to be general support for the proposed conditions relating to forecasts included in sales literature, although strenuous objections were voiced in the investment dealers' submission. The Commission's principal conclusion that the inclusion of earnings forecasts should be permitted, but should not be made mandatory, was generally supported by the majority of the respondents, although two of the ten opposed the move and even the supporters drew attention to significant practical problems and inherent dangers. A number of the respondents expressed concern about the requirement for written comments by the auditor on his review of the forecasts; the implication of unwarranted credibility and complications relative to the regular consent letter were the two major sources of dissatisfaction.

A major issue which must be considered in the context of forecasts is the appropriate extent of statutory liability. The point at issue is whether the Ontario securities legislation should be amended to provide some form of 'safe harbour' in favour of directors and signatories to the prospectus and to the auditors who review the earnings forecasts against liability claims if the actual results differ materially from the forecast. This is a significant and complicated legal matter which undoubtedly will involve considerable investigation and legal analyses. However, it is clear that the legal ramifications surrounding the public disclosure of earnings forecasts should be considered prior to the final ratification of the proposed regulations.

The regulations proposed by the Ontario Securities Commission have not yet been finalised and incorporated in law. Similar proposals have not been released to date by any of the other provincial securities commissions. The next opportunity for consideration of a uniform policy on this matter is the September 1982 meeting of the Canadian Securities Administrators.

Proposed accounting and auditing guidelines – 1980

Following the release of the Research Study *Earnings Forecasts* in 1976, the Accounting Research Committee of the Canadian Institute of Chartered Accountants put into process a project on 'Earnings Forecasts'. Initially, this project was related to the development of Accounting Recommendations (the Canadian equivalent of Accounting Standards) and dealt with forecasts included in published reports to shareholders and prospective shareholders (annual and interim reports to shareholders, prospectuses, circulars relating to takeovers and mergers, and so on.

Recognising the experimental nature of the various aspects of publishing and using forecasts and the need to allow a reasonable degree of flexibility during a transitional period, the Committee decided, very early in the project, that the development of Guidelines rather than Recommendations would be a more appropriate approach. It is important to point out that the authority for issuing Guidelines rests with the Steering Committee of the Accounting Research Committee and not with the Committee itself. Guidelines only express opinions of the Steering Committee and do not have the authority of Recommendations issued by the Committee.

In 1979, cognisant of the negative attitudes and strenuous opposition within the Canadian business community to the public disclosure of future oriented data, the Steering Committee decided that the scope of the project should be restricted to earnings forecasts included in prospectuses. The Steering Committee decided, also, that the project should be tied in with actions by the securities commissions and, in particular, by the Ontario Securities Commission. These decisions were influenced by the concern expressed by a number of persons and organisations, who had been asked to review draft material, that the Accounting Guideline, as then drafted, implied that the Accounting Research Committee was encouraging enterprises to issue earnings forecasts. The changes in the project were designed to avoid such implications.

At that time, the Steering Committee of the Auditing Standards Committee of the Canadian Institute of Chartered Accountants was working on an Auditing Guideline. Following the decisions with respect to the Accounting Guideline, the scope of the proposed Auditing Guideline was reduced correspondingly. During the ongoing development of these Guidelines, informal discussions were held with interested parties and the securities commissions and relevant documents were circulated for comment on a private and confidential basis.

In July 1980, the Accounting Research and Auditing Standards Steering Committees released drafts of the proposed Guidelines in conjunction with the release of the proposed Regulations by the Ontario Securities Commission. It is not the normal policy to circulate proposed Guidelines publicly; this practice is restricted to Recommendations, Exposure Drafts being released for comment before the finalisation of the standards for inclusion in the CICA Handbook. However, to provide those who received the draft Ontario Securities Commission's Regulations with a complete picture of the accounting and auditing implications of the inclusion of earnings forecasts in prospectuses, the Steering Committees agreed to the drafts of the Guidelines being circulated by the Ontario Securities Commission with its proposed Regulations in the Weekly Summary of the week ending 18th July, 1980.[6] Both the draft Guidelines and proposed Regulations were also reproduced in the Research column of the August 1980 issue of *CA Magazine.*

The Accounting Research Committee specifically stated that, in providing guidance on the presentation and disclosure of forecast data in prospectuses, it wished to make it clear that it neither recommends nor discourages the publication of future oriented data in prospectuses. The main features of this proposed Accounting Guideline are as follows:

(a) The decision on whether to include forecast data in a prospectus is up to the board of directors. They must determine whether there is a reasonable basis for issuing such data, whether the proposed form and content may be misleading and whether the data can be presented in an easily understood way.

(b) The adequacy of the forecast data is management's responsibility.

(c) An earnings forecast included in a prospectus should disclose sales or gross revenue, net income or loss and earnings per share. Revenues, net income and earnings per share data should be presented together to avoid any misleading inferences should individual items reflect contradictory trends.

(d) In some cases, management should consider also providing a forecast balance sheet and a forecast statement of changes in financial position.

(e) Forecast data should be prepared in accordance with the accounting policies expected to be used in the historical financial statements covering the forecast period. This fact, as well as a summary of significant accounting policies expected to be followed, should be disclosed.

(f) In some situations, forecast data covering a two or three year period may be entirely reasonable; in others, there may not be a reasonable basis for forecasts beyond the current year.

(g) To emphasise the uncertainties in the forecast data, the major assumptions on which the data are based should be disclosed and prefaced by a statement indicating that they are assumptions and may not materialise and that actual results may vary materially from the amounts forecasted.

(h) Forecast data should indicate that it has been approved by the board of directors.

(i) Earnings and financial forecasts should be presented separately or clearly distinguished from the historical financial statements or data included in the prospectus, and should be clearly labelled as 'Forecasts'.

The proposed Auditing Guideline sets out the procedures auditors would perform and the comments they would provide when reporting on earnings forecasts in prospectuses. It is important to note that the Auditing Standards Steering Committee is suggesting that the auditors, in their comments, should disclaim an opinion as to the likelihood of the forecast results being attained.

The main procedures proposed in the Auditing Guideline include the following:

(a) When reviewing forecasts, auditors should consider whether the assumptions appear reasonable, are adequately disclosed, and whether the forecast has been properly compiled.

(b) Auditors should have a clear agreement with their clients about the nature and extent of the engagement, preferably in writing.

(c) The review should be performed and the comments prepared 'with due care and objectivity' by persons having adequate technical training and proficiency in accounting and auditing.

(d) Auditors should disassociate themselves from any forecasts that they know are misleading.

(e) The review should consider the effects of both internal and external factors on the operations of the enterprise; for example, the intentions of management, the competitive climate, markets, resources and economic trends.

(f) A review of forecasts should also include procedures to ensure that management's assumptions − and the financial data and information underlying them − are consistent and appear to be reliable.

(g) If the forecast is presented as a range of earnings, auditors should consider whether the range makes disclosure meaningless and comparisons with historical results difficult.

(h) The auditor should obtain written representation from management stating that it is responsible for the preparation of the forecast and has developed it from reasonable and appropriate assumptions, and that all information relevant to the review of the forecast has been disclosed.

(i) Because the forecast assumptions relate to future events and cannot be independently verified, the Auditing Standards Steering Committee recommends that auditors should not comment on the plausibility or reasonableness of forecast assumptions.

The intention is that the Guidelines will be released in final form when the proposed Regulations are finalised. To date, the Steering Committees have received very few comments on, or reactions to, the draft Guidelines. They seem to have attracted even less attention than the Ontario Securities Commission's draft Regulations.

Quo Vadis?

Whether the Accounting and Auditing Guidelines are finalised and released depends upon the fate of the proposed Regulations relating to the inclusion of earnings forecasts in prospectuses.

Three possibilities exist:

(a) the Ontario Securities Commission could 'go it alone' and finalise its proposed Regulations without similar action by the other commissions.

(b) the securities commissions in some or all of the provinces could adopt a uniform policy, similar to or along the lines of the Ontario proposal.

(c) the Ontario proposed Regulations could be withdrawn.

In the first two instances, the Guidelines would be finalised but, if the proposed Regulations were withdrawn, no further work would be done on the Guidelines and the related accounting and auditing projects would be dropped. What will happen is a matter of conjecture. It is unfortunate that the second anniversary of the release of the Ontario Securities Commission's proposed Regulations (July, 1982) passed without a decision being taken by any of the securities commissions. Hopefully, the matter will be resolved, one way or the other, at the next semi-annual meeting of the Canadian Securities Administrators in October 1982.

References

[1] Section 7000, CICA Handbook, *Prospectuses,* Toronto, the Canadian Institute of Chartered Accountants, 1968, paragraph 7000.15.

[2] *Report on Mergers, Amalgamations and Certain Related Matters,* Select Committee on Company Law, to Ontario Legislature, Toronto, 1973, p. 56.

[3] R. H. Kidd, *Earnings Forecasts,* Toronto, the Canadian Institute of Chartered Accountants, 1976, Foreword.

[4] Ibid., p. 206

[5] *Draft Regulations, 'Earnings Forecasts',* Supplement to the Weekly Summary, Week Ending 18th July, 1980, Toronto, Ontario Securities Commission.

[6] *Draft Accounting and Auditing Guidelines,* Supplement to the Weekly Summary, Week ending 18th July, 1980, Toronto, Ontario Securities Commission.

Draft Regulations

Earnings Forecast: Request for comments

In its 1973 Report to the Legislative Assembly on Mergers, Amalgamations and Certain Related Matters the Select Committee on Company Law (Chapter 19 – Financial Forecast) recommended that the Ontario Securities Commission institute a study of this matter with the accounting profession and members of the financial community with a view to developing necessary guidelines and regulations.

During the intervening period there has been much discussion on the topic both here and in other jurisdictions including the Research Study commissioned by the Canadian Institute of Chartered Accountants in 1976. With the new Securities Act now in place the Commission has once again turned to the topic.

As a result of its discussions with interested parties over these years the Commission has concluded that earnings forecasts should not be made mandatory but that they should be permitted subject to appropriate guidelines or controls. Steering Committees of the CICA Accounting and Auditing Standards Committees have developed proposed accounting and auditing guidelines, copies of which are attached.

Attached is a copy of draft amendments to the regulations which would permit earnings forecasts in a prospectus. These can be read in the context of the CICA proposals.

Comments regarding the proposed regulations should be made in writing to the Commission by filing 15 copies of such comments by Friday, 26th September, 1980, with the Secretary, Ontario Securities Commission, 10 Wellesley Street East, Toronto, M7A 2H7.

Comments will be made available to the securities administrators of the provinces of Canada and for public inspection unless confidentiality is specifically requested.

Draft Regulation

Earnings and Financial Forecasts

Section 23a

(1)   In this section 23a,
(a) 'forecast' means a written estimate of the most probable results of operations of an issuer, alone or together with one or more of its affiliates, that includes an estimate of earnings or range of earnings, for one or more periods that are future periods or are periods not completed when the estimate is made, and also may include the most probable financial position and changes in financial position for the same period, but does not include an estimate that
(i) is prepared in the ordinary course of business and without reference to a specific distribution of securities, and
(ii) appears in a compendium of estimates relating to a number of issuers or in a publication that is distributed regularly to investors or prospective investors, who are not selected because of their potential interest in a specific issue of securities;
(b) 'distribution' means a distribution to the public of securities with respect to which a prospectus is filed under the Act and a receipt issued therefor under section 60 or section 61;
(c) 'distributing firm' means a registrant that is an underwriter with respect to a distribution, and includes the issuer of the securities being distributed if the issuer is registered as a security issuer.

(2)   A distributing firm shall not, during the course of a distribution and to assist in the sale of the securities being distributed, disseminate a forecast with respect to the issuer of those securities, unless the forecast is set out in the prospectus and what is disseminated by the distributing firm consists solely of that forecast or a reasonable extract therefrom or summary thereof.

Section 46
The Director may permit the inclusion in a prospectus of a forecast,

214

within the meaning of section 23a, but the forecast shall be identified as such and, when a forecast is permitted, the Director will require that the prospectus include the written comments of a public accountant concerning the accountant's review of the forecast.

15 Profit forecasts in the EEC

J M Renshall, Partner, Peat, Marwick, Mitchell & Co.

Community directives and proposals

There are no specific requirements in any EEC country for companies
to prepare and publish profit forecasts. However, as with the United
Kingdom, there are certain circumstances in which companies are
required to provide information about future prospects.

A firm distinction must be drawn between the practice of providing
information about future prospects, either in reports to shareholders or
in other company documents or circulars, and the publication of a
formal forecast. The most useful definition of a profit forecast is
probably that included in paragraph 7 of Practice Note 6 of the
February 1981 edition of the City Code on Takeovers and Mergers.
There, a profit forecast is taken broadly to include every situation in
which a form of words puts a floor under (or, in certain circumstances,
a ceiling on) the likely profits of a particular period, or whenever a
form of words contains the data necessary to ascertain an approximate
figure for future profits by an arithmetical process. Any indicator
referable to a quantified amount constitutes a forecast under this
definition — for example, such a statement as 'profits will be somewhat
higher than last year'.

As noted, there is no requirement, statutory or otherwise, in any
member state, for companies to include a profit forecast which falls
within the above definition in annual reports, prospectuses, offer
documents in connection with acquisitions or amalgamations with
other companies, or other circulars to shareholders relating to investment transactions. However, many provisions in the EEC Company
Law harmonisation programme are likely to affect present practice
relating to comments on future prospects. One provision of the Second
EEC Directive is likely, in certain circumstances, to make both companies and their professional advisers look for more formalised information about future prospects (although it does not impose any
requirement to publish a quantitative forecast). This provision requires

a report by its auditors, where a public company issues shares for a non-cash consideration. Where the non-cash consideration represents profit earning assets (although it should be noted that the provisions do not apply to takeovers and mergers) the auditor may need to form a view on the future profit earning potential of the assets acquired if he is to comment, as he is required to do, on whether the price is fair and reasonable. Simply to look at past results when valuing assets is unlikely to be sufficient. It may be necessary to investigate prospects. This may not call for a full profit forecast, but many of the disciplines involved in preparing a profit forecast will be used in assessing future prospects.

The Third EEC Directive was adopted on 9 October 1978. The directive applies to mergers between public companies that are governed by the laws of the same member state. It does not apply to mergers between companies registered in different member states. Such mergers are the subject of a draft convention on international mergers. The Third EEC Directive covers two types of merger virtually unknown in the UK:

'*Merger by acquisition*' — whereby one or more companies are wound up without going into liquidation (e.g. dissolution by order of a Court) and transfer to another all their assets and liabilities in exchange for the issue, to the shareholders of the company or companies being acquired, of shares in the acquiring company and a cash payment, if any, not exceeding 10 per cent of the nominal value of the shares so issued or, where they have no nominal value, of their accounting par value.

'*Merger by the formation of a new company*' — whereby several companies are wound up without going into liquidation and transfer to a company that they set up, all their assets and liabilities, in exchange for the issue to their shareholders of shares in the new company and a cash payment, if any, not exceeding 10 per cent of the nominal value of the shares so issued or, where they have no nominal value, of their accounting par value.

In prescribing the information which has to be made available to shareholders, the directive does not require any information to be provided on future prospects and does not require or envisage the publication of a profit forecast. However, certain detailed information will be required. The management bodies of each of the merging companies will be required to prepare a report setting out the draft merger terms, including their legal and economic justification. The report must include, in particular, the share exchange ratio and describe any special valuation difficulties which have arisen. Independent experts are required to prepare a report to the shareholders of the merging companies stating whether, in their opinion, the share exchange ratio is fair and reasonable. The report must indicate at least:

(a) the method or methods used to arrive at the proposed share exchange ratio;

(b) whether such methods are adequate;

(c) the values arrived at by each method and an opinion on the relative importance attributed to such methods in arriving at the value decided on;

(d) any special valuation difficulties which have arisen.

The significance of these requirements is that, although no formal profit forecast needs to be published, both the management and the independent expert must gain information about the future prospects of the merging companies. The management will need the information to prepare their management report and, in particular, to formulate their views on the economic justification for the merger. The independent expert will need some information on future prospects to enable him to report on whether the share exchange ratio is fair and reasonable. Because of these requirements, the need to adopt established procedures for preparing and documenting forecasts seems likely to become more apparent in EEC countries with the enactment of the Third Directive in member states. (Member states were required to enact legislation by October 1981.)

When the EEC Fourth Directive is implemented, the contents of the annual report and accounts of companies will be prescribed in member states' legislation in detail. Article 46.2(a) provides that the annual report (equivalent to the directors' report in the UK) of a company shall give an indication of the company's likely future development. It is probable, therefore, that legislative backing will be given in each of the member states to the practice of providing a broad indication of future prospects which has been adopted by many companies. But this is not construed as requiring any form of quantified forecast. The need to provide such information about a company's likely future development may prompt company management to seek assurance that their procedures for documenting their strategic long term plans and short term forecasts are adequate.

The EEC Sixth Directive, dealing with the contents of prospectuses issued by companies whose shares are to be admitted to official listing on a stock exchange, also contains provisions relating to future prospects. For example, chapter 7 of Schedule A to the annexe to the Sixth Directive provides that, normally, general information should be disclosed on the trend of the issuer's business since the end of the financial year to which the last published accounts relate, including in particular:

(a) significant recent trends in production, sales and stocks and the state of the order book;

(b) recent trends in costs and selling prices.

The Directive also envisages that information should be published on the issuer's prospects for at least the current financial year. Again, this is not construed as requiring more than broad indications — a quantified forecast is optional.

A high standard of care is required of those associated with prospectuses. Where information about future prospects is given, both directors and professional advisers must be satisfied that any statement made about future prospects is adequately supported and documented. This may involve the preparation of internal profit forecasts, properly supported and documented.

The proposed directive on the content of interim announcements by listed companies will also look for information about future developments and prospects. Specifically, it proposes that this information should be contained in an explanatory statement. The explanatory statement is designed to enable investors to make an informed assessment of the development of the company's business during the relevant period. The explanatory statement should provide at least the following items, to the extent that they are significant (giving supporting figures whenever appropriate):

(a) the number of persons employed;

(b) investments carried out and firm commitments made by the company's bodies concerning principal future investments, with the exception of interests to be acquired in other undertakings;

(c) state of the order book;

(d) the general situation regarding stocks of finished products;

(e) the degree of capacity utilisation;

(f) any new products or activities which have had a significant effect on turnover;

(g) the company's prospects for the current financial year.

Directors will wish to be satisfied that any information provided is properly supported, which again may involve the preparation of properly supported and documented internal forecasts.

The EEC preparatory study for a proposed directive on general bids for the acquisition of shares and securities of public companies also envisages that the publication of forecasts in the context of a bid should be regulated, if provided. Based largely on UK practice, the study suggests that if an offer document contains a forecast of the future profits of the offeror, the offeree company or any other company, it must set out the basis on which the forecast was made, and must be accompanied by a statement made by an accountant, who is qualified to audit the accounts of the company in question, 'that in his opinion the forecast is reasonable, having regard to the company's financial condition and past profits.'

Although there is little likelihood of early progress on the formulation of a draft directive, professional advisers in the EEC may have the prospect of legislation setting out a requirement for them to report on published forecasts.

Regulations in main EEC countries

Against the background of the company law harmonisation programme, it is useful to look briefly at the current regulatory background to profit forecasts in the main EEC countries (apart from the United Kingdom and Eire which have been dealt with earlier in this book).

France

The rules covering documents relating to the listing of securities in France are supervised by the Commission des Operations de Bourse (COB). This is a body that was set up by law in 1967. The members are appointed by the French Council of Ministers and also by the Chambre Syndicale des Agents de Change, which is an association of stockbrokers.

General bids for the shares of companies which have a stock exchange quotation or whose shares are dealt in on a stock exchange are regulated by law. In France, the relevant legislation stems from the *Arrêtes ministerials* of 21 January 1970, 22 February 1972 and 6 March 1973, by which the Minister of Economics and Financial Affairs added articles 68 and 96 to Title II of the *Règlement général de la compagnie des agents de change,* and this legislation has been supplemented by the *Decision générale* of the COB dated 13 January 1970 establishing a code of good conduct to be observed by parties to bids and their agents, which, despite its name, is supported by legal sanctions.

In 1973, the COB issued recommendations that the *Note d'Information* should include, inter alia, forecasts as regards:

(a) evolution of the market;
(b) forecast production and turnover figures, based, if possible, on the latest order book;
(c) latest information as to the forecast results for the year in progress.

In practical terms, the COB goes on to recommend that in all cases such information should be issued on the most prudent basis and, therefore, cover very short term information. In addition, the Company Law of 1967 requires that the annual directors' report to shareholders should include a comment as to future prospects. This comment is, however, normally made in the broadest terms. The COB considers that it is up to individual companies to choose how and when any such forecast information should be published, provided this is normally done on a consistent basis. It also considers that, where possible, the underlying bases for the forecast should be indicated, together with variations of actual from previous projection.

The preceding paragraphs summarise the broad guidelines contained in the law and recommendations of the COB as to both regularly required information and requirements as regards listings, takeovers, mergers and similar transactions. The only legal requirement is that directors comment on current prospects in their annual report to shareholders. This, however, in no way resembles a 'profit forecast'. It should be noted that the statutory auditor ('commissaire aux comptes') is required to give an opinion in his report as to the reasonableness of the financial information contained in the directors' report.

While the COB has issued recommendations on forecasts as regards official listings, takeovers, and mergers this has had little effect in practice. In any event, the recommendations are couched in such broad terms, that, even if enforced, they would not lead to profit forecasts in the accepted sense of this term. In practice, the related comments contained in the *Note d'Information* or prospectus are, in most cases, limited to half a dozen lines of general comment — somewhat similar to that frequently seen in the chairman's report of a UK company. The COB is considering the impact of the EEC Sixth Directive in this respect and expects to issue instructions in due course to ensure harmonisation.

Germany

The law establishing stock exchanges in Germany dates from 1896. Rules governing the admission of securities to listing on a German stock exchange were first introduced in 1910. Again, there are no specific requirements to publish profit forecasts and it is not German practice to publish such forecasts on the admission of securities to listing.

German company law is embodied in the Commercial Code, *Handelsgesetzbuch*, Stock Corporation Law, *Aktiengesetz*, Limited Companies Act, *GmbH-Gesetz* and Cooperative Law, *Genossenschaftsgesetz*. In addition, publication requirements with regard to companies of a certain minimum size are set out in the Publication Act, *Publizitats-gesetz.*

However, the only relevant provision is that, in statutory annual reports, the board of directors must at least comment on prospects for the next financial year. Usually such comments are very brief and generalised. They are reviewed by the auditor in the same manner as all other comments in annual reports; that is, to ensure that they do not conflict with the auditors' views of the company's position.

Italy

Under Law 216 of 7 June 1974, control over the Italian Stock Exchange passed to the Commissione Nazionale per le Società e la Borsa ('CONSOB'). This is an independent central administrative body based in Rome and it is responsible to the Italian Government. There are two types of market for securities in Italy. One of these is the authorised stock exchanges. The other is known as the over-the-counter market. CONSOB has issued rules governing the admission of securities to listing and has also set out the procedures to be followed in an application for admission to listing.

In Italy, regulation of takeover bids or offers for sale emerges from a code of conduct which does not have the force of law, but is enforced by professional sanctions. The relevant Code of Conduct (*Codice di comportamento per le offerte pubbliche di acquisto di titoli*) was issued by the Milan stock brokers' committee in December 1971, and applied only to companies whose shares were quoted or dealt in on that exchange, although it also established a pattern of conduct which could be followed by brokers who are members of other exchanges and by companies whose shares are either quoted on other stock exchanges or are not quoted at all. However, consistent with the position in other member states, no requirements in Italy related to the publication of quantitative profit forecasts. The practice of providing some indication on future prospects in a company's annual report is probably less well developed than in other EEC countries.

Netherlands

The rules governing the admission of securities to official stock exchange listing in the Netherlands are determined by the Amsterdam Stock Exchange – *Vereniging voor de Effectenhandel*. The exchange is an independent body working under a licence issued by the Finance Minister under the Beurswet of 1914. In other respects it is self-regulatory. The rules relating to listing applications are contained in the 'Rules and Regulations as to the inclusion of securities in the Official List of the Amsterdam Stock Exchange' – *Fondsenreglement*. The regulations are continuously updated. Supplementing these rules, in 1973 the Social and Economic Council published a voluntary code of conduct for companies to follow in merger and takeover situations. It also established a commission to monitor compliance. The code does not carry the force of law, and the Commission has no sanctions, other than the publication of its findings. As far as the content of annual reports are concerned, the Civil Code Book 2, Title 6 applies.

In the Netherlands there are, again, no requirements for the publication of profit forecasts. However, a forecast is usually given voluntarily in the context of admission of securities to official listing on the stock exchange. The format and contents of such forecasts vary considerably.

Although there is no legal requirement to provide forecasts, the practice of providing information on future prospects in annual reports is probably better developed in the Netherlands than in other EEC countries.

Belgium and Luxembourg

The admission to listing of shares in Belgium involves three different bodies, the Quotation Committee (Comité de la Cote/Comite der Beursnotering), the Banking Commission (Commission Bancaire/Bank Commissie) and, in certain cases, the direct participation of the Ministry of Finance.

A company that applies for a listing must first obtain the authorisation of the Banking Commission. The company must submit details of its objects, the members of its board of directors and its capital and financial statements. In examining the file of information the Commission may ask for more information and it has the power either to reduce, or to delay, the issue. The company also has to obtain the approval of the Quotation Committee. Information that may be requested from the Committee is not restricted. In practice, a company will consult the Quotation Committee before lodging application.

Regulations governing takeover bids emerge from the *Arrêté royal sur le contrôle des banques* of 9 July 1935, article 26 of which was amended by the Law of 10 June 1964 so as to extend the powers it conferred on the government appointed supervisory authority, the Commission Bancaire, in respect of new issues of shares and bonds to enable it to deal with all kinds of general bids as well. The content of annual reports in Belgium is governed by the law of 17 July 1975 supplemented by Royal Decree of 8 October 1976.

Although there are no formal legal requirements to publish forecasts in Belgium a few points of practice are worthy of note. First, there is a requirement (introduced in 1978) for the promoters of a new company to lodge a two year financial plan for registration with the relevant authorities. Secondly, if a public company decides to publish a profit

223

forecast (which it very rarely does) the circumstances will be subject to close scrutiny by the Banking Commission and the Stock Exchange.

In Luxembourg, provisions are somewhat similar to those of Belgium. The rules governing the admission of securities to official stock exchange listing are determined by the Luxembourg Stock Exchange, (Société Anonyme de la Bourse de Luxembourg), in conjunction with the Luxembourg Banking Control Commission. The former is a limited company, granted powers of administration by a Grand-Ducal decree. The latter is a government body responsible to the Ministry of Finance. Present rules relating to listing applications are governed by the Grand Ducal decree of 19 June 1965. The Banking Control Commission monitors the content of prospectuses. The legislation dealing with general bids emerges from the *Arrêté grand ducal concernant les operations de banque et de credit* of 19 June 1965. The content of annual reports is laid down in a Law of 10 August 1915.

Survey on statements about future prospects

One of the most useful surveys of current practice by major companies in Europe on the publication of information about future prospects is given by Lafferty, Carty and Cairns in their 1979 *Financial Times* Survey of *100 Major European Companies' Reports and Accounts.* Of the 100 companies surveyed in 1977, 62 companies made comments about future prospects compared with 38 which did not. The comments which were made tended to fall into one or more of six types:

(a) a broad description of the year ahead;
(b) a reference to the results for the first month of the financial year starting after the balance sheet date;
(c) a reference to one or more specific events which may affect the results for the new year. Such comments are often made in isolation and it may be difficult to measure the likely effect of the events;
(d) quantified forecasts about results expressed either in money terms or as a percentage change;
(e) details of capital expenditure or financing plans;
(f) reference to outstanding orders at the beginning of the new year and orders received since the balance sheet date.

The authors reach the conclusion that about 60 companies in the survey say something about their prospects, but few say anything of significance. Of the EEC countries, the authors conclude that the Netherlands leads the way in providing information in future prospects in annual accounts.

The authors pick out the information provided by one Netherlands company, KLM for special mention. In its annual report for 1977 KLM set the scene by noting the increases in passenger traffic and freight expected by IATA. KLM foresaw similar progress. After a paragraph on the need for new aircraft it forecast:

> '. . . . a traffic growth of approximately 6 per cent with a capacity increase of some 4 per cent. This will lead to a further improvement of the load factor. The continuing expansion entails a limited increase in the number of employees.
>
> We expect to be able to maintain the cost per unit produced at the same level this year as in the past year.'

Statistics for the current year for capacity, traffic, load factor and unit costs were given earlier in the report.

The conclusion they reached in 1979 was endorsed in the 1980 study by Lafferty and Cairns covering 200 leading international companies. In that study the authors single out Electrolux. Although Electrolux is a Swedish company and Sweden is not a member of the EEC, it is instructive to examine the approach adopted. The information contained in the 1979 accounts of Electrolux on the outlook for 1980 is reproduced in the Appendix to this chapter. As can be seen this statement includes a specific profit forecast in the following terms:

> 'Against the background of what is stated above it is expected that the result from current operations after depreciation according to plan and before taxes . . . will rise by 10 per cent in 1980 provided that no further serious disturbances affect the world economy.'

Elsewhere in the report a forecast of 1980 sales is included. The accounts are dated April 1980.

Information of this kind is no doubt useful to investors. There is no independent accountants' report on the statement in the Electrolux accounts. This approach accords with UK practice where a report will only be required on such a forecast if the company subsequently engages in a takeover or merger transaction (City Code on Takeovers and Mergers). In the context of Electrolux it is interesting to note that similar information was given in the previous report. The sales forecast was substantially accurate and the profit increase turned out to be of the order of 17 per cent compared with the forecast increase of 10 per cent, so falling within the margin of 10 per cent allowed by the Panel on Takeovers and Mergers in the United Kingdom when monitoring the accuracy of forecasts published in bid situations.

Conclusion

There is no statutory or regulatory requirement for the regular publication of quantitative profit forecasts in any of the EEC countries and no such requirement seems likely to flow from the harmonisation of EEC company law. In contrast, a more unified approach to the provision of information about future developments and future prospects will no doubt emerge as the EEC company law harmonisation programme develops. In particular, on the implementation of the EEC Fourth Directive, companies will be required to provide some information on future developments in their annual report and accounts. Similarly, information on future prospects will be required in prospectuses issued by companies whose shares are to be admitted to official listing on a stock exchange, and in interim announcements by listed companies. In the context of proposed requirements relating to valuations, independent experts may turn to companies for information about their future prospects. The proposal for a draft directive on takeover bids, although containing no definitive requirement to include a profit forecast, sets out the rules which must be followed where one is included.

Neither law nor regulation seems likely to anticipate practice on the provision of detailed information about future profits of a company. As in the past, commercial practice will dictate the amount of prospective information that companies disclose. This in turn, will be influenced by the stability of the economic conditions under which they operate. Obviously, companies will be less inclined to give detailed information about prospects when economic conditions are uncertain than in more stable times. It remains to be seen whether the harmonisation of company law in the EEC will lead to the development of accepted standards for the publication of meaningful information about the future prospects of companies.

Appendix: Extract from Electrolux Annual Report 1979

Outlook for 1980

As a result of the company acquisitions which have taken place in recent years Electrolux has strengthened its competitive position in several lines of business. In the household appliances sector, mainly vacuum-cleaners, refrigerators and freezers, as well as in chain saws, the Group has reached such a size that it is comparable to its principal competitors. This has involved increased exports at the same time as high volume production has created the conditions for integrated manufacturing. Automation and structural changes have played an important role, in the implementation of which the consistently positive attitude of the Swedish trade unions towards rationalization has contributed to the achievement of these results. In other product areas further growth and greater efficiency are necessary if the Group is to be able to meet the stiffening competition. Future efforts will therefore be concentrated partly on consolidating established strong positions and partly on strengthening the Group in sectors where our competitive edge needs further sharpening. The offer to acquire the share capital of Gränges AB, which will result in increased vertical integration in manufacturing, should be seen as one element in these efforts.

On the basis of the following factors sustained positive progress can be expected for the Group as a whole:

1 Electrolux is now one of the world's two leading manufacturers of vacuum-cleaners. The market for these products is expected to show sustained expansion.

2 The Group holds a pre-eminent position in the market for absorption refrigerators, which are principally used for leisure purposes. The decline in the sales of caravan refrigerators in 1979 is regarded as only temporary.

As far as other 'white products' are concerned production at the Group's European manufacturing facilities has been reviewed and will be restructured in the coming years with the object of gaining economies of large-scale production, such as have been achieved through the company acquisitions in the household appliances sector.

3   Electrolux has developed energy-saving products and is introducing electronics in order to increase the efficiency of its products and simplify their use, for example, in the case of sewing machines, vacuum-cleaners, electric cookers, washing machines and dishwashers.

4   Following the acquisition of The Tappan Company Electrolux has further strengthened its position as an important manufacturer of gas and electric cookers. In addition, the Group has obtained a new product, namely micro-wave ovens for cooking, in which the European market is displaying growing interest.

5   It has been possible to improve the profitability of the Husqvarna group more rapidly than originally estimated, partly owing to advantage being taken of the opportunities for co-ordination in the white products, commercial refrigeration and freezer equipment sections which existed between Electrolux and Husqvarna. Electrolux is now one of the leading commercial refrigeration and freezer equipment companies in Europe.

The market for sewing machines in the industrialized countries has shown slight decline. The results of the sewing machine operations have improved but are still not satisfactory.

Following the acquisition of Husqvarna the Group has made further investments in chain saws, which are expected to attract increasing demand. The Electrolux Group is now one of the world's three largest manufacturers of this product group.

6   The Group is one of the world's most widely diversified organizations in commercial cleaning services, the hire of linen and work apparel, laundry service and other servicee activities. It is the board's intention to expand further in this type of service on an international basis.

7   Facit's office products operations have been completely transformed, which has brought balance between the volume of demand and the necessary production capacity. This balance has led to an improvement in the results, which is expected to be sustained.

8   Expansion is also foreseen for several other activities not

228

mentioned above, for example, food service equipment, sterilisation products, materials handling equipment and lawnmowers.

As the Group's equity ratio is still at an acceptable level, despite further company acquisitions, etc., it is considered that the capital required for further expansion will be obtainable. The proposed acquisition of the share capital of Gränges AB will affect the Group's equity ratio. However, it should be observed that no cash will be needed for this acquisition, as payment will be through convertible debentures, which will normally be converted in due course into shares of AB Electrolux, with a higher equity ratio as the result. Gränges has relatively large liquid assets of its own, which means that no further long-term borrowing will be needed for the time being to finance the expansion of the Gränges group.

The Group intends to continue its active policy of disposing of assets which are not indispensable for the business, which will raise the equity ratio as well as liquid assets.

Dividends received from abroad are expected to remain largely sufficient to cover the amount that AB Electrolux pays out in dividends to its shareholders.

The Group has a well-diversified product program, and a wide geographical spread of markets throughout the world. This means that the effects of changes in the economic situation and currency fluctuations broadly cancel out.

Against the background of what is stated above it is expected that the result from current operations after depreciation according to plan and before taxes—excluding Gränges—will rise by 10% in 1980, provided that no further serious disturbances affect the world economy.

Bibliography

Books

Accountants International Study Group, *Published profit forecasts—current practices in Canada, the United Kingdom and the United States,* A.I.S.G., c. 1974.

American Institute of Certified Public Accountants, *Corporate financial reporting; ethical and other problems,* New York, A.I.C.P.A., 1972.

American Institute of Certified Public Accountants, *Guidelines for systems for the preparation of financial forecasts,* New York: A.I.C.P.A., c. 1975, (Management advisory services guidelines, no. 3).

American Institute of Certified Public Accountants, Accounting Standards Division, *Statement of position on presentation and disclosure of financial forecasts.* New York, A.I.C.P.A., 1975, (Statement of Position, 75-4).

American Institute of Certified Public Accountants, *The Financial Forecasts and Projections Task Force, Guide for a Review of a Financial Forecast;* New York, A.I.C.P.A., October, 1980.

Amey, L.R., *The Efficiency of Business Enterprises,* Allen and Unwin, 1969.

Anderson, O.D., *Time series analysis and forecasting – the Box-Jenkins approach,* Butterworths, 1976.

Anson, C.J., *Profit from figures,* McGraw-Hill, 1971.

Ashe, T.M., *Insider Trading,* Company Communications Centre, 1980.

Ashton, D., and Simister, L., *The Role of Forecasting in Corporate Planning,* Staples Press, 1970.

Association of Certified and Corporate Accountants, *The Planning and measurement of profit: a technique of management accounting,* A.C.C.A., 1957.

Australian Society of Accountants, *Forecasting, planning and control,* Melbourne, A.S.A., 1968.

Battersby, Albert, *Sales Forecasting,* Cassell, 1968.

Belew, Richard C., *How to win profits and influence bankers,* New York, Van Nostrand Reinhold, 1973.

Bierman, H., *Capital budgeting decision,* New York, Macmillan, 1971.

Bolt, G.J., *Market and sales forecasting – a total approach,* Kogan Page, c. 1971.

Bratt, E.C., *Business Forecasting,* McGraw-Hill, 1958.

Broster, E.J., *Planning profit strategies,* Longman, 1971.

Briston, R.J., *The Stock Exchange and investment analysis,* 2nd ed., Allen & Unwin, 1973.

Butler, W.F., Kavesh, R.A., and Platt, R.B., eds. *Methods and techniques of business forecasting,* 2nd ed., Prentice-Hall, 1974.

Carter, W.G.K., and Morland D.P., *Investigations and Reports,* Institute of Chartered Accountants in England and Wales, 1978.

Chambers, J.C., Mullick, S.K., and Smith, D.D., *An executive's guide to forecasting,* New York, Wiley, 1974.

Cohen, M.S., Ma, R., and Miller, M.C., *Disclosure of forecasts –* publication of forecasts by M.S. Cohen; forecasts and external reporting by R.Ma, and M.C. Miller, Melbourne, A.S.A., 1974.

Cooper-Jones, D., *Business planning and forecasting,* Business Books, 1974.

Copulsky, W., *Practical sales forecasting,* New York, A.M.A., 1970.

Council for the Securities Industry, *The City Code on Takeovers and Mergers,* February 1981.

Council for the Securities Industry, *Statement on Insider Dealing,* June 1981.

Coutie, G.A., et al., *Monograph No. 2 Short term Forecasting,* ICI and Oliver & Boyd, 1964.

Cox, B., *Value Added,* Heinemann, 1979.

Croxton, F.E. and Cowden D.J., *Practical Business Statistics*, Prentice-Hall, 1960.

Danos, P., and Imhoff, S.A., *The Auditor's Role in Financial Forecasts,* Ann Arbor, University of Michigan, 1979, (Working Paper, 198).

Dodd, T.F., *Sales forecasting – how to prepare and use market data and sales forecasts in profit planning,* Gower, 1974.

Enrick, N.L., *Market and sales forecasting – a quantitative approach,* Rev.ed., New York, Krieger, 1979.

Evans, E.C.D., *Profit planning and the measurement of return on capital employed,* Macdonald, 1964.

Fildes, R., and Wood, D., *Forecasting and Planning,* Saxon House/ Gower Press, 1978.

Financial Analysts Federation, *Disclosure of corporate forecasts to the investor.* New York, F.A.F., 1973. Contents – Part I: Proposals by the Federation for systematic disclosure of corporate forecasts by F.A.F. Special Committee on Corporate Forecasts. Part II: Legal aspects of corporate forecasts by J.G. Gillis. Part III: Research report on corporate forecasts by S.S. Stewart.

Financial Executives Research Foundation, *Public Disclosure of Business Forecasts,* FERF, New York, 1972.

Firth, M., *Forecasting methods in business and management,* Arnold, 1977.

Forrester, D.A.R. (Ed) *With Disclosed Intent – being readings on published accounting forecasts,* Strathclyde Convergencies, 1980.

Gilchrist, R.R., *Managing for profit: the added value concept,* Allen & Unwin, 1971.

Goodman, S.R., *Techniques of profitability analysis,* New York, Wiley-Interscience, c. 1970.

Graham, B., and Dodd, D.L., *Security analysis: principles and technique,* 4th ed., New York, McGraw-Hill, 1962.

Grinyer, P.H. and Wooller, J., *Corporate Models Today,* Institute of Chartered Accountants in England & Wales, 2nd Edn., 1978.

Halford, D.R.C., *Business Planning – A Practical Guide to Management,* David & Charles, 1971.

Hill, R.W., *Cash management techniques,* New York, American Management Accounting, 1970.

Humphreys, R.G., *Forecasts for plans and decisions,* Institute of Chartered Accountants in England and Wales, 1977, (Accountants Digest, no. 48).

IBM: *Retail IMPACT I.B.M. Application Programme,* IBM, 1967.

IBM: *Concepts and Applications of Regression Analysis,* IBM Data Processing Application, 1967.

Institute of Chartered Accountants in Australia, *Professional development – the reporting accountants responsibility for profit forecasts?* Sydney, ICAA, 1976.

Institute of Chartered Accountants in England and Wales, *Accountants' Reports on Profit Forecasts (Statement S23),* November 1978.

The Institute of Cost and Works Accountants, *An Introduction to Business Forecasting,* ICWA, 1968.

Irwin, P.H., *How to make a profit plan,* Hamilton, Ontario, Society of Industrial and Cost Accountants of Canada, 1961.

Johnston, A., *The City Takeover Code,* Clarendon Press, 1980.

Jones, C.J., *Financial planning and control: A survey of practices by UK Companies,* Institute of Cost and Management Accountants, 1980.

Kidd, R.H., *Earnings forecasts,* Toronto, Canadian Institute of Chartered Accountants, c. 1976.

Kofstede, G.H., *The Game of Budget Control,* Van Gorcum, 1967.

Laventhol, Krekstein, Horwath & Horwath., *Publishing financial forecasts: benefits, alternatives, risks– a guide to interpretation and implementation of the SEC ruling on financial forecasts,* Philadelphia: LKHH., c. 1974.

Lees, F.A., *Public Disclosure of Corporate Earnings Forecasts,* Report no. 804, the Conference Board, New York, 1981.

Lesseps, M., and Morrell, J., *Forecasting exchange rates: theory and practice,* Institute of Cost and Management Accountants in association with the Henley Centre for Forecasting, 1977.

Levich, R.M., *The international money market: an assessment of forecasting techniques and market efficiency,* (Contemporary studies in economic and financial analysis, vol. 22), Greenwich, Conn.: Jai Press, c.1979.

McAlpine, T.S., *Profit planning and control,* Business Books, 1969.

McConkey, D.D., *Planning next year's profits,* American Management Assoc., 1968.

Milne, T.E., *Business forecasting – a managerial approach,* Longman, 1975.

Morrell, J., *An approach to short-term business forecasting,* Henley-on-Thames, Administrative Staff College, 1968.

Morrell, J., *Business forecasting for finance and industry,* Gower Press, 1969.

Morrell, J., (ed.), *Management decisions and the role of forecasting,* Penguin, 1972.

Morrell, J., *A Short Guide to Business Forecasting*, Henley Centre for Forecasting, 1976.

Morrell, J., Nutall, C., and Tyrrell, R., *Forecasting costs and prices – theory and practice.* Institute of Cost and Management Accountants, in association with the Henley Centre for Forecasting, (Management accounting in inflation series), 1977.

National Association of Accountants, *Long-range profit planning,* Research Report no. 42, New York, NAA., 1964.

National Industrial Conference Board, *Forecasting Sales Business Policy Study,* No. 106, 1964.

Powell, R.W., *Profit by control; management controls for smaller companies,* British Broadcasting Corporation, 1972.

Prakash, P., and Rappaport, A., *Public reporting of corporate financial forecasts,* Proceedings of a conference held on 18-19th October 1971 at: Northwestern University. Graduate School of Management. Centre for Advanced Study in Accounting and Information Systems, Commerce Clearing House, Chicago. c.1974.

Prescott, J.M., *Profit and cash flow forecasting,* Industrial and Commercial Finance Corporation, 1980.

Reichard, Roberts, *Practical Techniques of Sales Forecasting,* Prentice-Hall, 1966.

Robinson, C., *Business forecasting: an economic approach,* Nelson, 1971.

Samuels, J.M. *Readings on mergers and takeovers,* Elek, 1972.

Scott-Armstrong, J., *Long-Range Forecasting from Crystal Ball to Computer,* Wiley- Interscience, 1978.

Simon, H.A., *Models of Man,* John Wiley and Sons, 1957.

The Society of Investment Analysts, *Guidelines to insider dealing,* May 1981.

Spencer, H., Clark, Colin, and Hoguet, P.W., *Business and Economic Forecasting,* Irwin, 1961.

Stamp, E. and Marley, C., *Accounting Principles and the City Code,* Butterworths, 1970.

Steiner, G.A., *Top management planning,* New York, Macmillan, 1969.

Stock Exchange, The, *Admission of Securities to Listing.*

Turner, J., *Forecasting practices in British industry,* Surrey University Press, 1974.

Theil, H., *Applied Economic Forecasting,* North Holland, 1966.

Ward, A.J. *Forecasting practices and techniques,* Industrial and Commercial Techniques Ltd., 1970.

Wheelwright, S.C., and Makridakis, S., *Forecasting methods for management,* 2nd ed., Wiley, c. 1977.

Whittington, G., *Prediction of profitability and other studies of company behaviour.* CUP, (Dept. of Applied Economics, Occasional Paper 22).

Wills, G., Ashton, D., and Taylor, B., *Technological Forecasting and Corporate Strategy*, Bradford University Press and Crosby Lockwood & Son Ltd., 1969.

Willsmore, A.W., *Business budgets in practice,* Pitman, 1973.

Wood, D., and Fildes, R., *Forecasting for business: methods and applications,* Longman, 1976.

Woy, J.B., (ed.) *Business trends and forecasting information sources,* Management Information Guide no. 9, Gale Research Company, Michigan, 1965.

Articles

Adelberg, A.H., 'Forecasting the U.S. dilemma', *Accountancy,* October 1976, p.83.

Albrecht, W.S. & others, 'Comparison of the accuracy of corporate and security analysts' forecasts of earnings: a comment', *Accounting Review,* July 1977, p.736.

Alexander, M.O., 'Financial forecasting – a part of the accountant's professional work,' *Canadian Chartered Accountant,* October 1969, p.259.

Amey, L.R., 'Budget Planning: A Dynamic Reformulation', *Accounting and Business Research,* Winter 1979.

Anderson, W.R., 'Financial forecasting', *The Accountant,* 6 January 1972, p.7.

Anderson, P.K., 'Financial planning: a model approach', *Canadian Chartered Accountant,* May 1973, p.54.

Asebrook, R.J., and Carmichael, D.R., 'Reporting on forecasts: a survey of attitudes', *Journal of Accountancy,* August 1973, p.38.

'Assumptions and Profit Forecasts', *Accountants Magazine,* (Scot.), January 1972, p.13.

Backer, M., 'Reporting profit expectations', *Management Accounting,* NAA, February 1972, p.33.

Baker, H.K., and Tralins, S.M., 'An analysis of published financial forecasts', *Atlanta Economic Review,* July/August 1976, p.42.

Barnea, A., 'Published profit forecasts', *Financial Executive,* November 1977, p.52.

Bart, John T., 'Single vs. multiple-value earnings forecasts: one or the others?', *CA Magazine,* March 1980, p.50.

Bartholomew, E.G., 'Proposed directive on company prospectuses', *Journal UEC,* October 1973, p.249.

Basi, B.A., Carey, K.J., & Twark, R.D., 'Comparison of the accuracy of corporate and security analysts' forecasts of earnings', *Accounting Review,* April 1976, p.244.

Basi, B.A., Carey, H.J., & Twark, R.D., 'Comparison of the accuracy of corporate and security analysts' forecasts of earnings: a reply', *Accounting Review,* July 1977, p.741.

Baumann, W.S., 'Scientific investment analysis', *Financial Analysts Journal,* p.93.

Beckman, R.W., 'Accountants sales forecasts — partners for profit', *Australian Accountant,* March 1970, p.65.

Beehler, P.J., 'Cash Management: forecasting for profit', *Management Advisor,* July-August, 1973, p.35.

Belda, B.J., 'Reporting on forecasts of future developments', *Journal of Accountancy,* December 1970, p.54.

Benjamin, James J., and Strawser, Robert A., 'The Canadian accountant and changes in financial reporting, *CGA Magazine,* May-June 1973, p.4.

Bhaskar, K., 'A Multiple Objective Approach to Capital Budgeting', *Accounting and Business Research,* Winter 1979.

Bissell, G.S., 'Professional investor looks at earnings forecasts', *Financial Analysts Journal,* May-June 1972, p.73.

Black, T., 'Profit planning for action and results', *Management Accounting,* NAA, January 1971, p.9.

Bleasdale, F.E., 'Ascertainment of periodic financial results', *Accountant,* November 2, 1972, p.548.

Body, J.P., 'Planning and forecasting in industry-finance', *Management Accounting,* June 1967, p.219.

Bowers, R.L., 'Managing the company's cash', *Management Accounting,* NAA, September 1971, p.22.

Boothman, D., 'Whither forecasts', *Accountancy Age,* 15 July 1975, p.8.

Bradbury, M.E., 'Cash flow forecasts', *Accountants' Journal,* N.Z. November 1978, p.384; December 1978, p.427.

Briston, R.J., and Fawthrop, R.A., 'Accounting principles and investor protection', *Journal of Business Finance,* Summer 1971, p.10.

'Britons Measure Profit Forecasts', *Journal of Accountancy,* November 1971, p.14.

Broster, E.J., 'Trend forecasting — a proposed new technique', *Accountant,* 25 February 1967, p.207.

Broster, E.J., 'Trend forecasting for planning', *Certified Accountant,* April 1974, p.157.

Brown, A.D., & Rozeff, M.S., 'Superiority of analyst forecasts as measures of expectations: evidence from earnings', *Journal of Finance,* March 1978, p.1.

Buckley, A., 'Planning estimates — a summary of their accuracy', *Accountancy,* June 1973, p.56.

Burton, John C., 'Financial forecasts', *CA Magazine,* Nov. 1973, p.34.

Busch, G.A., 'Prudent Manager Forecasting', *Harvard Business Review,* May-June 1961.

Carey, K.J., 'Accuracy of estimates of earnings from naive models', *Journal of Economics and Business,* Spring/Summer 1978, p.182.

Carlson, J.A. 'Forecasting Errors and Business Cycles', *American Economic Review*, 57 No. 3, 1967.

Carmichael, D.R., 'Reporting on forecasts: an UK perspective,' *Journal of Accountancy*, January 1973, p.36.

Carper, W.B., 'The future of forecasting', *Management Accounting*, NAA, August 1979. p.27.

Carroll, J., 'Managing Director and the profit plan', *Chartered Accountant in Australia*, September 1971, p.31.

Casey, Frank C., 'Earnings forecasts and the management accountant,' *Cost and Management*, May-June 1977, p.42.

Chambers, A., 'Business appraisal in first phase in planning profitability,' *Management Accounting*, January 1973, p.15.

Chambers, J.C., 'How to choose the right forecasting tool', *Harvard Business Review*, Winter 1971, p.45.

Chang, D.L.S., and Liao, S.S., 'Measuring and disclosing forecast reliability', *Journal of Accountancy*, May 1977, p.76.

Chapin, D.K., 'Earnings forecasts – where do we go from here and why?', *Journal of Commercial Bank Lending*, April 1973, p.2.

Coldicott, T., 'Forecasting in the long-term', *Accountancy*, October 1973, p.23.

Collins, W.A., and Hopwood, W.S., 'Multivariate analysis of annual earnings forecasts generated from quarterly forecasts of financial analysts and univariate time series models,' *Journal of Accounting Research*, Autumn 1980, p.390.

Copeland, R.M., and Marioni, R.L., 'Executives' forecasts of earnings per share versus forecasts of naive models,' *Journal of Business*, October 1972, p.497.

Cousland, R.C., 'Forecasting for a future,' *Accountants Magazine*, Scots., March 1969, p.162.

Crichfield, T., Dyckman, T., and Lakonishok, J., 'Evaluation of security analysts' forecasts,' *Accounting Review*, July 1978, p.651.

Daily, R.A., 'The feasibility of reporting forecasted information', *Accounting Review*, October 1971, p.686.

Damant, D.C., 'Financial forecasting by companies – a note on UK practice', *Financial Analysts Journal*, September-October 1972, p.44.

Davison, I.H., 'Budgetary control and long-range planning', *Management Accounting,* NAA, October 1967, p.406.

Demski, J.S., 'Forecast evaluation', *Accounting Review,* July 1972, p.533.

Dev, S., 'Problems in interpreting prospectus profit forecasts', *Accounting & Business Research,* Spring 1973, p.110.

Dev, S., 'Statements of company prospects', *Accounting & Business Research,* Autumn 1974, p.270.

Dev, S., & Webb, M., 'The accuracy of company profit forecasts', *Journal of Business Finance,* Autumn 1972, p.26.

Dickerson, Robert W.V., (ed.), 'Might isn't always right' (Legal Cases), *CA Magazine,* June 1978, p.60.

Dohrn, P., 'Forecasting in the short term', *Accountancy,* July 1973, p.15.

Dudick, T.S., 'Planning for profit: focusing on the big picture', *Management Accounting,* NAA, August 1970, p.15.

Dyckman, T.R., and Steckler, H.O., 'Probabilistic turning point forecast', *Review of Economics and Statistics,* 48 No. 3, 1966.

Edwards, James Don., 'The impact of new dimensions in financial reporting − on management, the management accountant and the auditor,' *Cost and Management,* March-April 1974, p.6.

Elgers, P., 'Inclusion of budgets in financial reports: investor needs v. management disclosure', *Accounting & Business Research,* Winter 1972, p.53.

Elgers, P., 'The role of assumptions in financial forecasts', *Journal of Accountancy,* July 1974, p.63.

Elgers, P.T., and May, G.S., 'Forecast guidelines', *CPA Journal,* March 1978, p.21.

Emmanuel, C.R., and Pick, R.H., 'The predictive ability of UK segment reports', *Journal of Business Finance and Accounting,* Vol 7 No. 2, 1980, p.201.

Ferris, K.R., 'Profit forecast disclosure: the effect on managerial behaviour', *Accounting & Business Research,* Spring 1975, p.133.

Ferris, K.R., 'The apparent effects of profit forecast disclosure on managerial behaviour: an empirical examination', *Journal of Business Finance & Accounting,* vol. 3, no. 3, 1976, p.53.

Ferris, K.R., and Hayes, D.C., 'Some evidence on the determinants of profit forecast accuracy in the UK', *International Journal of Accounting,* Spring 1977, p.27.

Fess, P.E., 'Company forecasts and the independent auditor's inexorable involvement', *The CPA Journal,* October 1973, p.868.

Firth, M., 'The forecasting of company profits', *Accountants Review,* March 1975, p.35.

Folie, G.M., 'Role of forecasting in the decision making process', *Australian Accountant,* March 1973, p.86.

Fraser, D.R., and Richards, R.M., 'Accuracy of earnings forecasts for public utilities', *Public Utilities Fortnightly,* 23 November 1978, p.27.

Fraser, I.J., 'Accountancy and the merger movement', *The Accountants Magazine,* Scot., August 1971, p.405.

Ghosh, T.K., 'Sales forecasting', *The Chartered Accountant,* India, June 1972, p.1036.

Gibson, C.J., 'Can the auditor's opinion be extended to include budgets?', *Chartered Accountant in Australia,* September 1971, p.17.

Gleeson-White, M.A., 'The public use of profit forecasts', *Chartered Accountant in Australia,* July 1975, p.50.

Gray, S.J., 'Managerial forecasts and European multinational reporting', *Journal of International Business Studies,* Vol. 9 No. 2, 1979, p.21.

Grenside, J.P., 'Accountants reports on profit forecasts in the UK', *Journal of Accountancy,* May 1970, p.47.

Gunders, H., 'Better profit planning', *Management Accounting,* NAA, August 1965, p.3.

Guy, D.M., 'Auditing procedures for projected financial statements: a suggested approach', *Canadian Chartered Accountant,* June 1972, p.20.

Hagaman, T.C., 'Forecasting in financial planning', *Financial Executive,* July 1968, p.28.

Hagerman, R.J., & Ruland, W., 'Accuracy of management forecasts and forecasts of simple alternative models', *Journal of Economics & Business,* Spring 1979, p.172.

Halford, D.R.C., 'Profit planning and forecasting', *The Accountant,* 2, 9, 16 October 1965, pp.404, 441, 472.

240

Henderson, R., 'Improving the performance of capital project planning', *Cost and Management,* Canada, September-October 1971, p.24.

Hicks, C.F., 'Post-auditing the capital investment decision', *Management Accounting,* NAA, August 1971, p.24.

Hill, C., 'Introduction to planning and forecasting', *Management Accounting,* May 1967, p.171.

Hodson, D., 'Cash forecasting — a vital treasurer's tool', *Treasurer,* February 1981, p.27.

Hoogeveen, H., 'Computer-assisted profit analysis', *Canadian Chartered Accountant,* February 1972, p.63.

How Accurate are Forecasts? *Financial Executive,* March 1973, p.26.

Imhoff, E.A., 'Representativeness of management earnings forecasts', *Accounting Review,* October 1978, p.836.

Jaggi, B., 'Comparative accuracy of management's annual earnings forecasts', *Financial Management,* Winter 1978, p.24.

Jantsch, E., 'Forecasting the Future', *Science Journal,* October 1967.

Kapnick, H.E., 'Will financial forecasts really help investors?', *Financial Executive,* August 1972, p.50.

Kell, W.G., 'The SEC's new disclosure rule on forecasts', *Michigan Business Review,* May 1973, p.17.

Killough, L.N., 'An argument for published forecasted financial data', *National Public Accountant,* December 1973, p.15.

Kinney, W.R., 'Predicting earnings: entity versus subentity data', *Journal of Accounting Research,* Spring 1971, p.127.

Lefrançois, R., 'Published earnings forecasts: why they deserve reconsideration', *Cost and Management,* May-June 1979, p.11.

Levine, L.H., 'Forecasting techniques', *Management Accounting,* NAA, January 1967, p.31.

Lorek, K.S., McDonald, C.L., & Patz, D.H., 'Comparative examination of management forecasts and Box-Jenkins forecasts of earnings', *Accounting Review,* April 1976, p.321.

Lorenz, C., 'How Shell plans to cope with an era of surprise', *Financial Times,* Wednesday, 14 November, 1979.

Lowe, E.A., 'Budgetary control: an evaluation in a wider managerial perspective', *Accountancy,* November 1970, p.764.

Lowes, B., 'Budgeting to meet problems of uncertainty', *Management Accounting,* January 1973, p.10.

Luk, M.J., 'Forecasting and budgeting in a research firm', *Management Accounting,* NAA, June 1972, p.35.

Mallinson, A.H., 'A risk analysis approach to profit forecasts', *Accounting & Business Research,* Spring 1974, p.83.

Manthey, P.S., 'Profit planning using forecast schedules', *Management Accounting,* NAA, January 1967, p.13.

Markwalder, A.S., 'Profit forecasting: an overview', *National Public Accountant,* April 1974, p.27.

Matheson, C.B., 'Earnings statements in prospectuses', *Canadian Chartered Accountant,* February 1969, p.95.

Maxwell, T.B., 'Cash flow forecast', *Accountancy Ireland,* April 1973, p.27.

McDonald, C.L., 'An empirical investigation of the reliability of published predictions of future earnings', *Accounting Review,* July 1973, p.502.

McLaughlin, R.L., 'The Breakthrough in Sales Forecasting', *Journal of Marketing,* 27, 1963, p.46.

Meier, A., 'Framework of a budgetary system', *Journal,* UEC, October 1971, p.259.

Moore, J.F., 'How to prepare and use cash forecasts', *Practical Accountant,* July/August 1972, p.37.

Moore, L.J., 'Long range planning and the decentralised firm', *Management Accounting,* NAA, November 1971, p.35.

Morris, D.E.A., 'A case of forecasting', *P.M.M. World,* Autumn 1978, p.10.

Morris, R.C., & Breakwell, G.H., 'Manipulation of earnings figures in the UK', *Accounting & Business Research,* Summer 1975, p.177.

Newhouse, B.S., 'Short-term cash forecasting', New York, *C.P.A.,* August 1969, p.597.

Nichols, D.R., and Groomer, S.M., 'The accuracy of estimates of earnings', *Abacus,* December 1979, p.113.

Norby, W.C., 'Budget forecasts in first offering prospectuses', *Financial Analysts Journal,* July/August 1972, p.90.

Offord, J., 'Evaluation of profit and risk using D.C.F. criteria', *Management Accounting,* September 1967, p.353.

Omlor, J.J., 'Management information system for planning, forecasting, and budgeting', *Management Accounting,* NAA, March 1970. p.13.

Oszer, P.W., 'Long range forecasts: where do we go from here?', *Management Accounting,* NAA, January 1971, p.21.

Parker, G.G.C., 'How to get a better forecast', *Harvard Business Review,* March-April 1971, p.99

Penman, S.H., 'Empirical investigation of the voluntary disclosure of corporate earnings forecasts', *Journal of Accounting Research,* Spring 1980, p.132.

Platt, C.J., 'How reliable are profit forecasts?', *Accountancy,* April 1979, p.95.

Quinn, J.B., 'Technological forecasting', *Harvard Business Review,* March/April 1967.

Reckers, P.M.J., and Taylor, Martin E., 'The U.S. takes a new look at financial forecasts', *Cost and Management,* March-April 1980, p.26.

Richards, R.M. 'Analysts' performance and the accuracy of corporate earnings forecasts', *Journal of Business,* July 1976, p.350.

Richards, R.M., Benjamin, J.J., and Strawser, R.H., 'Examination of the accuracy of earnings forecasts', *Financial Management,* Fall 1977, p.78.

Richards, R.M., and Fraser, D.R., 'Further evidence on the accuracy of analysts' earnings forecasts: a comparison among analysts', *Journal of Economics and Business,* Spring/Summer 1977, p.193.

Richards, R.M., and Fraser, D.R., 'Predictability of corporate earnings', *Atlanta Economic Review,* March-April 1978, p.43.

Robinson, C., 'Some principals of forecasting in business', *Journal of Industrial Economics,* 14, (1) 1965.

Ruff, F.H., 'Planning for profit', *Financial Executive,* July 1969, p.31.

Ruland, W., 'Accuracy of forecasts by management and financial analysts', *Accounting Review,* April 1978, p.439.

Ruland, W., 'Forecasting and the stability of earnings', *Journal of Business Finance & Accounting,* Summer 1979, p.187.

Sautter, W., 'Projected cash needs', *Management Accounting,* NAA, February 1971, p.11.

Schachner, L., 'Published forecasts and internal budgets', *CPA Journal*, January 1975, p.19.

Simister, L.J., and Turner, J., 'Systematic forecasting in British industry', *Journal of Business Policy,* Winter 1972, p.43.

Slater, A.G., 'The Potential from Profit Planning', *Managerial Finance,* Volume 3, No. 1, 1977, p.1.

Stewart, S.S., 'Research on corporate forecasts', *Financial Analysts Journal,* January/February 1973, p.77.

Sycamore, R.J., 'Public disclosure of earnings forecasts by companies', (Research), *CA Magazine,* May 1974, p.72.

Terrara, W.L., 'Toward probabilistic profit budgets', *Management Accountant,* NAA, October 1970, p.23.

Van Arsdell, S.C., 'Forecasting: a view from England', *CPA Journal,* January 1974, p.20.

Vancil, R.F., 'The accuracy of long-range planning', *Harvard Business Review,* September-October 1970, p.98.

Valenta, J.R., 'Implementation of a financial forecasting system', *Managerial Planning,* November/December 1980, p.23.

Wall Street Journal, The, 'Forecast standards for firms proposed by accounting body', 15 April, 1974.

Welsch, G.A., 'Fundamental appraisal of profit planning and control', *Management Accounting,* NAA, March 1969, p.22.

Westwick, C.A., 'Profit forecasts in bid situations', *Accountancy,* July 1972, p.10.

Wilkins, E., 'Forecasting cash flows: some problems and some applications', *Management Accounting,* NAA, October 1967, p.26.

Wheelwright, S., 'Selecting a forecasting technique', *Management Decision,* Spring 1972, p.71.

Index